DISAGREEING VIRTUOUSLY

Disagreeing Virtuously

Religious Conflict in
Interdisciplinary Perspective

Olli-Pekka Vainio

WILLIAM B. EERDMANS PUBLISHING COMPANY
GRAND RAPIDS, MICHIGAN

Wm. B. Eerdmans Publishing Co.
2140 Oak Industrial Drive NE, Grand Rapids, Michigan 49505
www.eerdmans.com

23 22 21 20 19 18 17   1 2 3 4 5 6 7

ISBN 978-0-8028-7504-4

Library of Congress Cataloging-in-Publication Data

Names: Vainio, Olli-Pekka, author.
Title: Disagreeing virtuously : religious conflict in interdisciplinary
  perspective / Olli-Pekka Vainio.
Description: Grand Rapids : Eerdmans Publishing Co., 2017. | Includes
  bibliographical references and index.
Identifiers: LCCN 2016059252 | ISBN 9780802875044 (pbk. : alk. paper)
Subjects: LCSH: Virtue. | Virtues. | Conflict management--Religious aspects.
  | Interpersonal relations.
Classification: LCC BJ1531 .V35 2017 | DDC 201/.5--dc23 LC record available at https://lccn.
  loc.gov/2016059252

Contents

List of Tables and Figures   vii

Foreword, by Rob Barrett   viii

Acknowledgments   xii

Abbreviations   xiii

Introduction: We Are All Heretics Now   xv

The Heretical Imperative   xv

Defining Disagreement   xviii

Structure of the Book   xx

1. We Have Been Here Before   1

  1.1. Malleable Men and the Council of the Wise:
Plato and Aristotle   2

  1.2. Varieties of Goodness: Augustine and Aquinas   10

  1.3. Method Men: Bacon and Descartes   20

  1.4. From Natural War to Perpetual Peace:
Hobbes, Locke, and Kant   25

  1.5. Beyond Enlightenment: Nietzsche, Hamann,
and Contemporary Voices   33

2. Programmed to Disagree?   46

  2.1. Constrained and Confused Minds   47

2.2. The Nature of Human Rationality and Decision-Making   59

2.3. Cognitive Biases   69

2.4. Two Hemispheres, Two Ways of Thinking   73

2.5. On Being Right(eous)   76

2.6. Human Cognition and Religious Disagreement   80

3. Science, Philosophy, and Religious Disagreement   85

3.1. Scientific Perspectives on Religion   86

3.2. Naturalistic Accounts of Religion   91

3.3. Religion and Violence   99

3.4. Philosophy of Religious Disagreement   115

3.5. Reacting to Disagreement: A Dynamic View   133

4. Disagreeing Virtuously   138

4.1. The Nature of Virtue   139

4.2. Virtues of Disagreement   157

4.3. Tolerance as a Virtue   169

4.4. Religious Disagreement and Virtue   176

Bibliography   187

Index   204

List of Tables and Figures

Table 1   Theological and philosophical reasons for disagreement and
            suggested cures   45

Table 2   Two types of cognitive processing   63

Table 3   McGilchrist's model of cognition: the master and the
            emissary   74

Figure 1   Disagreement and various types of inquiry   xix

Figure 2   Stanovich's model of the dual-process account   66

Figure 3   Haidt's three ways of ethical deliberation   80

Figure 4   The process of debiasing   155

Figure 5   Bootstrapping   155

Foreword

Disagreement is part of life. Sometimes far too much a part of life.

Polarization and conflict plague us at every level, whether in global conflicts, national politics, struggles within churches and denominations, or among families and friends. We are increasingly unable to work together on the important problems we face. As Edward Wasserman, Knight Professor in Journalism Ethics at Washington and Lee University, observed, "Mainstream media have made a fortune teaching people the wrong ways to talk to each other."[1] Wherever the teaching has come from, we have learned all too well how to disagree poorly. We have all watched—and unfortunately, experienced—disagreement devolve into lasting enmity.

And so this phenomenon of disagreement threatens us. Along the journey of life, we are confronted with forks in the road. We stop and look left and right. Our co-travelers do the same. I point left and she points right. What now? How will our difference affect our shared life? Will we be able to continue the journey together? How can we help one another?

I work for The Colossian Forum, a Christian organization committed to transforming our most difficult conflicts into opportunities for good. In other words, we're committed to the possibility that forks in the road can be gifts. Positive results can come out of our most pressured disagreements. This might seem an audacious hope as we look at our bitter divisions over faith and science, same-sex sexuality, and so on. But it is possible. I've seen it. And this book will help me do it better.

At one level we all know that disagreement need not be a problem. When I want to vacation at the seaside and you prefer the mountains, we

---

1. Edward Wassermann, "Why News Media Must Embrace Online Rules," September 22, 2015, https://www.scu.edu/ethics/focus-areas/journalism-ethics/resources/why-news-media-must-embrace-online-rules/.

disagree. But such disagreements need not be destructive. In fact, your preference may well bring me the joy of discovering a part of the world I would never otherwise experience.

But this is not how we typically think of disagreement. We reserve this term for encounters that threaten our relationships. Such destructive disagreements are vicious. This most often happens when the stakes are high, but it can happen at any time. The deciding factor is less the character of the disagreement than the character of those who are disagreeing. As we like to say at The Colossian Forum, "We need to become the kind of people who can handle this conflict well."

Which brings us to Olli-Pekka Vainio's project. As the title of this book suggests, the solution to destructive, vicious disagreement stares us in the face, for the opposite of "vicious" is "virtuous." If disagreement is to be constructive, we need to handle it virtuously. Vainio lays before us a vision for virtuous disagreement, a handling of disagreement that moves us forward.

As one who deals with seemingly intractable conflicts both in theory and in practice, I believe this book moves us forward in two significant ways.

First, it creates a space for the interdisciplinary, scholarly consideration of disagreement. By gathering together work on disagreement from a range of disciplines, Vainio invites us to treat disagreement as a topic in its own right. It is a thing we can study from many different perspectives. He has begun the work of charting a map of disagreement as an interdisciplinary field, drawing from philosophy (classical, Enlightenment, and modern political), psychology and cognitive science, the particularities of religious disagreement, and virtue theory. By defining disagreement as a field of study, Vainio offers us a place for such integrated work. From my experience with The Colossian Forum, I believe this book is the tip of an important iceberg. I look forward to others' contributions to this new field, whether from the theory of wicked problems, business approaches to navigating disagreement in business, the practices associated with attaining the requisite virtues for disagreeing well, or any of countless other studies that illuminate the topic of disagreement. Vainio has defined a space and taken a first, significant step toward filling it, but there remains much more to be done. May many others contribute to an expanding interdisciplinary field of disagreement.

Second, this book lands at the proper place: the need for virtue. He closes his work with careful and nuanced considerations of some of the virtues required for handling disagreement well: open-mindedness, humility, courage, and tolerance. I believe Vainio is completely right in pointing us to virtue. Unfortunately, learning about virtue is not the same as attaining virtue.

We must realize the limitations of this—and any—book about virtue. It can bring us only so far. It can bring us to a better understanding of the nature of disagreement, the philosophical unavoidability of disagreement, the psychological factors that drive our disagreements, the social forces that exacerbate our disagreements, and the virtues we need in order to navigate our disagreements well. But it cannot confer upon us those virtues. It is the wish-dream of many of us with a tendency toward the academic that reading the right book or attending the right conference will give us the information that will solve our problems. But in this case, what we lack is more than information. We lack the formation into people who can live it out. We lack the habits and impulses that enable us to navigate disagreement in constructive ways.

So where does this leave us? Has Vainio failed us in the end? By no means. The information is necessary. We must understand disagreement and the role of virtue better. The work begun here must continue to mature and develop. But we must not stop with improving our information. We must pursue better formation—even re-formation—out of our vices and into the virtues. As Vainio and all of the classic virtue theorists have observed, such formation depends on two difficult activities: imitating the best exemplars of virtue and taking up formational practices that reshape us.

But we should pause before launching into a virtue-building campaign. We must clarify our goal, for there is no single, objective form of the virtues. So it is important to note that Vainio's project is a Christian one. He works within a Christian framework and ultimately addresses Christian readers. His work is not narrowly Christian, drawing as he does upon a wide variety of intellectual disciplines. But once we land in the realm of virtue, different pathways to human flourishing diverge, and Vainio's focus is on the Christian understanding of flourishing displayed in the life, death, and resurrection of Christ. All of the virtues gain their form from the dominant virtue of charity, self-giving love. So virtue for Christians is oriented around the very particular form of Christ's love. Our exemplars come from the community of the Church. Our formational practices are, at their root, spiritual practices that participate in the work of the Holy Spirit in and among us. We understand Christian growth to be a process of sanctification that brings glory to God, and we depend upon God to provide all that we need in order to accomplish this. Others will pursue virtue out of their own traditions, and so take up different practices aimed at different goals. And, yes, there will always be disagreements between the traditions—specifically, religious disagreements. But it is important to realize that Vainio's foundation is a Christian one.

With that clarification, I am thrilled with the great service Vainio has done us in bringing together this study of virtuous disagreement. I must admit, though, that his project will end in failure if his readers consider themselves done when they finish the book. It is inherent to the nature of virtue that learning is only a part of the process. This book can be only a starting point for recommitting ourselves to the practices that form us into people who can disagree well.

Fortunately, as we have observed at The Colossian Forum, our very disagreements provide a most excellent context for taking up the formational practices that give us the capacities we need to engage disagreement well. In other words, our world of polarization and conflict—as threatening as it can be—is also a world of great opportunity. As we stand at innumerable forks in the road, pointing in different directions, we are being confronted by opportunities to take up the practices that lead to attaining the virtues that Christians have commended throughout the ages, such things as the fruit of the Spirit in Galatians 5:22-23: love, joy, peace, forbearance, kindness, goodness, faithfulness, gentleness, and self-control (NIV).

Further, by the very nature of virtue, as we gain the capacity to engage disagreement well, we are gaining riches beyond measure. For the virtues are not highly specialized, but broadly tuned toward flourishing in all of life. So disagreement, when understood as a classroom and testing ground for our virtue-mettle, can be received as a gift, even along with the discomfort and difficulty it brings. This lands us in a place of hope.

So I encourage you to take up the work in your hand and read it well. Then read it again. But in-between readings, take up the practices that orient your life and form your character into the shape that can disagree virtuously. Search out exemplars, whether living and proximate or long gone and distant, and imitate them. Do this hard work in community alongside others who share the vision. Measure yourselves based on the quality of your disagreements. Contribute what you are learning back to this newly defined interdisciplinary field of the study of disagreement.

Our world will be a better place for it. And we will be better people. So may we Christians who take up the spiritual disciplines that lead to better disagreement thereby contribute more positively to the building up of Christ's church, testifying to the glory of God, and serving the needs of the world.

Rob Barrett, *Director of Forums and Scholarship*
The Colossian Forum
Grand Rapids, Michigan

Acknowledgments

I wish to express my gratitude to the following people who helped me with their comments, critiques, and discussions: Max Baker-Hytch, Phillip Cary, Helen de Cruz, Timo Nisula, Rich Park, Tim Pawl, Ryan Pemberton, Andrew Pinsent, Jeroen de Ridder, Johan de Smedt, Nathanael Smith, Joshua Thurow, Roger Trigg, Aku Visala, Joseph Wolyniak, and Hetty Zock. Special thanks are due to Simo Knuuttila and Risto Saarinen, who were in charge of the Academy of Finland's Political Philosophy, Morality and Psychology Centre of Excellence, which enabled me to pursue this project. I also thank two anonymous reviewers for their comments.

I have presented parts of this book in several academic settings. I am very grateful to the hosts and participants of the following gatherings: Ian Ramsey Centre Seminar at the University of Oxford; the conference of European Society of Philosophy of Religion; Williamson Conference at Austin Theological Seminary, Texas; and the research seminar at the Faculty of Philosophy, Umeå University, Sweden.

The work has been financially supported by the Faculty of Theology (University of Helsinki); the Academy of Finland; the Finnish Association of Non-fiction Writers; and Kellogg College, Oxford.

Parts of chapter 5.4 have been printed before in *Religion in Public Life*, edited by Niek Brunsveld and Roger Trigg, Ars Disputandi Supplement Series 5 (Utrecht: Ars Disputandi, 2011). Reprinted by permission.

Abbreviations

Acad.	Augustine, *Contra Academicos*
Catech.	Augustine, *De catechizandis rudibus*
Civ.	Augustine, *De civitate Dei*
Doctr. chr.	Augustine, *De doctrina Christiana*
Enchir.	Augustine, *Enchiridion*
Ep.	*Epistulae*
KRS	G. S. Kirk, J. E. Raven, and M. Schofield, *The Presocratic Philosophers: A Critical History with a Selection of Texts.* 2nd ed. Cambridge: Cambridge University Press, 1983 (numbers refer to fragments)
PA	St. Thomas Aquinas, *Sententia super Posteriora Analytica*
ST	St. Thomas Aquinas, *Summa Theologiae*
WA	*D. Martin Luthers Werke* [Weimarer Ausgabe]. Weimar: Böhlau, 1883–1993

We Are All Heretics Now

The Heretical Imperative

The general fragmentation of our societies creates a challenge concerning how to deal with the plurality of worldviews and values in politics, religion, ethics, and aesthetics. As a result of this fragmentation and the inherent plurality of our society, we are faced with the "heretical imperative": we are always heretics to a vast number of people.[1] Disagreement is something we cannot escape in late-modern society. The question remains, then: How to deal with it?

Answering this question calls for an interdisciplinary approach. In this book, I seek to combine the history of ideas, cognitive sciences, analytic philosophy of religion, and virtue theories to provide a new way to look at the nature of disagreement. The general aim of the project is to understand the ways in which our thinking, more precisely our cognitive setup, affects the reasoning, judgments, and ultimately our behavior in the state of disagreement. The dynamics of disagreement are relatively similar in all cases, be they moral, political, or religious in nature. I thus aim at a metalevel analysis, which can be applied to multiple instances of disagreement. A further aim is to use these results to draw lessons about the nature and the ethically acceptable management of interpersonal and intercommunal disagreements and conflicts.

In brief, this book has the following as its main goals:

---

1. Peter Berger, *The Heretical Imperative: Contemporary Possibilities of Religious Affirmation* (Garden City, NY: Anchor, 1980). John Locke expressed this in inverted form in *A Letter Concerning Toleration* 1: "Everyone is orthodox to himself."

1. Analyze how disagreement has been portrayed in historical traditions.
2. Map out the current discussion on disagreement among different disciplines.
3. Offer ways to understand the complicated nature of human disagreement and recommend ways to manage it in ethically sustainable ways.

A distinctive feature of recent discussion about disagreement has been the lack of holistic approaches. Research in general has been relatively restricted within particular disciplines. My attempt is to bring together some of these discussions. For example, there is a lively debate within analytic philosophy on the epistemology of disagreement, but so far it has been extremely theoretical and conceptually orientated.[2] One of the central topics in this discussion has been the notion of epistemic peerage and its effects on our beliefs. Should we give up our beliefs or can we retain them? Despite meticulous analysis, suggestions for the wider scientific community have been scant.[3] However, religious disagreement has received special attention, representing one of the main fields in which the results of this discussion have been applied.

In the field of psychology, the study of human rationality has seen several interesting new theories in the last twenty years, such as the debates on heuristics and biases, and the consequences of our cognitive limitations for our reasoning. But what do these findings actually mean? Is rational judgment natural despite (or because) of our biases, or is our thinking in the need of constant debiasing? This field of problems is sometimes called "Rationality War," where different theorists frame our cognitive life in at least partially mutually excluding ways.[4] This is an important debate because it touches on the very notion of "rationality," which, particularly after the Enlightenment, has been

2. These two volumes gather together the central voices in the discussion: Richard Feldman and Ted A. Warfield, eds., *Disagreement* (Oxford: Oxford University Press, 2010); David Christensen and Jennifer Lackey, eds., *The Epistemology of Disagreement: New Essays* (Oxford: Oxford University Press, 2013).

3. There have been very few attempts to discuss how disagreements are dealt with in the scientific community and in the philosophy of science, and how that might help expand reasonable philosophical policies on disagreement. In the hard sciences, disagreements are usually solved when enough time is given, which is not always the case with value disagreements. However, climate-change debates, for example, have fueled the recent discussion on how we can "argue the facts." See Dan M. Kahan et al., "The Polarizing Impact of Science Literacy and Numeracy on Perceived Climate Change Risks," *Nature Climate Change* 2 (2012): 732–35.

4. See, e.g., the essays of Gerd Gigerenzer and David Matheson in Stainton, ed., *Contemporary Debates in Cognitive Science* (Oxford: Blackwell, 2006) and Daniel Kahneman, *Thinking, Fast and Slow* (London: Allen Lane, 2011).

the main source of hoped-for consensus: if we just act reasonably, disagreements will be solved. The current discussion frustrates these expectations.

Especially after 9/11, religion's role in conflicts has been a subject of renewed interest. However, the evaluation of religion varies a great deal, from purely negative (New Atheist critiques in general) to positive (where religion is seen as a major tool for reconciliation).[5] Scientific inquiry concerning religion and its ability either to prevent or cause violent clashes is still young, contains many prejudices, and lacks sufficient data.[6] The role of religion in conflicts gives rise to a set of interesting debates, for example, regarding the notion of religion per se and our ability to assess the role religion plays in human conduct.

But disagreements are not something that humans have encountered only recently. The history of the human race is a series of different kinds of disagreements. Recently, our story has been written from viewpoints particularly focused on food, drink, and of course weapons.[7] The story of humanity is one in which we have fought over food, got drunk, and invented more efficient weapons to solve our disputes. If this is what our kings and queens achieved, our philosophers have not fared any better. The history of Western philosophy starts with elemental disagreements and develops into more complex forms of divergence as time goes on. The cynical question is, why bother with philosophy in the first place? The quick answer: there really is no other option for us. Everything we do is affected by philosophy. Even if the history of philosophy cannot provide us with clear answers, that does not mean we cannot learn any lessons from it. Here my attempt is to examine how our predecessors have encountered the problem of disagreement and to propose ways to benefit from those discussions.

5. For discussion see, e.g., Scott Atran, *Talking to the Enemy: Violent Extremism, Sacred Values and What It Means to Be Human* (London: Allen Lane, 2010); Desmond Tutu, *No Future without Forgiveness* (London: Rider, 2000).

6. It appears that there is a pervasive trend to emphasize the negative effects of religion. See, e.g., John Perry and Nigel Biggar, "Religion and Intolerance: A Critical Commentary," in *Religion, Intolerance, and Conflict: A Scientific and Conceptual Investigation*, ed. Steve Clarke et al. (Oxford: Oxford University Press, 2012), 253–61. William T. Cavanaugh has analyzed how the notion of religious violence functions as a mythic notion that is invoked to support certain antireligious public policies. See William T. Cavanaugh, *The Myth of Religious Violence* (Oxford: Oxford University Press, 2009). Also Atran (*Talking to the Enemy*) has argued that religion has actually very little to do with contemporary acts of terrorism.

7. Tom Standage, *A History of the World in Six Glasses* (New York: Atlantic Books, 2005); Standage, *An Edible History of Humanity* (New York: Atlantic Books, 2010); Chris McNab, *The History of the World in 100 Weapons* (London: Osprey, 2014).

The ambiguous state of discussion in the sciences that analyze human conduct and thinking, and the human race's relatively poor track record in problem-solving, leaves us with few choices. To spoil the end of this book: disagreement is a natural part of human existence, and it is highly probable that most of our disagreements can never be solved. Furthermore, there are cases when we should favor disagreement over consensus, since disagreement is not necessarily negative. However, if disagreements are solved (and by this I mean genuinely resolved, not brushed aside or treated with mere force), the resulting reconciliation is always an act of virtue.

After these admittedly pessimistic accounts of the human condition, I turn to virtue theories, which manifest no less variety than all the other fields of human theorization. Nevertheless, I argue that we have access to virtues that may help us to survive persistent disagreements. Of course, few of us succeed in living virtuous lives, and often our attempts to become more virtuous are frustrated by severe failings. Despite this possibility of failure, I see no other way to treat the persistent existence of disagreement since the other options attribute a morally subpar ideal for human conduct.

Defining Disagreement

In contemporary intellectual contexts we tend to isolate disagreements to different types within their respective spheres, such as scientific, philosophical, political, moral, religious, or aesthetic disagreement. Even if human conduct in all of these instantiations of disagreement is similar, the reasons why we disagree are different. Figure 1 below illustrates how different causes bring about disagreement in a given stratum of reality. The point of the figure is not to suggest that the three levels are so sealed from each other that, for example, biases would not affect the reasoning of mathematicians. Instead, in the upper levels it is reasonable to hope that time and effort will bring about an increase in knowledge, which will eventually put the disagreements behind us. However, in the lower levels, we cannot reasonably hope that simply adding "more reason" will resolve disagreements.[8] Although reasoning is necessary, it alone does not suffice; reason needs to be balanced with wisdom.

8. For example, C. S. Lewis expresses his hesitation with the suggestion that the solution to the problems of human knowledge is simply "more reason." Increasing reason does not necessarily help because reality is often too complicated to be known in the first place. See C. S. Lewis, "De Futilitate," in *Essay Collection: Literature, Philosophy and Short Stories* (London: HarperCollins 2000), 270.

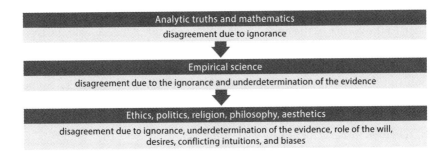

Figure 1. Disagreement and various types of inquiry

At this point, it suffices to note that disagreements about ethics, politics, religion, philosophy, and aesthetics can be causally very complex. There are several causes that bring about conflict in these areas, which makes simple explanations unwise. My intention is not to offer a total explanation but simply to point out some things that need to be taken into account when we discuss the reality of disagreements in these spheres.

In this book, I wish to concentrate on religious disagreements, though the discussion is applicable beyond religion. In order to give an accurate account of what we are talking about, the following distinctions need to be made:

1. Religious disagreements in the public sphere
   a. Violent clashes between religions and worldviews (ideologically motivated violence and war)
   b. Clashes between ideologically motivated values (arguments about abortion, euthanasia, marriage, etc.)
2. Intrareligious disagreements
   a. Disagreements between members of the same community in a smaller scale (such as the Anglican Communion crisis or the Great Schism of 1054)
   b. Disagreements between the members of neighboring communities (ecumenical debates)
3. Personal conflicts
   a. Disagreements among family members and other close peers
   b. Individual feelings of cognitive dissonance

First, I would like to point out that we could easily replace the word *religion* with *politics*. Religion is one more thing that we can disagree about;

whether it is a cause of especially problematic disagreement will be discussed later. In the course of the book, I will (when appropriate) designate the type of disagreement using the aforementioned scale. This taxonomy functions as a heuristic reminder of all the various instantiations of disagreement. Some of these forms of disagreement are more serious than others. Some may be, even if painful, ultimately beneficial. Not all disagreements are bad. Often we need disagreements to make progress. In principle, all three types of religious disagreement can have some positive value. The challenge, of course, is to gain the skills to see this and manage the disagreement so that the negative effects are mitigated.

Type 1 disagreements are more serious and usually draw more media attention. For example, the New Atheists are more concerned with type 1 religious disagreements, while the religious institutions themselves are usually more concerned with type 2 disagreements. As they concern the life of religious communities, and therefore concern the least number of people outside the communities, type 2 disagreements seldom appear in secular media but are often highly important for the members of the communities themselves.

Type 3 disagreements, in contrast, typically manifest as individual feelings or in close interpersonal relations. These disagreements interest secular media more than type 2 because the story involved often draws curious attention to the effects of a religion on its adherents. Covering all the forms of religious disagreement is beyond the scope of this book. Instead, I will concentrate on general dynamics of disagreement, while offering deeper analyses of some of these more particular types of disagreements.

Structure of the Book

The first chapter of this book explores how the nature of disagreement has been viewed in the history of Western philosophy. I will briefly examine the accounts and proposed solutions from pre-Socratic philosophers to recent postmodern thinkers. History offers a comical lesson here: our greatest thinkers disagree not only about *how* we should solve our disagreements but also about what disagreement essentially is, that is, why we disagree in the first place, and about the role of disagreement as part of the human condition.

The book's second chapter introduces several social, psychological, and cognitive factors that create disagreements. Human life is limited by these factors, which effectively disable our knowledge acquisition. Time and resources are among the most crucial material factors and, along with the structure of human psychological and cognitive makeup, set us within a relatively well-sealed bubble, which distorts everything outside of our immediate surroundings. The overview of the limiting factors of the human psyche point toward the fact that disagreement is an integral part of human existence. We can escape from it as effectively as we can live without breathing—or thinking.

In the third chapter, I will examine the nature of religious disagreement from cognitive and philosophical perspectives. There is a lively conversation on the nature of disagreement among analytic philosophers, and there have been some applications of this discussion in the philosophy of religion as well. I shall build on this existing discussion and attempt to move it forward by offering some perspectives from the cognitive science of religion, which helps us to understand, first, the factors that cause religious disagreements and, second, the practical constraints that need to be taken into account when we are searching for possible solutions to inevitable disagreements.

The fourth chapter investigates the nature of virtue and whether we can be trained in moral and epistemic virtues. Recent studies in psychology suggest that learning virtues is indeed possible, though highly difficult. Religions have a dual role in virtue formation, as they tend to foster some epistemic vices while simultaneously enabling habituation in many beneficial virtues. Last, I offer a model of tolerance that is able to accommodate thick religious convictions and enable conviviality of mutually contradicting identities.

CHAPTER 1

We Have Been Here Before

But what differences are there which cannot be thus decided, and which therefore make us angry and set us at enmity with one another? I dare say the answer does not occur to you at the moment, and therefore I will suggest that these enmities arise when the matters of difference are the just and unjust, good and evil, honorable and dishonorable. Are not these the points about which men differ, and about which when we are unable satisfactorily to decide our differences, you and I and all of us quarrel, when we do quarrel?

Plato, *Euthyphro* 7

For human reason is very deficient in things concerning God. A sign of this is that philosophers in their researches, by natural investigation, into human affairs, have fallen into many errors, and have disagreed among themselves.

St. Thomas Aquinas, *ST* II-IIae.2.4

The first philosophical writings that have been preserved for us give mutually conflicting accounts of the nature of ultimate reality and the possibility of knowledge. Although history does not offer consensus, there are multiple lessons to be drawn from the writings of our predecessors. The philosophical problem of disagreement has been with us from the beginning, and over the centuries we have tried to solve the problem in myriad ways, some of which I will summarize in the following pages. Against this background, we may come to understand our own disagreements and proposed solutions more clearly.

1.1. Malleable Men and the Council of the Wise: Plato and Aristotle

One of the first philosophical treatises from the pre-Socratic period comes from Parmenides of Elea (515–445 BC), whose *Poem* focuses on the opinions of simple men who are misled by naively following their senses. Because the world of senses is in a constant state of flux, we are not able to form correct opinions about what is and what is not and we are therefore doomed to form contradictory convictions. Philosophers, instead, know a better way: the meditation of "uncreated and imperishable . . . whole and of single kind and unshaken and perfect."[1]

Here, among the early Greek philosophers, we observe that a question about knowledge is immediately transformed into a question about metaphysics.[2] Heraclitus (fl. 500 BC), Parmenides's contemporary, argued that unchanged and motionless being is not the object of true knowledge; instead *change* is eternal. For Heraclitus, the ultimate nature of reality is not static and harmonious in the way Parmenides thought. The underlying harmony is to be found in corresponding states that are in eternal opposition. This leads him to conclude, "It is necessary to know that war is common and right is strife, and that all things happen by strife and necessity."[3] This river-like constant change shows people their true place in the world: "War is the father of all and king of all, and some he shows as gods, others as men, some he makes slaves, others free."[4] War and strife are eternal; their cessation would indicate the end of the world.

Here we have two basic stances that were to become the two opposite poles of stability and change, being and nothingness, toward which all metaphysical solutions gravitate in the history of Western philosophy. These disputes, which go back to the first serious attempts to philosophize, illustrate the complexity of disagreement. If our disagreements were only about

---

1. KRS 293–95; A. H. Coxon, *The Fragments of Parmenides* (Assen: Van Gorcum, 1986), 193–226.

2. It is part of our post-Enlightenment methodological mind-set that it is easy for us to treat various disagreements within certain boundaries. For example, we discuss disagreement within epistemology so that it does not have immediate bearing on our political or metaphysical convictions. In ancient philosophy and medieval scholasticism, however, the different aspects of philosophy were more tightly connected. In this philosophical style it is impossible to separate metaphysics from epistemology, and these two from political philosophy. This explains why the ancients were more prone to give holistic explanations to disagreements (such as humanity's corruption), whereas moderns tend to refer to the lack of method.

3. KRS 211.

4. KRS 212.

perception, things might not be that serious.[5] However, we are immediately faced with metaphysical questions, which are consequently linked to questions of value. In ancient philosophy the different topics of philosophy were so intermingled that it was not possible to distinguish between epistemology, metaphysics, philosophy of mind, and political philosophy, as happens in modern philosophy.

Plato

Plato's epistemology is tied directly to his metaphysical views. In the *Republic*, for example, Plato argues that perceptible things cannot be the object of proper knowledge since perceptible things can present themselves in ways that contradict each other. That is why convictions regarding perceptible objects are just opinions (*doxa*). Knowledge (*epistēmē*) is possible only in relation to Ideas. Sometimes it seems that Plato restricts knowledge only to the knowing of the One (*hen*) and immediately related ideas, with the result that one actually "knows" very few things. Consequently, if knowledge proper is only about *hen*, epistemology regarding ordinary things loses much of its value as a reasonable pursuit. We should not let the shadows on the wall drag us into senseless disputes because our opinions about them are necessarily deficient.[6]

Nevertheless, even if Plato is not interested in the justification of beliefs in a modern sense, he believes that things such as goodness and justice are worth serious examination. In Plato's *Phaedrus*, Socrates points out that we tend to agree on simple things but get easily confused when faced with issues like justice and goodness, especially if we fall under the influence of a master rhetorician.[7]

5. For pre-Socratic philosophers, the problem of perception was the central issue in epistemology. See Anthony Kenny, *A New History of Western Philosophy* (Oxford: Oxford University Press, 2011), 118–29.

6. Plato, *Republic* 475–80; *Symposium* 210e–211a. See also Nicholas White, "Plato's Metaphysical Epistemology," in *The Cambridge Companion to Plato*, ed. Richard Kraut (Cambridge: Cambridge University Press, 1992), 277–310.

7. Also in *Euthyphro* (8a), Plato acknowledges that in more mundane cases you can always "resort to a weighing machine," but wonders how you measure values when "people regard the same things, some as just and others as unjust,—about these they dispute; and so there arise wars and fightings among them." And, of course, the problem is not only with people but also with gods who disapprove and approve of the same things. Here it is also important to note Plato's general distaste for rhetoric and the negative influence it has on dem-

Socrates: Every one is aware that about some things we are agreed, whereas about other things we differ.

Phaedrus: I think that I understand you; but will you explain yourself?

Socrates: When any one speaks of iron and silver, is not the same thing present in the minds of all?

Phaedrus: Certainly.

Socrates: But when any one speaks of justice and goodness we part company and are at odds with one another and with ourselves?

Phaedrus: Precisely.

Socrates: Then in some things we agree, but not in others?

Phaedrus: That is true.

Socrates: In which are we more likely to be deceived, and in which has rhetoric the greater power?

Phaedrus: Clearly, in the uncertain class.[8]

The above dialogue underlines the need for criteria and standards against which values are evaluated. The criticism of rhetoric arises from the debaters' analysis of Lysia's speech on love. Socrates and Phaedrus criticize Lysia for not defining the concepts he is using. This way Lysia "begins at the end": from the conclusions without properly introducing his arguments, necessary concepts, and their definitions. Consequently, masses are led astray by rhetoricians who make complicated things look simple. Against this view, Socrates argues that dialectic (philosophy) is greater than rhetoric because it leads people to understand the things as they are.[9]

---

ocratic decision making. This comes to the fore in other dialogues as well. See, e.g., *Gorgias*, *Symposium*, and *Phaedrus*.

8. Plato, *Phaedrus*, in *The Dialogues of Plato*, trans. Benjamin Jowett, 3rd ed. (New York: Oxford University Press, 1892), 263a–b.

9. The method of collection and division proceeds as follows. If, for example, we judge a thing to be both good and bad, we are in effect conflating two different objects and basing our judgment on the conflated entity. Instead, we need to make a correct distinction between particular objects and our dispositions. See Nicholas P. White, *Plato on Knowledge and Reality* (Indianapolis: Hackett, 1976), 122. In the conclusion of the dialogue, Socrates states: "Until a man knows the truth of the several particulars of which he is writing or speaking, and is able to define them as they are, and having defined them again to divide them until they can be no longer divided, and until in like manner he is able to discern the nature of the soul, and discover the different modes of discourse which are adapted to different natures, and to arrange and dispose them in such a way that the simple form of speech may be addressed to the simpler nature, and the complex and composite to the more complex nature—until he has accomplished all this, he will be unable to handle arguments according to rules of art, as

Nicholas White notes that the peculiarity of Plato's "metaphysical epistemology" is found in the cases of puzzlement regarding particular goods. There is no talk about different contexts or ways of knowing (because the context is always less than ideal for humans). Plato simply goes on to explain what this particular good consists of *in reality*.[10] In the *Republic*, Plato's suggested solution to value disagreements is the meditation of Ideas. But is our knowledge of Ideas more secure?

Plato's imagined republic reflects the human soul's ideal condition: the rational part of the soul rules over the irrational part. In like manner, society's lower classes behave rationally when they submit themselves to the upper classes, and the upper classes are rational when they rule wisely over the lower classes.[11] The utopian state is needed to educate people in the right way; namely, if people are subjected to a substandard moral environment in their youth, it is almost impossible to correct them later. As an example of perfection, Plato envisions an ideal judge who has not been familiarized with crimes in his youth, but who "should have learned to know evil, not from his own soul, but from late and long observation of the nature of evil in others."[12]

Plato has no rosy view of humanity.[13] Truth is easily corrupted, and human nature is prone to go astray if not properly tutored. This leads him to create a utopian (and totalitarian) state, which enables humans to achieve harmony and happiness (*eudaimonia*). Plato argues that conflicts typically arise in situations when there is some question of ownership. As a result, conflicts can be avoided by removing standard family structures and private property. This radical reorganization of social life should lead to equitable treatment. However, the sense of ownership extends to one's own body and makes the complete uprooting of the notion of the private (*idion*) impossible. Here we face the crucial moment in Plato's theory, summarized by Martha Nussbaum: "For the body is not only the biggest obstacle to stable life and to

---

far as their nature allows them to be subjected to art, either for the purpose of teaching or persuading—such is the view implied in the preceding argument."

10. White, "Plato's Metaphysical Epistemology," 297. For examples, see *Republic* 583b–586e; *Theatetus* 170a–c.

11. Plato, *Republic* 431a.

12. Plato, *Republic* 409b.

13. And his opinion becomes even grimmer in his later dialogues. Although the *Republic* is taken to be Plato's major political work, his belief in the possibility of good rule by philosopher-kings diminishes in his later thought and is replaced by immutable laws, formulated by philosophers. See *Laws* 874e–875d. See also George Klosko, "Plato's Political Philosophy," in *The Routledge Companion to Social and Political Philosophy*, ed. Gerald Gaus and Fred D'Agostino (London: Routledge, 2013), 10–12.

true evaluation; it is also the most dangerous source of conflict, and therefore the biggest obstacle to impartial and harmonious civic justice."[14]

It is not only the commoners who suffer from their bodily restrictions; philosophers are subject to it as well. In Plato's utopian state, philosophers rule the other classes, who willingly submit themselves to philosophers' tutelage. For this reason, philosophers cannot have any private property either; honor is their only salary. However, other classes do not easily yield to philosophers' rule. Even if philosophical knowledge is available for all, it is easily lost, and it cannot be promulgated to the society as a whole if the correct system, namely, a utopian state, is not in place.

Plato senses that even philosophers can become corrupt, which consequently makes it harder to use the Ideas as the starting point from which to start intellectual enquiry.[15] This underscores the fragility of his utopian state, and eventually leads him to conclude that such a state will never come into being. Instead, we should strive for the *Republic*'s ideals without the state's support. Even in the less-than-ideal state, it is the philosophers' task to enter the cave they have left behind and educate the cave dwellers.[16]

Plato offers several enduring pieces of advice on managing disagreement in our time. The rhetoricians are still among us and continue to lead people in multiple directions. However, the means of bringing the desired state about are not well suited for contemporary democracies. For Plato, politics is not about coming together from different backgrounds and trying to find a common way; the common people have nothing worthwhile to say. Knowledge is restricted to the philosophical elite. Plato's state is an intellectual aristocracy, which, sadly, is not able to secure its own internal consensus, as the later history of philosophy demonstrates, and which Plato himself also anticipates.

14. Martha Nussbaum, *The Fragility of Goodness: Luck and Ethics in Greek Tragedy and Philosophy* (Cambridge: Cambridge University Press, 1986), 160.

15. Jason Xenasis ("Plato on Ethical Disagreement," *Phronesis* 1 [1955], 50–57) has suggested that Plato offers a hierarchy of criteria, which helps navigate among different judgments. In *Philebus* 66a–c, there appears a set of desiderata in which five goods appear in a particular order. These are, first, right measure and moderation; second, beauty and adequateness; third, practical wisdom; fourth, science and skills; and finally, "painless" pleasures. Xenasis argues that the Platonic hierarchy is superior to "horizontal" commandments, such as the Decalogue, where all commandments have equal value and can thus mutually contradict each other. However, one must ask, do not the vertical and hierarchical systems suffer from different kinds of problems? In our technological age, why should we favor practical reason or beauty over effectiveness? Who tells us which one of two beautiful things is more desirable? What is the correct measure of moderation, and so on?

16. Plato, *Republic* 591e–592b; 520b–d.

Aristotle

Aristotle follows the basic division of the parts of the soul that was assumed in Plato's Academy. According to Aristotle, the human soul consists of three parts: vegetative, appetitive or animal, and rational. The vegetative soul joins us together with the world of nature, and it does not actually have an effect on our actions. The animal soul is responsible for those actions that we have in common with living beings, such as sensations, desires, and emotions. The properly human part is the rational soul, and it is divided into theoretical and calculative parts. The theoretical part deals with scientific reasoning, while the calculative part determines which actions we should perform.[17]

An action (and the person who performs it) can be regarded as good when the rational and appetitive parts work together harmoniously so that the action resonates with the particular good that is the action's goal.[18] If the calculative part does not rule over the appetitive part, the person in question behaves like an animal driven by its involuntary desires.

How, then, does the person engage with the world in a rational way? Aristotle's philosophy of mind is simple and even optimistic: the world appears to the observer simply as it is. The standard model of Aristotelian knowledge acquisition operates with the following sequence: sense perception, apprehension of single essences, and discursive reasoning. The central notion in any act of perception is the intelligible species (*species intelligibilis*), or the "secondary form." The classic passage in Aristotle's *De anima* reads as follows:

> In general, with regard to all sense-perception, we must take it that the sense is that which can receive perceptible forms without their matter, as wax receives the imprint of the ring without the iron or gold, and it takes the imprint which is of gold or bronze, but not *qua* gold or bronze.[19]

This species (*eidos, forma*), or form,[20] was taken to be something that is present in the soul of the observer; that is to say, this species somehow shapes the intellect so that they share the same form with the object.[21] This makes

---

17. Aristotle, *Nicomachean Ethics* 1102a26–1103a1.

18. 1139a22–35.

19. Aristotle, *De anima*, trans. D. W. Hamlyn (Oxford: Clarendon, 1968), 424a17–a20.

20. The Greek word *eidos* can be translated both as "species" and "form."

21. See Leen Spruit, *Species Intelligibilis: From Perception to Knowledge*, vol. 1, *Classical Roots and Medieval Discussions* (Leiden: Brill, 1994), 37–38, 45–46. Aristotle, *De anima* 429a13–17.

knowledge acquisition sound easy. Aristotle's view is more optimistic than Plato's, as he thinks that humans are generally well equipped to perceive reality as it is. The world's weight on our shoulders is so overwhelming that it necessarily pushes us in the right direction. Perception, however, is not without obstacles, and this apparent simplicity should not lead us to think that knowledge acquisition is free from errors.

In addition to appearances (*phainomena*), our knowledge is based on "credible, received opinions" (*endoxa*). *Endoxa* is a central Aristotelian epistemological concept that has recently received scholarly attention, and it has been suggested that instead of being an uncomplicated empiricist, Aristotle might be part constructivist.[22] Aristotle goes to great lengths to argue that *endoxa* are to be taken seriously in knowledge acquisition, as appearances can be deceiving, which may lead to puzzlement (*aporia*).

> As in other cases, we must set out the appearances [*phainomena*] and run through all the puzzles regarding them. In this way we must prove the credible opinions [*endoxa*] about these sorts of experiences—ideally, all the credible opinions, but if not all, then most of them, those which are the most important. For if the objections are answered and the credible opinions remain, we shall have an adequate proof.[23]

In other words, Aristotle aims at collecting together all respectable opinions about the disputed matter and representing them in a way that does justice to diverse opinions. This demonstrates how every perspective has intrinsic value in the ongoing process that aims toward greater truth.[24] Nicholas Denyer sums up Aristotle's method for overcoming disagreements aptly:

> We thus assemble into a systematic and harmonious synthesis as much as possible of the opinions and impressions with which we began. This synthesis will incorporate all the insights that anyone has ever had on the subject, and yet be free of all their errors. The idea is that truth will survive the dialectical process that results in this synthesis, whereas falsehood cannot. And because all parties will be able to recognise in this synthesis a statement of the truth that they were getting at, and an

22. See, e.g., Ekaterina Haskins, "Endoxa, Epistemological Optimism, and Aristotle's Rhetorical Project," *Philosophy and Rhetoric* 37 (2004).

23. Aristotle, *Nicomachean Ethics*, trans. J. A. K. Thomson (London: Penguin, 1955), 1145b2–7.

24. Aristotle, *Nicomachean Ethics* 1154a22–25.

explanation of any falsehoods into which they might have lapsed, this synthesis should command universal assent. It will have something of the authority over us of a treaty negotiated by the good offices of a master diplomat: everybody will be able to recognise that the synthesis has done justice to everybody's legitimate concerns. And finally, once we have reached such a synthesis, our investigations need go no further. The synthesis will provide an account of our subject matter that is correct, complete, and justified.[25]

Ekaterina Haskins concludes that Aristotle makes the "human race as a whole the measure of how things are absolutely."[26] Here Aristotle's philosophy of mind comes again to the fore; if the individual soul mirrors the world, how much greater is the power of all human souls working together? Yet he still holds an appreciation for the value of the "wise" (*phronimoi*) in contrast to ordinary people.[27] This effectively sets Aristotle against the strongest constructivist readings. In *Topics*, he defines *endoxa* as "the things believed by everyone or by most people or by the wise (and among the wise by all or by most or by those most known and commonly recognized)."[28] Disagreements are thus resolvable, given enough time, through common reasoning.

Aristotle's teleological reading of nature and his political theory, which stresses humanity's natural inclination to form stable communities, is the scaffolding that supports his optimistic view. While Plato seeks maximal unity within the state based on the destruction of ownership and the rule of philosopher-kings, Aristotle thinks that seeking this kind of unity is against the nature of both polis and humanity. Societies are inherently plural since their citizens are plural. We must learn to live with that fact unless we want to obliterate politics altogether.[29]

25. Nicholas Denyer, *Language, Thought and Falsehood in Ancient Greek Philosophy* (London: Routledge, 1990), 210.

26. Haskins, "Endoxa, Epistemological Optimism, and Aristotle's Rhetorical Project," 5–6.

27. Nussbaum, *Fragility of Goodness*, 261; Carrie-Ann Biondi Khan, "Aristotle's Moral Expert: The *Phronimos*," in *Ethics Expertise: History, Contemporary Perspectives and Applications*, ed. Lisa Rasmussen (Dordrecht: Springer, 2005), 39–53.

28. Aristotle, *Topics*, 100b20. Quoted from Aristotle, *Introductory Readings*, trans. Terence Irwin (Indianapolis: Hackett Publishing, 1966).

29. Aristotle, *Politics*, trans. Benjamin Jowett (Blacksburg: Virginia Tech, 2001), 1261a1–34: "We ought not to attain this greatest unity even if we could, for it would be the destruction of the state. Again, a state is not made up only of so many men, but of different kinds of men."

Aristotle also criticizes Plato's suggestion that conflicts are a result of structural elements that make people do bad or unwise things. Against this view, Aristotle points out that it is not necessarily structural inequality that drives people to become highwaymen but their inordinate desires that seek pleasure.[30] Thus Aristotle more strongly emphasizes individual duties toward other citizens than Plato does in the *Republic*: it is up to each one to strive to become a moral person, regardless of external circumstances.

1.2. Varieties of Goodness: Augustine and Aquinas

Augustine

For Augustine, the question of disagreement arose naturally at several junctures in his intellectual life. In his convoluted journey from Manichaeanism to Catholic Christianity, he experienced various ruptures with the traditions he was engaged in. Most notably, on several occasions Augustine ponders the fact that philosophers continue to disagree with each other while they claim that the use of reason will lead them to truth.[31] In the early phase of his career, he tackled the skeptical challenge in his *Contra Academicos*, where he steers away from skepticism by demonstrating that it leads to performative contradictions: in order to doubt, you must know.[32] The same problem took

---

30. Aristotle, *Politics* 1267a4–5.

31. See, e.g., Augustine, *Civ.* 4.8–32; 8.1–4. Augustine's account of Socrates in *Civ.* 8.3 is illustrative: "Both in his life and in his death, Socrates left very many disciples of his philosophy, who vied with one another in desire for proficiency in handling those moral questions which concern the chief good [*summum bonum*], the possession of which can make a man blessed; and because, in the disputations of Socrates, where he raises all manner of questions, makes assertions, and then demolishes them, it did not evidently appear what he held to be the chief good, every one took from these disputations what pleased him best, and every one placed the final good in whatever it appeared to himself to consist. Now, that which is called the final good is that at which, when one has arrived, he is blessed. But so diverse were the opinions held by those followers of Socrates concerning this final good, that (a thing scarcely to be credited with respect to the followers of one master) some placed the chief good in pleasure, as Aristippus, others in virtue, as Antisthenes. Indeed, it were tedious to recount the various opinions of various disciples" (all translations of *De civitate Dei* are from Augustine, *The City of God*, in *A Select Library of Nicene and Post-Nicene Fathers of the Church*, vol. 2, series 1, *St. Augustin's "City of God" and "Christian Doctrine,"* ed. Philip Schaff, trans. Marcus Dods [1886–1889; repr., Peabody, MA: Hendrickson, 1994]).

32. Augustine, *Acad.* 151. An example of philosophical skepticism was Sextus Empiricus (fl. second/third century), whose *Outlines of Pyrrhonism* has had a significant impact in later

form within the church in bitter controversies with the Donatists: Why did these apparently sincere people refuse to follow what Augustine perceived to be the legitimate form of church government?

Paul J. Griffiths sees two reasons why Augustine thinks our reasoning often leads us astray.[33] First, we might not be adequately catechized; that is to say, we do not have enough knowledge about the matter, which makes us unable to properly understand the issue at hand. Second, our depraved will prevents us from even wanting to know the truth. Let us take a closer look at each of these points.

In *Enchiridion*, Augustine acknowledges that is it simply impossible for us to avoid ignorance, which is one of the main sources of error.[34] In *De catechizandis rudibus* he approaches the problem from the viewpoint of semantics. Why do we feel bored when we teach about things that should be wonderful and set our hearts on fire? Surely, if the teacher is not passionate, the listeners will find the material uninteresting. Augustine offers the following explanation. The words used to teach are already two steps removed from the subject being taught. The divine truth has been illumined and realized in the teacher's mind (step one), and it is being communicated to the hearers through words (step two). This distance from the thing being taught understandably results in a lack of interest.[35] As a result, in Augustine's theological epistemology, words and proofs become largely irrelevant. Words are pointers toward something that they do not essentially contain. Consequently, merely hearing the words is not going to help anyone if one does not already know what the words signify. The one reading Scripture needs to be illumined by God *before* reading, otherwise one's understanding is destined to be erroneous.[36]

In *De doctrina Christiana*, Augustine explains that some signs are natural. In the case of sensing smoke, for example, we take it to mean there's fire

---

Western philosophy, especially during the Renaissance, when his works were rediscovered. Sextus suggests that for every philosophical point argued, one can find equally good reasons to oppose it. Therefore one should not form beliefs about matters that are contested in this way, but should suspend one's judgment. This leads to tranquility (*ataraxia*), which frees the person from troubling thoughts and consequent anxiety. On Augustine and the skeptical tradition, see Phillip Cary, *Outward Signs: The Powerlessness of External Things in Augustine's Thought* (Oxford: Oxford University Press, 2008), 39–55.

33. Paul J. Griffiths, "How Reasoning Goes Wrong: A Quasi-Augustinian Account of Error and Its Implications," in *Reason and the Reasons of Faith*, ed. Paul J. Griffiths and Reinhard Hütter (New York: T&T Clark, 2005), 145–59.

34. Augustine, *Enchir.* 5.17.

35. Augustine, *Catech.* 3. See Cary, *Outward Signs*, 11.

36. Cary, *Outward Signs*, 102–5.

somewhere. However, some signs are given, rather than natural, and therefore ambiguous. This pertains to the names of things that conscious beings use to communicate with each other.[37] Interestingly, Augustine expands the ambiguous nature of sign-giving to God's revelation as well, claiming that "even the divinely given signs contained in the holy scriptures have been communicated to us by the human beings who wrote them."[38] Thus signs are not the same in every context. Augustine refers to the tower of Babel as a sign of artificial unity, which was torn down in order to cure humans of their pride: "Wicked men justly received incompatible languages to match their incompatible minds."[39] Consequently, even the reading of the Scriptures inevitably leads to disagreement. But Augustine sees a divine plan behind this: Exertion and toil in interpretation is good for humans as it cures their souls of harmful attitudes.

> Casual readers are misled by problems and ambiguities of many kinds, mistaking one thing for another. In some passages they find no meaning at all that they can grasp at, even falsely, so thick is the fog created by some obscure phrases. I have no doubt that this is all divinely predetermined, so that pride may be subdued by hard work and intellects which tend to despise things that are easily discovered may be rescued from boredom and reinvigorated.[40]

But sometimes the increase of knowledge as such is not enough, as is evident in the case of mutually disagreeing philosophers. At this point of history, Augustine is already wrestling with substantial philosophical traditions. The novelty that he introduces to the ancient theory of knowledge is the role of love and sin in decision-making. According to some later Stoics, our scattered actions and convictions result from the weakness of our will (*akrasia*), but for Augustine this is not enough to explain the widespread disagreements among equally intelligent thinkers. The analysis of will, as provided by the ancients, does not penetrate deep enough. It is not only what we want but also what we love or hate that directs our course of action.

37. Augustine, *Doctr. chr.* 2.1–15. Numbering and all translations for *De doctrina Christiana* are from Saint Augustine, *On Christian Teaching*, trans. R. P. H. Green (Oxford: Oxford University Press, 1997).

38. Augustine, *Doctr. chr.* 2.3.

39. Augustine, *Doctr. chr.* 2.8.

40. *Doctr. chr.* 2.10. Augustine also makes similar claims in *Doctr. chr.* 4.27; *Ep.* 55.11.21; *Ep.* 137.18.

Our actions are teleological, formed by our loves, which aim for some ulti-mate end.[41] Consequently societies are formed by shared love among their members.[42] This emphasis on will and love gives Augustine's social theory a special twist: perverted love creates disagreement, and purified love, unity. In *Confessions*, Augustine writes:

> For just as in violent acts, if the emotion of the soul from whence the violent impulse springs is depraved and asserts itself insolently and mu-tinously—and just as in the acts of passion, if the affection of the soul which gives rise to carnal desires is unrestrained—so also, in the same way, errors and false opinions contaminate life if the rational soul itself is depraved. Thus it was then with me, for I was ignorant that my soul had to be enlightened by another light, if it was to be partaker of the truth, since it is not itself the essence of truth.[43]

In this way, Augustine introduces explicitly religious considerations. If we were to follow the advice of philosophers, we should be able to bring about a state of harmony by using our reason alone. But observing their arguments and conclusions only leads to mutually excluding positions. This disagree-ment Augustine takes to be a result of inner convictions that connect indi-viduals with higher ends.[44]

Augustine thus is aligned closer with Plato than Aristotle: an optimis-tic right method and an optimistic view of human knowledge-acquisition skills are not going to resolve all disagreement. However, he does not follow Plato's utopian ideals, and is rather pessimistic regarding the possibility of a long-lasting state of harmony because of the perverted order of love, which cannot be fully mended in this life.[45] This does not mean, however, that

41. For a detailed treatment, see Luigi Gioia, *The Theological Epistemology of Augustine's "De Trinitate"* (Oxford: Oxford University Press, 2008), 190–218; John Rist, "Faith and Rea-son," in *The Cambridge Companion to Augustine*, ed. Norman Kretzman and Eleonore Stump (Cambridge: Cambridge University Press, 2001), 32–37; Risto Saarinen, *Weakness of the Will in Medieval Thought: From Augustine to Buridan* (Leiden: Brill, 1994), 20–43; Timo Nisula, *Augustine and the Functions of Concupiscence* (Leiden: Brill, 2012).

42. Augustine, *Civ.* 19.24.

43. Augustine, *Confessions*, trans. Albert C. Outler (1955; repr., New York: Barnes & Noble Classics, 2007), 4.15.25.

44. For a brief exposition on how will functions in the decision-making process, see Griffiths, "How Reasoning Goes Wrong," 154–57.

45. For detailed, and various, accounts of Augustine's political vision, see Eric Gregory, *Politics and the Order of Love* (Chicago: University of Chicago Press, 2010), 75–125, 363–84;

attempts at reconciliation are futile. With proper instruction things can be changed. In *De Doctrina Christiana*, for example, Augustine offers an amusing anecdote.

> I was once appealing to the people in Caesarea of Mauretania to abandon their civil strife, or rather that conflict worse than civil strife which they called *caterva*, in which regularly at a particular time of the year not merely citizens, but even close relatives, brothers, and even parents and sons used to split into opposing gangs and fight with stones continuously for several days, slaughtering whomever they could. I spoke, to the best of my ability, in the grand style, in order to eradicate and eliminate such a cruel and chronic evil from their hearts and their habits by my words. I did not think that I had achieved anything when I heard them applaud, but only when I saw them in tears. Their applause showed that they were receiving instruction and experiencing delight; their tears that they were moved. It was when I saw this—and before they showed it in their actions—that I believed that this brutal practice, inherited from their fathers and grandfathers and remoter ancestors, which so fatally obsessed, or rather possessed, their hearts, had been overcome. Quickly finishing my speech, I occupied their hearts and mouths in giving thanks to God.[46]

These momentary glimpses of peace are set in context in *De civitate Dei*, where Augustine draws a picture of two cities, earthly and heavenly. Almost in Heraclitean tones, he depicts how these cities have always been, and always will be, in enmity with each other.[47] The earthly city is characterized by violence and strife: "The society of mortals spread abroad through the earth everywhere, and in the most diverse places, although bound together by a certain fellowship of our common nature, is yet for the most part divided against itself, and the strongest oppress the others, because all

---

Charles Mathewes, *A Theology of Public Life*, Cambridge Studies in Christian Doctrine (Cambridge: Cambridge University Press, 2008); Phillip Cary, "United Inwardly by Love: Augustine's Social Ontology," in *Augustine and Politics*, ed. John Doody, Kevin L. Hughes, and Kim Paffenroth (Lanham, MD: Lexington, 2004), 3–33; John Milbank, *Theology and Social Theory* (Oxford: Blackwell, 1990), 389–92; Nicholas Wolterstorff, *The Mighty and the Almighty: An Essay in Political Theology* (Cambridge: Cambridge University Press, 2012), 35–46.

46. Augustine, *Doctr. chr.* 4.139–40.

47. See the first ten books of *De civitate Dei*, as well as *Civ.* 18.1. However, Augustine rejects metaphysical dualism. See *Civ.* 4.15.24.

follow after their own interests and lusts."[48] In the earthly city, everyone seeks their own happiness, which inevitably leads to conflict. The earthly city can reach the state of peace only through war. This peace is good in itself, as it enables the enjoyment of earthly goods, yet it is ontologically distinct from the heavenly peace that consists of the unity of souls existing in participation with God and experiencing total transparency to each other. In this heavenly state there can be no disagreement, because everyone wills the same thing. Inversely, earthly peace is not based on the unity of will and on a shared object of love, but in the fear of punishment. Nevertheless, this peace is worth pursuing even if it is not perfect.[49]

Earthly peace is always contingent and fragile. Members of the heavenly city can share this peace as long as they do not have to compromise their faith and loyalty to the heavenly city. In this life they share the eternal peace only by faith. In the next life, this peace will be perfected as our wills will be conjoined in harmony with the divine will, which makes conflicts cease once and for all.[50]

Thomas Aquinas

In order to examine what Aquinas has to say about disagreement, we need to first explain how he perceives human cognitive processes. Aquinas's theory of judgment and action is deeply nuanced, and it changes throughout the

---

48. Augustine, *Civ.* 18.2.

49. Cary, "Inwardly United," 30–33. Augustine, *Civ.* 15.4: "But the things which this city desires cannot justly be said to be evil, for it is itself, in its own kind, better than all other human good. For it desires earthly peace for the sake of enjoying earthly goods, and it makes war in order to attain to this peace; since, if it has conquered, and there remains no one to resist it, it enjoys a peace which it had not while there were opposing parties who contested for the enjoyment of those things which were too small to satisfy both. This peace is purchased by toilsome wars; it is obtained by what they style a glorious victory." See also *Civ.* 19.12.

50. Augustine, *Civ.* 19.17: "Even the heavenly city, therefore, while in its state of pilgrimage, avails itself of the peace of earth, and, so far as it can without injuring faith and godliness, desires and maintains a common agreement among men regarding the acquisition of the necessaries of life, and makes this earthly peace bear upon the peace of heaven; for this alone can be truly called and esteemed the peace of the reasonable creatures, consisting as it does in the perfectly ordered and harmonious enjoyment of God and of one another in God. When we shall have reached that peace, this mortal life shall give place to one that is eternal, and our body shall be no more this animal body which by its corruption weighs down the soul, but a spiritual body feeling no want, and in all its members subjected to the will."

Summa theologiae's volumes. I do not hope to offer a complete overview of this issue, but instead try to concentrate on the essentials.

Aquinas adopts a broadly Aristotelian theory of cognition: knowledge is based on the forms of objects present in one's soul. More detailed exposition of this theory of action reveals the complexities of knowledge acquisition. In Aquinas's philosophy of mind, action is performed as follows: First, a sense experience evokes a desire. Desires have a cognitive component that makes them processable by the will and, consequently, by reason. The will, having experienced a desire, asks reason for guidance: is this apparent good a genuine good? Then reason, based on its acquired notion of goodness and happiness, either affirms or denies the will's proposal. The will is ultimately dependent on reason and its evaluations of what is good and promotes happiness. If reason does not have the correct understanding of the good, it leads us astray.[51] In this way, intellect and will work together and are interrelated.[52]

According to Aquinas, reality, as God's creation, is a harmonious unity. Like Aristotle, Aquinas believes the world is presented to us as it is, and the problem of radical skepticism does not appear to him as a real problem that needs addressing. Additionally, there is no conflict between faith and reason. Even if he recognizes the real possibility of superficial conflict, for Aquinas there can be no real, irresolvable value-judgment conflicts.[53]

Value judgments are based on the knowledge of first principles, which are abstract, action-guiding propositions, such as "good must be done and evil avoided."[54] First principles are both immediate and indemonstrable. By this Aquinas means that when one encounters first principles, one immediately understands that they are necessarily and universally true; their falsehood is incomprehensible. Even if first principles are in principle knowable to all, it is not necessary that everyone in fact is able to know them. For in-

51. *ST* I.82.2; 85.6 See also Eleonore Stump, *Aquinas* (London: Routledge, 2013), 233. Jean Porter, *Nature as Reason* (Grand Rapids: Eerdmans, 2005), 255–57; Alasdair MacIntyre, "Aquinas and the Extent of Moral Disagreement," in *Selected Essays*, vol. 2, *Ethics and Politics* (Cambridge: Cambridge University Press, 2006), 64–84.

52. In *ST* I.82. Aquinas still has intellectualist emphasis: intellect is able to move the will as its final cause. Later in *ST* I-II.9.1 intellect appears as a formal cause, that is to say, it merely presents objects to the will. This moves Aquinas in a more voluntaristic direction. See Reinhard Hütter, "The Directedness of Reasoning and the Metaphysics of Creation," in Griffiths and Hütter, *Reason and the Reasons of Faith*, 174–76; Stump, *Aquinas*, 289–90.

53. For an extensive treatment of various cases of conflict, see Daniel McInerny, *The Difficult Good: A Thomistic Approach to Moral Conflict and Human Happiness* (New York: Fordham University Press, 2006).

54. *ST* I-II.2.94.2.

stance, it is possible to misunderstand the nature of subject and predicate in a given proposition. Disagreeing with first principles is possible if one does not understand what they mean. Additionally, due to the complexity of some issues, it is occasionally difficult to understand the proposition. Some degree of uncertainty remains as a result.[55] In other words, some disagreements are merely due to our limited knowledge and can be resolved through better comprehension of the matter at hand.[56]

55. Scott MacDonald, "Theory of Knowledge," in *The Cambridge Companion to Aquinas*, ed. Norman Kretzman and Eleonore Stump (Cambridge: Cambridge University Press, 1993), 178. *PA* 1.5.7. "To clarify this division it should be noted that any proposition whose predicate is included within the notion of its subject is immediate and known in virtue of itself as it stands. However, in the case of some of these propositions the terms are such that they are understood by everyone, as *being* and *one* and those other notions that are characteristic of being precisely as being: for *being* is the first concept in the intellect. Hence it is necessary that propositions of this kind be held as known in virtue of themselves not only as they stand but also in reference to us. Examples of these are the propositions that 'It does not occur that the same thing is and is not,' and that 'The whole is greater than its part,' and others like these. Hence all the sciences take principles of this kind from metaphysics, whose task it is to consider being absolutely and the characteristics of being. On the other hand, there are some immediate propositions whose terms are not known by everyone. Hence, although their predicate may be included in the very notion of their subject, yet because the definition of the subject is not known to everyone, it is not necessary that such propositions be conceded by everyone. (Thus the proposition, 'All right angles are equal,' is in itself a proposition which is immediate and known in virtue of itself, because equality appears in the definition of a right angle. For a right angle is one which a straight line forms when it meets another straight line in such a way that the angles on each side are equal.) Therefore, such principles are received as being posited or laid down" (translation from Thomas Aquinas, *Commentary on the "Posterior Analytics" of Aristotle*, trans. Fabian R. Larcher, OP [Albany, NY: Magi Books, 1970]).

56. It is well known that medieval schools and individual thinkers occasionally disagreed with each other. Novel views or those that contradicted prevailing orthodoxy were typically treated with iron gloves. For a good overview on how differing views were handled in general, see Robert Pasnau, *Metaphysical Themes, 1274–1671* (New York: Oxford University Press, 2011), 428–58. One clear exception was Nicholas of Autrecourt's *Tractatus*, which tried to lay out some rules on how to deal with disagreements. Pasnau explains (*Metaphysical Themes*, 447–48): "[Autrecourt's] first step is to offer a general rule for the conditions under which it is permissible to offer a new doctrine that clashes with the majority view. The rule is that if someone grasps all the concepts pertinent to some question as well as does the majority, and also clearly grasps further concepts that permit one to see more into the truth of that question, then one can 'without presumption' and 'with sufficient certitude' reach conclusions contrary to the majority. As an example he describes how the majority of young men abandon the intellectual virtues in pursuit of riches, honors, and carnal pleasures. What is one to do in the light of how the majority conduct themselves? Should one reason that the majority is likely to know best? Of course not—instead, one should follow the rule just described, and reason

According to Aquinas, the sin's presence in the soul does not alter the basic functions of the intellect; it continues to apprehend reality in a reliable manner. But while sin does not affect reason's basic cognitive function, it can turn reason away from the highest good, and this may lead reason to perform various errors, listed below, which are also potential causes of disagreement.

First, reason may not comprehend how particular knowledge or action can be accidentally linked to evil. This can be the case when we seek knowledge to learn something in order to sin, or we are unable to see the true nature of our actions; for example, when one desires something and is unable to weigh the proper consequences of the actions that satisfy the desire. Second, our appetite for knowledge can be inordinate, which can lead, for example, to acquiring knowledge through illicit means. Third, we may want to know things that exceed our capacity, and this can lead us to err. Most serious, however, is knowledge acquisition that is unable to relate itself to the highest good, that is, God.[57] Aquinas states that the corruption of *theoria* is possible "when a man desires to know the truth about creatures, without referring his knowledge to its due end, namely, the knowledge of God. Hence, Augustine says (*De Vera Relig.* 29) that 'in studying creatures, we must not be moved by empty and perishable curiosity; but we should ever mount toward immortal and abiding things.'"[58]

But why is disregarding God, or the ultimate order of things, in knowledge acquisition so serious? Aquinas links his answer to the hierarchy of goods. If God is not loved above everything else, and all other good things in relation to the supreme good, the goodness of these created things is lost because our desires do not conform to reality. In other words, we perceive

---

that one sees perfectly well what the attraction of these sensual pleasures is, and has further concepts as well, regarding 'the good that lies in the contemplation of God and in the use of the moral virtues.' This makes it permissible to ignore the masses, and follow one's own, superior judgment. Autrecourt quickly clarifies that he does not mean to apply this rule to himself: he claims no such superiority in grasping philosophical concepts. But there is a second rule that applies to his own case. If someone develops unorthodox ideas in some domain, and if that person discusses these ideas with others of good judgment, and if that person deliberates for a long time about these ideas, and they continue to seem correct, 'then he can and should—especially in merely speculative matters—reveal faithfully his view and set out his claims [not] as true, but so that his view may be considered in light of these claims.'" However, Autrecourt's advice was not well received, and in 1347 he was required to burn his writings.

57. This list is given by Hütter ("Directedness of Reasoning," 180–82), who comments here on *ST* II-II.167.1 (On Curiosity).

58. *ST* II-II.167.Resp.

the reality in a truncated or false way. Depending on the case, this may lead to harmless miscalculations or, in the worst case, harm to one's soul.[59]

Alasdair MacIntyre discusses this problem in relation to the nature of philosophical enquiry from a broadly Thomistic perspective.[60] Philosophy is in constant danger of committing two opposite vices. On the one hand, it is possible to proceed in one's enquiry in a piecemeal fashion so that the examined topics remain disconnected from other bodies of knowledge. This MacIntyre calls the "analytical vice." On the other hand, we are in danger of committing the "idealist vice" when we gloss over the difficulties in our grand system that could possibly challenge it. Both these vices are problematic because they inevitably hinder knowledge acquisition and make it more difficult to ask proper philosophical questions about the nature of the human good. For Aquinas, these questions cannot be answered properly without the inclusion of God within the hierarchy of goods.

Based on the above, we can see how disagreement can be both a result of our limited cognition (when we are not culpable in a real sense) and our distorted will that follows the wrong order of love. For Aquinas, disagreement is realized when we lack adequate knowledge or when our love directs either our reason or our will toward an end that is not the highest good.[61]

But let us return to first principles. The first, nonspeculative principles function as the primary precepts of natural law.[62] The primary precepts are the same for everyone: unchanging, self-evident, and, in principle, known to all. The knowledge of first principles can never be undone from the human heart. However, as already noted, these precepts include only very basic principles, such as "good is to be done, and evil avoided." But if knowledge of the first principles is so pervasive, why do we quarrel about beliefs and morals?

---

59. Aquinas, however, thinks that people who do not have faith are able to perform genuine virtues, whereas Augustine thinks that pagan virtues are only splendid vices. Augustine thus has the more pessimistic view of human performance than Aquinas. For discussion, see Jennifer Herdt, *Putting on Virtue: The Legacy of the Splendid Vices* (Chicago: University of Chicago Press, 2008).

60. Alasdair MacIntyre, "Philosophy Recalled to Its Tasks: A Thomistic Reading of 'Fides et Ratio,'" in *Selected Essays*, vol. 1, *The Tasks of Philosophy* (Cambridge: Cambridge University Press, 2006), 180–82. See also MacIntyre, *God, Philosophy, Universities: A Selective History of the Catholic Philosophical Tradition* (London: Continuum, 2009), 175.

61. Given that Aquinas's theory of knowledge is so optimistic, Stump (*Aquinas*, 234) argues that "error, deception, and false opinion have to be explained as either guilt or punishment." In the original state, Adam could not err (and thus there could be no disagreements either). After the fall, disagreement can be seen as a form of punishment.

62. *ST* Ia-IIae.94.

Things get murky when first principles are applied to particular situations. Although primary principles are universal, their application always takes place in a cultural setting, which gives them a certain shape. Furthermore, we may lack adequate experience and knowledge, or practical wisdom (*phronē-sis*), which could guide our judgment.[63]

The notion was explained earlier that happiness gives direction to reason and will. Aquinas readily acknowledges that it is possible to define good and happiness in manifold ways. In the *Summa theologiae*, he lists as possible candidates things such as wealth, honor, fame, glory, power, bodily or spiritual goods, and pleasure.[64] If any of these is taken as the goal of one's actions, a particular way of life follows, where actions, moral deliberation, and preferences resonate with the respective ultimate goal. It is easy to see how this gives rise to conflicts.[65] In his defense of Aquinas's natural law theory, MacIntyre offers several ways to adjudicate between various goods and reach for agreement, which includes spelling out in more detail the central beliefs about human nature and ultimate value and so on.[66] (These suggestions will be discussed later in this book.) However, he concedes that even with Aquinas's lights, we should not expect "reasonable" discussion to lead inevitably to agreement.

1.3. Method Men: Bacon and Descartes

The chaotic state of late medieval philosophy and the Protestant Reformation disrupted the fragile and superficial consensus of the early sixteenth century, and a new search for sure foundations was launched. From Francis Bacon's *New Organon* through René Descartes's *Meditations* to Locke's praise of "reasonability," the hearts of the philosophers were filled with the hope that we would soon possess the necessary tools for determining the foundations of the universe.

In the seventeenth century, Western civilization had to face the reality of disagreement in multiple spheres of life. The New World had been "dis-

---

63. MacIntyre, "Aquinas," 65–67.

64. *ST* I-II.2. Of course, Aquinas denies that these are genuine definitions of happiness, even if they can be regarded as good things per se if they are in proper relation to the ultimate good.

65. MacIntyre, "Aquinas," 71.

66. Aquinas himself does not offer a single solution for how to solve actual disagreement. Instead, depending on the case, disagreements should be solved by individuals' own judgment, or by rulers or ecclesial authority's command.

covered" one hundred years earlier, and the knowledge of other civilizations and religions had become an accepted fact. Martin Luther had opened the spiritual Pandora's box, and new ways of practicing faith were introduced everywhere in Europe. The Scientific Revolution was already underway. Change was in the air, but how to ensure that this change was for the better?

Francis Bacon

Shortly after the Thirty Years' War began, Francis Bacon (1561–1626) published a programmatic treatise, *The New Organon* (1620), which laid out the plan for the renewal of science and philosophy. Looking back at the history of science, Bacon sees only philosophers waging war against each other. Bacon was distrustful of "pure" reason; he sought a more trustworthy method. After the fall, humankind's epistemic abilities were marred (along with a host of other deleterious effects within creation). What was needed was not a haughty reliance on mere reason, but a method producing knowledge that could be taken up as a communal enterprise successively transmitted from one generation to another. In *The Great Instauration*, Bacon locates the problem in the human mind's limitations, which will continue to lead us into errors if something radical is not done.[67]

> Now that the errors which have hitherto prevailed, and which will prevail for ever, should (if the mind be left to go its own way) either by the natural force of the understanding or by help of the aids and instruments of logic, one by one, correct themselves, was a thing not to be hoped for, because the primary notions of things which the mind readily and passively imbibes, stores up, and accumulates (and it is from them that all the rest flow) are false, confused, and overhastily abstracted from the facts; nor are the secondary and subsequent notions less arbitrary and inconstant; whence it follows that the entire fabric of human reason which we employ in the inquisition of nature is badly put together and built up, and like some magnificent structure without any foundation.[68]

67. Bacon's *Advancement of Learning* (1605), however, is an earlier and more comprehensive (yet less known) vision than *Organon*, and the first major work in which he lays out the outline for the renewal of science and philosophy.

68. Francis Bacon, *The Great Instauration*, in *Selected Philosophical Works*, ed. Rose-Mary Sargent (Indianapolis: Hackett, 1999), 66. All following in-text references in this section are page numbers to this edition.

Bacon takes the human soul to be a thoroughly corrupted instrument, fundamentally damaged by Adam's fall from what was humanity's original righteousness. The fall had a profound effect on human cognitive powers: unaided, human senses are not trustworthy. Our limited condition leads us to misperceive reality; even if we perceive something correctly, we do not necessarily understand it properly (*Great Instauration*, 79).[69] Nor is the intellect free from sin. This is proved by the incompetence of ancient philosophers and schoolmen. Bacon laments that "formerly there existed among philosophers such great disagreement, and such diversities in the schools themselves, a fact which sufficiently shows that the road from the senses to the understanding was not skillfully laid out, when the same groundwork of philosophy (the nature of things to wit) was torn and split up into such vague and multifarious errors" (*New Organon*, 114). The rule of philosophy over science leads to a sad state, in which "what is now done in the matter of science there is only a whirling round about, and perpetual agitation, ending where it began" (*Great Instauration*, 66–67). Bacon uses colorful, sexual imagery to prove the infertility of philosophy, as he claims that the knowledge of Greeks "is but like the boyhood of knowledge, and has the characteristic property of boys: it can talk, but it cannot generate, for it is fruitful of controversies but barren of works" (*Great Instauration*, 69). He also likens philosophy to Scylla, who had the face of a virgin but in the place of a womb she had heads of horrible monsters. Respectively, "when they [philosophers] should produce fruit and works, then arise contentions and barking disputations, which are the end of the matter and all the issue they can yield" (*Great Instauration*, 69).

Bacon's most well-known image is of four idols that lead people astray: the idols of the tribe, idols of the cave, idols of the marketplace, and idols of the theater (*New Organon*, 95–108). The idols of the tribe are habitual inclinations to make false inferences. The human mind is "like a false mirror, which, receiving rays irregularly, distorts and discolors the nature of things by mingling its own nature with it" (*New Organon*, 96). Such things as imagination, emotions, irrational will, and lack of conscientiousness impede our reasoning.

The idols of the cave are limitations that result from one's personal perspective and location in the world. Each of us has our own background,

---

69. Bacon, *Selected Philosophical Writings*. See also Peter Harrison, "Original Sin and the Problem of Knowledge in Early Modern Europe," *Journal of the History of Ideas* 63 (2002): 171–72.

experiences, and education, all of which narrow and fix our gaze on certain things. The idols of the marketplace are weaknesses of human language. By this Bacon means that we can use words that have no real meaning, or more precisely, we cannot fix the meaning of the words through empirical means. These "lead men away into numberless empty controversies and idle fancies" (*New Organon*, 96). These three idols are our natural companions, and it is hard to resist their power over us. However, we can fight the fourth idol, the idols of theater, which refers to false authorities. First and foremost, these are philosophical systems, which in one way or another shackle our thoughts.

The suggested cure for this malaise is the introduction of *method*. Bacon characterizes philosophers as spiders who do not create new knowledge but only restructure the old, and contemporary scientists as ants who collect knowledge but lack the overall picture. The ideal mode of inquiry is that of bees, who both collect knowledge and structure it (*New Organon*, 128). Bacon goes on to argue that instead of seeking valid proofs through deductive syllogisms, we should employ induction, which progressively directs us nearer the truth. Other instruments that Bacon introduces are communal inquiry, which is able to correct the mistakes of individual scientists—and offer spiritual and moral renewal (*Great Instauration*, 74–75).[70] Bacon points out that sinful affections and intentions caused both the fall of humanity and angels, producing such effects as lust for power, fame, and profit, and the prideful desire for knowledge, which cause us to fall under the influence of the idols.

René Descartes

Echoing Bacon's sentiments, René Descartes (1596–1650) tells in his *Discourse on the Method* how he had dedicated his life to the pursuit of knowledge since his childhood. He studied in the best universities of his time and absorbed everything he could in all branches of science. The result, however, was confusion. He expresses his skeptical conclusion especially regarding philosophy: "Philosophy has been pursued for many centuries by the best minds, and yet everything in it is still disputed and hence doubtful; and I wasn't so arrogant as to hope to achieve more in philosophy than others had

---

70. Bacon's utopian work *New Atlantis* tells about a perfect island, where both technology and moral spiritual virtues are practiced in harmony. See Stephen A. McKnight, "Religion and Francis Bacon's Scientific Utopianism," *Zygon* 42 (2007): 463–86.

done. . . . I had no confidence in any of philosophy's 'results' or in my ability to improve that situation" (*Discourse on the Method* 1).[71] Descartes describes his journeys across Europe at some length, all of which points toward cynicism. Nevertheless, he observes that the buildings designed and constructed by multiple architects exhibit "less perfection" and that those made by one person are "finer and better organized." This observation does not, of course, pertain only to the field of architecture. "I believe that if Sparta was at one time very flourishing, this wasn't because each of its laws was good (seeing that many were very strange and even contrary to good morals), but because they were devised by a single man and hence were all conducive to the same end" (*Discourse on the Method* 2). Instead of consulting the multitude of philosophers, Descartes suggests, we are better off pursuing the truth by ourselves, guided by our reason (*Discourse on the Method* 4).[72]

From here, Descartes presents his famous method of doubt, which follows four simple principles. First, we should not accept anything as true unless we are sure that it is evidently true, which means there is no way in which we can imagine having made a mistake. The words Descartes uses here are "clear and distinct," which he explains more thoroughly elsewhere (*Principles of Philosophy* 1.45–46).[73] In effect, "clear" (*clara*) means something that is seen in bright daylight, and "distinct" (*distincta*) is something that we cannot mistake for something else. The latter term illustrates his second principle, in which problems are divided into smaller parts so that they might be easier to solve. The third principle requires particular order that proceeds from easier questions toward more complicated ones. Fourth, the inquirer should aim at the largest possible scope so that nothing is overlooked or forgotten.

Descartes insists that these principles for his method of doubt should not be taken to imply skepticism or vain sophism but a sincere desire to know the truth. Famously, the surest thing is one's own existence: "Observing that this truth *I am thinking, therefore I exist* was so firm and sure that not even the most extravagant suppositions of the skeptics could shake it,

71. In-text references are from René Descartes, *Discourse on the Method of Rightly Conducting One's Reason and Seeking Truth in the Sciences*, trans. Jonathan Bennett, Some Texts from Early Modern Philosophy, last revised 2007, http://earlymoderntexts.com/assets/pdfs/descartes1637.pdf.

72. "We ought never to let ourselves be convinced except by the evidentness of our reason."

73. See *Principles of Philosophy*, trans. Jonathan Bennett, Some Texts from Early Modern Philosophy, last revised 2012, http://earlymoderntexts.com/assets/pdfs/descartes1644.pdf.

I decided that I could accept it without scruple as the first principle of the philosophy I was seeking" (*Discourse on the Method* 4). The acuity of this perception is ultimately guaranteed by the perfect being, God, who cannot create a human being and then let him or her be led astray. Therefore we can take our perceptions as true accounts of our own existence, and consequently the structure of the world.

What lies behind this account of human nature and our access to knowledge? Peter Harrison has argued that Descartes's theory of knowledge is broadly Thomistic.[74] Descartes was introduced to the principles of Thomism, which had started to gain momentum at the time, during his studies at La Flèche. Along these lines, human reason and the skills of judgment are not seriously corrupted by the fall. Instead, "our opinions differ not because some of us are more reasonable than others, but solely because we take our thoughts along different paths and don't attend to the same things" (*Discourse on the Method* 1). If we form diverse opinions it is only because we lack proper methodology, not because we are corrupted. We simply need to be told how to use our reason. Descartes's view of human knowledge is therefore optimistic. Because of our lofty status, we have, at least in principle, access to the "Adamic science," the prelapsarian perfect knowledge of nature. Harrison, however, notes that this optimistic view was not widely welcomed. In an atmosphere where Reformers' critique of worldly wisdom and philosophy were gaining popularity, this optimism was received with suspicion.[75]

1.4. From Natural War to Perpetual Peace: Hobbes, Locke, and Kant

Thomas Hobbes

In *Leviathan*, Thomas Hobbes (1588–1679) famously states, "Hereby it is manifest, that during the time men live without a common power to keep them all in awe, they are in that condition which is called war; and such a war, as is of every man, against every man" (8).[76] In this "state of nature" where no government exists, human life is "solitary, poor, nasty, brutish,

---

74. Harrison, "Original Sin and the Problem of Knowledge," 246–47.

75. Peter Harrison, *Fall of Man and the Foundations of Science* (Cambridge: Cambridge University Press, 2007).

76. In-text references are to section numbers in Thomas Hobbes, *Leviathan*, ed. J. C. A. Gaskin (Oxford: Oxford University Press, 1996).

and short" (13). This is the background against which Hobbes builds his own proposal for a more functional human society, the commonwealth.

It is natural for humans to disagree, because their desires cause them to pursue things in ways that reveal their poor judgment skills. For example, Hobbes thinks that blind-spot bias is widespread in humanity: "For such is the nature of men that howsoever they may acknowledge many others to be more witty, or more eloquent, or more learned, yet they will hardly believe there be many so wise as themselves; for they see their own wit at hand, and other men's at a distance" (8). Despite all kinds of individual deficits and whims, virtually every human being values life over death. This universal self-preservation, when combined with poor judgment, creates the state of nature.

But it is not just human will that causes us to disagree; it is the use of language. Hobbes was a radical nominalist: he did not believe that there are universal essences behind words. The names of things are mere conventions, and are attributed to objects by human will. This pertains also to central ethical notions such as "good" and "evil."[77]

> But whatsoever is the object of any man's appetite or desire; that is it, which he for his part calleth good: and the object of his hate, and aversion, evil; and of his contempt, vile and inconsiderable. For these words of good, evil, and contemptible, are ever used with relation to the person that useth them: there being nothing simply and absolutely so; nor any common rule of good and evil, to be taken from the nature of the objects themselves; but from the person of the man (where there is no commonwealth;) or, (in a commonwealth,) from the person that representeth it; or from an arbitrator or judge, whom men disagreeing shall by consent set up, and make his sentence the rule thereof. (6)

Now we can observe the central problem Hobbes attributes to the pluralism he saw emerging in his time. Because disagreements go to the root of our language, which is controlled by will without anything to check against it, it is futile to hope that disagreements could be solved by discussion and reason.

Hobbes's absolutist solution is well known. Given the state of human

---

77. For a thorough treatment, see Philip Pettit, *Made with Words: Hobbes on Language, Mind, and Politics* (Princeton: Princeton University Press, 2008); Simone Chambers, "Who Shall Judge? Hobbes, Locke and Kant on the Construction of Public Reason," *Ethics and Global Politics* 2, no. 4 (2009): 349–68.

nature, the rational thing to do is to submit oneself to the rule of the absolute sovereign one, who by his absolute power guarantees that everyone follows the law, even when it goes against one's immediate self-interest (18). The word *absolute* needs to be taken here in its strictest possible sense. Namely, if the sovereign does not have *everything* in his hands, then power has been delegated to lower levels, which naturally and necessarily creates the possibility of disagreement (18). Under the sovereign's rule, there is no room for dissent "because the major part hath by consenting voices declared a sovereign, he that dissented must now consent with the rest; that is, be contented to avow all the actions he shall do, or else justly be destroyed by the rest" (18).

Hobbes's solution to religious disagreement is straightforward. The sovereign has the power to define the form and content of spirituality, and everyone else must follow his lead in their public practice. This means that everyone must stay loyal to official state religion in public, while in their minds and in private they may disagree with it (42).

Hobbes's theory is an interesting mix of pessimism and optimism. On the one hand, humans do not easily act rationally. Contrary to Aristotle, humans are not by nature teleologically orientated to strive for higher goods and form political structures. Hobbes claims that polis is not natural but always a contingent convention, and it does not come into existence except by power. Alan Ryan argues that instead of the Aristotelian *summum bonum*, Hobbes bows before the *summum malum*, which he posits as the natural goal of human beings.[78]

On the other hand, Hobbes's political theory attempts to build everything on purely scientific grounds. The problem of earlier generations, for Hobbes, is that they lacked proper scientific methods. The only token of pure science is mathematics, which is now supposed to be the foundation of politics as well (5).[79]

> When a man reasoneth, he does nothing else but conceive a sum total, from addition of parcels; or conceive a remainder, from subtraction of one sum from another: which (if it be done by words,) is conceiving of the consequence from the names of all the parts, to the name of the whole; or from the names of the whole and one part, to the name of

78. Alan Ryan, "Hobbes's Political Philosophy," in *The Cambridge Companion to Hobbes*, ed. Tom Sorell (Cambridge: Cambridge University Press, 1996), 216–17.

79. See also Tom Sorell, "The Science in Hobbes's Politics," in *Perspectives on Thomas Hobbes*, ed. G. A. J. Rogers and Alan Ryan (Oxford: Clarendon, 1998), 67–80.

the other part. And though in some things, (as in numbers,) besides adding and subtracting, men name other operations, as multiplying and dividing; yet they are the same; for multiplication, is but adding together of things equal; and division, but subtracting of one thing, as often as we can. These operations are not incident to numbers only, but to all manner of things that can be added together, and taken one out of another. (5)

The nature of this new political science is opaque in *Leviathan*. It seems that Hobbes wishes to use utility values and decision theory to accurately define the relevant concepts, therefore offering analytic truths that function as the foundation of human reasoning. Hobbes wants his theory to be as self-evident and irresistible as mathematical proof.[80]

But why would anyone trust his or her life in the hands of a sovereign? Hobbes argues that this is required of us by the laws of nature. These laws are duties that are binding at all times and everywhere, even in cases when we haven't consciously signed on to them (14–15). The exact argument Hobbes provides for the laws is, however, a bit obscure, and there are several different understandings of how it should work. The general line of his argument runs as follows: Everyone desires as their goal freedom from violence. The best way to achieve this goal is to follow the golden rule—"Whatsoever you require that others should do to you, that do ye to them" (14.5). Therefore this proves that the most rational thing to do is to follow the golden rule.[81]

Hobbes's political vision is crystal clear, even if his argument for it (contrary to his wishes) is open to debate. He belongs to the tradition of theorists who claimed to be able to ground political life in the modern scientific method. Instead of the previous generation's seemingly endless debates about metaphysics, the new method should lead us out of the philosophers' damp dungeons and into the light.[82]

80. Emmanuel Ugwudi Eze (*On Reason: Rationality in a World of Cultural Conflict and Racism* [Durham: Duke University Press, 2008], 28–32, [31]) colorfully defines this hoped-for result as "an epistemological slam dunk." Interestingly, Hobbes disregarded arts and literature because they corrupt the culture and manifest mere irrationality.

81. S. A. Lloyd, "Hobbes," in *The Routledge Companion to Social and Political Philosophy*, ed. Gerald Gaus and Fred D'Agostino (New York: Routledge, 2013), 65–66.

82. *Leviathan* contains a chapter (46, "Of Darkness from Vain Philosophy and Fabulous Traditions") that resembles Bacon's account of idols. Here, Hobbes turns his criticisms against the philosophy of the ancient Greeks, claiming, "Their moral philosophy is but a description of their own passions. . . . They make the rules of good and bad by their own liking and disliking;

John Locke

John Locke (1632–1704) shared Hobbes's concerns. The English Civil War (1642–1651) and Thirty Years' War (1618–1648) in Europe were still fresh in the minds of the populace when he wrote his *A Letter Concerning Toleration* (1689).[83] The Reformation had caused the collapse of religiously uniform culture, which now added an additional element to the ongoing birth process of modern nation-states. Locke's *Letter* aimed to end the persecution religious communities were inflicting on one another and to find a reasonable way for the state to manage religious disagreements.

Locke approached the religious disputes from a completely different perspective than Hobbes did. In his view, Hobbes's proposal would lead to more, not less, civil unrest. For Locke, religious disagreements were largely *caused* by the state, which tried to control something that cannot be controlled. Allowing more room for religious expression would eventually lead to a better outcome.

In his *Letter*, Locke grounds his idea of toleration on the observation that people cannot change their convictions by external force because "the life and power of true religion consists in faith, faith involves believing, and no-one can just believe what someone else tells him to believe, even if he wants to." Consequently,

> it can't be up to the magistrate to take care of souls, because his power consists only in outward force, whereas true and saving religion consists in the inward faith of the soul, without which nothing can be acceptable to God, and which the nature of the human mind won't allow to be compelled by any outward force. Confiscation of goods, imprisonment, torture—nothing like that can make men change their inward judgments about things.[84]

---

by which means, in so great diversity of taste, there is nothing generally agreed on; but every one doth, as far as he dares, whatsoever seemeth good in his own eyes, to the subversion of Commonwealth."

83. John Wiedhoft Gough, "The Development of Locke's Belief in Toleration," in *John Locke, "A Letter Concerning Toleration" in Focus*, ed. John Horton and Susan Mendus (London: Routledge, 1991), 57–77.

84. John Locke, *A Letter Concerning Toleration*, ed. Jonathan Bennett, Some Texts from Early Modern Philosophy, 2010, 2, http://earlymoderntexts.com/assets/pdfs/locke1689b.pdf (numbered references to Locke's *Letter* are to section number).

Locke's *Letter* contains two distinct arguments for toleration. The first is based on the involuntary nature of belief. The second concerns the nature of earthly government, the magistrate, which can use only force and does not possess reliable religious expertise that could evoke our trust in its judgments regarding religious matters.

The nature of belief formation in Locke's theory needs further elucidation. In his *Letter* and in *An Essay Concerning Human Understanding* (1689), Locke underscores the centrality of reason in belief formation: "Reason must be our guide in everything."[85] The obvious question then is, If belief is involuntary, how can it be assessed by reason? Are we not responsible for our beliefs? Maria Van Der Schaar points out that Locke faces a dilemma: in order to make his case for toleration, he needs to underscore the involuntary aspect of belief. But in order to cast blame on those who believe falsehoods or otherwise use their reason lazily, belief needs to be voluntary.[86]

Locke's point, however, is not that we have absolutely no control over our beliefs, only that we cannot force people into believing things they have no reason to believe. In his *Letter*, Locke points out that there are ways for changing one's beliefs: "It is one thing to persuade, another to command; one thing to press with arguments, another with judicial rulings"; and "The only way to change men's opinions is through light, and you can't produce light in someone's mind by torturing him."[87] In his *Essay*, Locke offers a more complete overview of belief formation, and sets its voluntary and involuntary aspects in their proper context.

> All that is voluntary in our Knowledge, is the employing, or with-holding any of our Faculties from this or that sort of Objects, and a more, or less accurate survey of them: But they being employed, our Will hath no Power to determine the Knowledge of the Mind one way or another; that is done only by the Objects themselves, as far as they are clearly discovered.[88]

In other words, we have power over faculties regarding which things we pay attention to and which we put out of the mind. We can choose, for example,

85. John Locke, *An Essay Concerning Human Understanding* (New York: Dover, 1959), 4.19.14.

86. Maria Van Der Schaar, "Locke on Judgment and Religious Toleration," *British Journal for the History of Philosophy* 20, no. 1 (2012): 46–47.

87. Locke, *Letter* 2.

88. Locke, *Essay* 4.13.2. See also Van Der Schaar, "Locke on Judgment and Religious Toleration," 48–50.

whether we enter the garden or not, but when we have passed the gates and opened our eyes we cannot but perceive the trees and flowers that grow in the garden. This relative freedom is enough to attribute personal blame if we perform cognitive actions that exhibit ignorance and error.[89]

In Locke's theory, humans are born with natural reasoning capabilities, but they need education to use their cognitive faculties well.[90] Typical errors that the human mind displays are, for example, not using one's reason at all, following others rather than using one's own judgment (conformism), resorting to emotions instead of reason, and using reason too narrowly. This last manifests itself as confirmation bias: we tend to consult only those sources that confirm our existing beliefs.[91]

Finding truth in religious matters is challenging, Locke admits, but his belief in the possibility of human reason to arrive at truth compels him to encourage us to keep looking. We will find religious truth when we use our reason as well as we can and when we believe only those things that are highly likely to be true.[92] Regarding religious disagreement, Locke makes a startling claim: disagreement is not necessarily a bad thing. Conversation between diverse standpoints helps us to avoid the aforementioned mistakes in reasoning by challenging our conventions, which are not necessarily based on solid reasoning, and by offering alternative viewpoints that can improve our knowledge.[93]

Immanuel Kant

For Immanuel Kant (1724–1804), Hobbes is almost right in his account of the natural state. However, Kant corrects Hobbes by claiming not that people are

89. Locke, *Essay* 4.20.16. In modern political discourse, tolerance and relativism are usually taken to be part of the same package. Contemporary tolerance is to a large extent motivated by skepticism about the possibilities of reasonable conversation. This is not the case with Locke, as he thinks that tolerance and disagreement can help us to achieve the truth. Additionally, tolerance is not based on the equality of all truth claims but on individuals' right to judge religious matters by themselves, not relying on external authorities. Thus, e.g., Adam Wolfson, "Toleration and Relativism: The Locke-Proast Exchange," *Review of Politics* 59 (1997): 213–31.

90. See, e.g., John Locke, *Some Thoughts Concerning Education*, ed. John W. Yolton and Jean S. Yolton (Oxford: Clarendon, 2000).

91. Locke, *Essay* 4.20; Van Der Schaar, "Locke on Judgment and Religious Toleration," 55.

92. For an overview of Locke's theory of knowledge, see Nicholas Wolterstorff, *John Locke and the Ethics of Belief*, Cambridge Studies in Religion and Critical Thought (Cambridge: Cambridge University Press, 1996).

93. Van Der Schaar, "Locke on Judgment and Religious Toleration," 62–65.

constantly in the state of war but that there is always a *chance* of war.[94] There are pure spatial reasons behind this: people feel that they have rights to particular property or conduct. The natural way to deal with disagreements is to spread out, but we soon realize that we cannot expand endlessly. Therefore we need some rules to help determine how to live in the same space so that we can avoid war but still maintain our fundamental rights as human beings.[95]

Kant observed that disagreements have to do mostly with things that people strive for in order to become happy and satisfied. Traditional philosophy, in Kant's mind, could not settle this problem. As Simone Chambers states, "Kant thought that that disagreement reflected the fact that there were no universal truths about happiness except for the completely empty principle that everyone wants it."[96]

The only way to prevent this fundamental disagreement from developing into a conflict is to establish a state that in many ways is similar to Hobbes's. In a commonwealth, each citizen retains their fundamental rights and freedoms without the fear that others might take away these freedoms. The state, in contrast, is built on the following three principles. First, every citizen should act so that they do not treat others as means to some further goal, such as personal gain or pleasure. Second, every citizen is equal; they have the same rights as all other citizens. The ruler is excused, however, as they have the right to coerce the subjects without their being coerced in return. Third, every citizen has an equal right to act as a co-legislator. In a commonwealth, laws are merely a reflection of the general will of the people. In the case of disagreements (which are inevitable), the minority position must yield to the will of the majority. This principle of yielding, however, must be accepted unanimously because it is the very basis on which the commonwealth is constructed.[97]

From here, the conversation about the possibility to resist the ruler or sovereign emerges naturally. On the surface, there does not seem to be any

94. Immanuel Kant, *Toward Perpetual Peace*, in *"Toward Perpetual Peace" and Other Writings on Politics, Peace, and History*, ed. Pauline Kleingeld, trans. David L. Colclasure (New Haven: Yale University Press, 2006), app. 4.

95. Kant, *Toward Perpetual Peace*, app. 2.

96. Chambers, "Who Shall Judge," 361.

97. John R. Goodreau, "Kant's Contribution to the Idea of Democratic Pluralism," in *Reassessing the Liberal State: Reading Maritain's "Man and the State,"* ed. Timothy Fuller and John P. Hittinger (Washington, DC: Catholic University of America Press, 2006), 99–126. Immanuel Kant, *Political Writings*, ed. H. S. Reiss, Cambridge Texts in the History of Political Thought (Cambridge: Cambridge University Press, 1991), 74–79.

fundamental difference between Hobbes and Kant: they both rule out the possibility of revolt. Kant, however, leaves room for dissent. In *Critique of Pure Reason* he claims that "reason has no dictatorial authority: its verdict is always simply the agreement of free citizens, of whom each one must be permitted to express, without let or hindrance, his objections or even his veto."[98] The people have the right and freedom to express their views, but their role is limited to making arguments in the public arena. If they want to change things, they should do so through public persuasion. This freedom of expression guarantees that the state acts and rules justly. Reasoning is thus a communal matter for Kant. To quote Onora O'Neill: "By Kant's own standards we will not reason or even think correctly unless we think in common with others."[99]

Kant's thinking is driven by his optimistic hope concerning the development of the human race. People may not yet be rational, but we are progressing toward that end.[100] One of the factors Kant perceived to be a cause of strife is religion. In *Religion within the Bounds of Reason Alone*, he remarks how ecclesial creeds naturally create a division between orthodox and heretic.[101] His vision of reasonable religion would survive without these distinctions and thereby decrease the likelihood of conflict.

1.5. Beyond Enlightenment: Nietzsche, Hamann, and Contemporary Voices

The project of Enlightenment started out as an attempt to root out uncertainty and disagreement. Ironically, the original optimistic belief in reason

98. Immanuel Kant, *Critique of Pure Reason*, trans. Francis Haywood (London: Living Time Press, 2004), A739/B767.

99. Quoted in Van Der Schaar, "Locke on Judgment and Religious Toleration," 365. Onora O'Neill, "The Public Use of Reason," *Political Theory* 14, no. 4 (1986): 546.

100. Immanuel Kant, *What Is Enlightenment?*, in *Political Writings*, 58: "If we are asked, 'Do we now live in an enlightened age?' the answer is, 'No,' but we do live in an age of enlightenment. As things now stand, much is lacking which prevents men from being, or easily becoming, capable of correctly using their own reason in religious matters with assurance and free from outside direction. But on the other hand, we have clear indications that the field has now been opened wherein men may freely deal with these things and that the obstacles to general enlightenment or the release from self-imposed tutelage are gradually being reduced. In this respect, this is the age of enlightenment, or the century of Frederick."

101. Immanuel Kant, *Religion within the Bounds of Bare Reason Alone*, trans. Werner S. Pluhar (Indianapolis: Hackett, 2009), 3.5.

was immediately contested, and it soon fragmented to various camps and ideologies that had very little to do with each other.[102] Nevertheless, the demand of reason is alive and well in contemporary culture, where it takes both sophisticated and naive forms. Alasdair MacIntyre, a vocal contemporary critic of the Enlightenment, points out the performative failure of the Enlightenment's central ideals.

> Notice then that it is not just in its inability to provide rationally justifiable and agreed moral values and principles that the Enlightenment and its heirs have failed. The failure of those modern institutions that have been the embodiment of the best social and political hopes of the Enlightenment is quite as striking. And those institutions fail by Enlightenment standards. For they do not provide—in fact they render impossible—the kinds of institutionalized reading, talking and arguing public necessary for effective practical rational thought about just those principles and decisions involved in answering such questions as: "How is a human life to be valued?" or "What does accountability in our social relationships require of us?" or "Whom, if anyone, may I legitimately deceive?"—questions to which we need shared answers. And there is no type of institutional arena in our society in which plain persons—not academic philosophers or academic political theorists—are able to engage together in systematic reasoned debate designed to arrive at a rationally well-founded common mind on these matters, a common mind which might then be given political expression. Indeed the dominant forms of organization of contemporary social life militate against the coming into existence of this type of institutional arena. And so do the dominant modes of what passes for political discourse. We do not have the kinds of reading public necessary to sustain practically effective social thought.[103]

102. Arthur A. Lovejoy (*The Great Chain of Being* [Cambridge, MA: Harvard University Press, 1978], 9) aptly describes the Enlightenment naïveté: "Assuming human nature to be a simple thing, the Enlightenment also, as a rule, assumed political and social problems to be simple, and therefore easy of solution. Rid man's mind of a few ancient errors, purge his beliefs of the artificial complications of metaphysical 'systems' and theological dogmas, restore to his social relations something like the simplicity of the state of nature, and his natural excellence would, it was assumed, be realized, and mankind would live happily ever after."

103. Alasdair MacIntyre, "Some Enlightenment Projects Considered," in Alasdair MacIntyre, *Selected Essays*, vol. 2, *Ethics and Politics* (Cambridge: Cambridge University Press, 2006), 185.

Even if some may see MacIntyre's evaluation as too pessimistic, there have been philosophers who have criticized the Enlightenment from the start. The problems MacIntyre articulates did not go unnoticed among Enlightenment contemporaries.

Friedrich Nietzsche

Nietzsche had very little patience for philosophies that aimed for consensus by means of reason or the sovereign's absolute power. One of his central contributions to epistemic theorization is his notion of perspectivism, which has had an enormous influence, especially in postmodern philosophy. Unsurprisingly, what Nietzsche meant is not beyond debate, and there are several perspectives from which to approach his perspectivism.[104] But it is best to start with Nietzsche's own claims. In *Genealogy of Morals*, he makes the following assertion:

> Precisely because we are people who seek knowledge, we should finally not be ungrateful for such determined reversals of customary perspectives and evaluations with which the spirit has for so long raged against itself with such apparent wickedness and futility. To use this for once to see differently, the will to see things differently, is no small discipline and preparation of the intellect for its coming "objectivity"—the latter meant not in the sense of "disinterested contemplation" (which is inconceivable nonsense), but as the capability of having power over one's positive and negative arguments and of raising them and disposing of them so that one knows how to make the very variety of perspectives and interpretations of emotions useful for knowledge. From now on, my philosophical gentlemen, let us protect ourselves better from the dangerous old conceptual fantasy which posits a "pure, will-less, painless, timeless subject of cognition"; let's guard ourselves against the tentacles of such contradictory ideas as "pure reason," "absolute spirituality," "knowledge in itself"—those things which demand that we think of an eye which simply cannot be imagined, an eye which is to have no direction at all, in which the active and interpretative forces are supposed to stop or

104. For an overview of discussion, see Brian Leiter, "Perspectivism in Nietzsche's *Genealogy of Morals*," in *Nietzsche, Genealogy, Morality: Essays on Nietzsche's "On the Genealogy of Morals*," ed. Richard Schacht (Berkeley: University of California Press, 1994), 334–54.

be absent—the very things through which seeing first becomes seeing something. Hence, these things always demand from the eye something conceptually absurd and incomprehensible. The only seeing we have is seeing from a perspective; the only knowledge we have is knowledge from a perspective; and the more emotions we allow to be expressed in words concerning something, the more eyes, different eyes, we know how to train on the same thing, the more complete our "idea" of this thing, our "objectivity," will be. But to eliminate the will in general, to suspend all our emotions without exception—even if we were capable of that—what would that be? Wouldn't we call that castrating the intellect?[105]

To summarize, perspectivism means denial of simple foundationalism: there are no indubitable, universally shared foundations on which to build our claims of knowledge. Everything is based on contextual and contingent claims, which receive their justification from that very moment and situation where they take place. This is a broadly antifoundationalist position.[106] According to Brian Leiter, the typical account of Nietzsche's perspectivism is formulated along the following lines:[107]

(i) the world has no determinate nature or structure;

(ii) our concepts and theories do not describe or correspond to this world because it has no determinate character;

(iii) our concepts and theories are mere interpretations or mere perspectives (reflecting our pragmatic needs, at least on some accounts); and

(iv) no perspective can enjoy an epistemic privilege over any other, because there is no epistemically privileged mode of access to the characterless world.

Leiter points out that a great number of scholars read Nietzsche through the lenses of this received view.[108] Furthermore, Reinhard Hütter argues that this

---

105. Friedrich Nietzsche, *On the Genealogy of Morals*, trans. Ian Johnston (Arlington, VA: Richer Resources, 2010), 3.12.

106. Maudemarie Clark, *Nietzsche on Truth and Philosophy* (Cambridge: Cambridge University Press, 1990), 130.

107. Leiter, "Perspectivism in Nietzsche's *Genealogy of Morals*," 334.

108. Leiter himself regards this to be an incorrect reading, and he tries to save Nietzsche from the obvious inconsistency that arises from the aforementioned tenets. The central inconsistency is between i, ii, and iv, as the two latter tenets offer a determinate description of the

received view has been taken as "an unexamined yet normative" account in contemporary humanities.[109]

What does Nietzsche have to say about the conflict of opinions, then? The question is especially interesting with regard to Nietzsche's philosophical theory and practice since he, on the one hand, seems to deny objective standpoints and, on the other hand, engages in full-scale criticisms of other standpoints. So how does he manage to do this without contradiction? Nietzsche's perspectivism has several problems. I will follow here Bernard Reginster's interpretation because it appears to offer the most consistent reading of Nietzsche's own position.[110]

Nietzsche's perspectivism allows for so-called reasonable disagreement, where both parties are rational in holding their respective views. If they, however, wish to criticize each other, what can they do? The evident option is to engage in internal criticism. This entails that one show how the rival view is somehow incoherent by its own standards. For example, Nietzsche may wish to show how the Christian commitment to minimizing suffering does not sit well with the pursuit of truth, which often requires suffering. The point here is to show that the rejection of suffering and the commitment to truth are mutually contradictory.

Reginster correctly points out that this does not offer Nietzsche a reason to accept his own view. In other words, demonstrating inconsistency in a rival view does not yet give reason to reject the alien belief as false or accept one's own belief as true. On perspectivism, there seems to be no way to persuade someone else of one's own view.

However, the purpose of Nietzsche's critique can be interpreted in a variety of ways. First, he may want to urge his antagonists to become more self-reflective regarding their intellectual commitments. Second, he may want to make them reconsider their commitments. Third, he may want his critique to expose the underlying power structures of truth claims. But again, this does not say anything about the truth of the respective positions.[111]

---

world. Leiter's suggestion is to read Nietzsche as a coherentist and antirealist. However, this goes against several of Nietzsche's own points, not least his criticisms of other views.

109. Hütter, "Directedness of Reasoning," 162.

110. Bernard Reginster, "Perspectivism, Criticism and Freedom of Spirit," *European Journal of Philosophy* 8 (2000): 40–62.

111. Brian Lightbody, "Nietzsche, Perspectivism, Anti-Realism: An Inconsistent Triad," *European Legacy* 15, no. 4 (2010): 425–38; Reginster, "Perspectivism."

Johann Georg Hamann

Johan Georg Hamann (1730–1788) is not customarily included in the Western philosophical canon. The reason behind this dismissal is a (falsely attributed) charge of irrationalism. One of the central figures in the Counter-Enlightenment, Hamann was painted as persona non grata in the higher philosophical echelons.[112] Only recently has he received more serious academic attention, as the rationale of his thought has become more transparent.

Especially noteworthy is his relation to Nietzsche. John Betz describes him as Nietzsche's good twin, of a sort.[113] They hold almost the same beliefs but within drastically different frameworks. Nietzsche is a misotheist; Hamann is a Lutheran Christian. Both accept the perspectival nature of human knowledge, but Nietzsche believes we should never try to get beyond perspectivism to "absolute knowledge" and Hamann believes that if this happens, it is always a miracle.

Large portions of Hamann's literary work serves as a radical alternative to Kant's philosophy.[114] Hamann observes that Kant is trying to achieve something that he cannot in all honesty achieve: to somehow get beyond language because "the indissolubility of the distance and the contingency of participation is constitutive."[115] He admits that in human history the unity was achieved once, in the form of tower of Babel, which, in his view, was a monstrosity born out of evil desire. It achieved superficial equality, unity, and harmony, but it was maleficent from the start and, luckily, short-lived. Hamann concludes that attempts to do away with the present plurality of languages are instances merely of self-deception and forgetfulness.

"To speak is to translate," Hamann writes, "from an angelic language to a human language, i.e. to transpose thoughts into words—things into names—images into signs." By this cryptic progression, he joins poetry, history, and philosophy together as specific instances of the same process of

---

112. For a critical account of Hamann, see Isaiah Berlin, *The Magus of the North: J. G. Hamann and the Origins of Modern Irrationalism* (London: Fontana, 1994). During the Counter-Enlightenment the criticism of Enlightenment reason was aimed at the uses of reason, which were perceived as illegitimate or even self-contradictory, not at reason as such.

113. John Betz, *After Enlightenment: The Post-Secular Vision of J. G. Hamann* (Oxford: Wiley-Blackwell, 2009), 319–26.

114. See especially Oswald Bayer, *A Contemporary in Dissent: Johann Georg Hamann as a Radical Enlightener* (Grand Rapids: Eerdmans, 2012), 156–70.

115. Quoted in Bayer, *A Contemporary in Dissent*, 160.

thought.[116] Language, in fact, is what enables us to philosophize in the first place. All philosophies have histories (including Kant's). Consequently, asking for reasons in some particular situation is only a subset of asking what the spoken language is.[117] According to Oswald Bayer, "The various languages and reasons are not systems that would harmoniously interplay, be variously joined, or happily subordinated to each other. Hearing and understanding, speaking and being understood occur in the intersecting of various perspectives, in the rivalry of various prejudices, the conflict of various languages."[118]

In other words, Hamann considers disagreement to be a noncontingent feature of our fallen world. Attempts to remove the plurality (if successful) are either acts of violence or of miracles. Ultimately, the only case where disunity was undone was at the moment of the incarnation, when the eternal divine nature assumed the form of man and became vulnerable. This is an eschatological icon through which we can observe a reality where disunity is overcome without violence, something that we can occasionally experience in this life but never in its full extent.

Contemporary Voices

In contemporary Western societies, we cannot avoid discussing themes that would have seemed totally foreign and even peculiar to our culture not long ago. The Western mind-set is to a large extent consensual, but the reaching of consensus seems increasingly more difficult as the plurality of views and practices within them grows. In his book *Political Liberalism*, John Rawls described the situation this way: "A modern democratic society is characterized not simply by a pluralism of comprehensive religious, philosophical, and moral doctrines but by a pluralism of incompatible yet reasonable comprehensive doctrines. No one of these doctrines is affirmed by citizens generally. Nor should one expect that in the foreseeable future one of them, or some other reasonable doctrine, will ever be affirmed by all, or nearly all, citizens."[119] Ironically, when the Renaissance and Enlightenment thinkers formulated their views about human nature and reasonability, they thought

---

116. Johann Georg Hamann, *Aesthetica in Nuce*, in *Writings on Philosophy and Language*, trans. Kenneth Hayes, Cambridge Texts in the History of Philosophy (Cambridge: Cambridge University Press, 2007), 66n23.

117. Bayer, *A Contemporary in Dissent*, 164–65.

118. Bayer, *A Contemporary in Dissent*, 159.

119. John Rawls, *Political Liberalism* (New York: Columbia University Press, 1996), xviii.

that removing authoritative hierarchies would bring about a harmonious state. Exactly the opposite ensued. In Rawls's mind, it is the *freedom* of late modern society that produces more and more options from which people can choose their worldviews and values. The freer people are, the more room they have for disagreement.

After the Enlightenment, reason has been a fundamental feature of Western thought. Today, however, no concept is more widely contested and disputed than reason.[120] This is due partly to the acknowledgment of the *histories* of our ways of reasoning, underlined by Nietzsche and Hamann, and picked up in various forms by postmodern theorists. The postmodern turn solidified the earlier historicist and antiessentialist ontologies, and made reference to abstract and universal reason if not impossible, at least much more difficult. There was nothing new in this new postmodern condition, however, as it only made visible the preexisting diversity and rehabilitated certain ancient forms of thought that we explored at the beginning of this chapter. The surplus of reasonabilities has been present since the beginning of Western civilization.

Interestingly, this has led to a strange dichotomy: in contemporary Western culture, reason is at the same time adored and distrusted.[121] On the one hand, reason has been attacked in academia by postmodernists who see it as a tool of oppression. On the other hand, we now have scientistic atheists and naturalists who think that hard science is able to provide us with all the necessary answers humans need to live flourishing lives. Never in the history of humanity have we seen such a variety of intellectual stances, which are also gaining support outside senior common rooms.

This disagreement has created heated debate about the role of religion, or for that matter any comprehensive tradition or doctrine, in public life. "Comprehensive doctrine" is Rawls's term; it denotes a particular set of beliefs that give form to a clearly distinguishable intellectual form of life. Modern Western society's problem, according to Rawls and many so-called liberal democrats, is the plurality and mutual exclusivity of these

---

120. The classic in this respect is, of course, Alasdair MacIntyre, *Whose Justice? Which Rationality?* (Notre Dame: University of Notre Dame Press, 1988). For more recent approaches, see, e.g., Robert Audi, *The Architecture of Reason: The Structure and Substance of Rationality* (Oxford: Oxford University Press, 2001); Emmanuel Ugwudi Eze, *On Reason: Rationality in a World of Cultural Conflict and Racism* (Durham: Duke University Press, 2008).

121. Audi, *Rationality*, 4. See also Pope John Paul II, *Fides et Ratio*, the Vatican website, 1998, §5, http://w2.vatican.va/content/john-paul-ii/en/encyclicals/documents/hf_jp-ii_enc_14091998_fides-et-ratio.html.

doctrines. In the following, I will briefly introduce the main moves in this debate.

Liberal democrats typically believe that political actions should be based on neutral and generally agreed-on principles, which, according to Rawls, "all citizens can reasonably be expected to endorse in the light of their common human reason."[122] Liberal democrats differ on how easily we can access these reasons. If for Locke and Hobbes this was relatively uncomplicated, contemporary theorists admit that one needs to put quite a lot of effort into finding these principles. Virtually no one believes that these values are self-evident and immediately accessible to all and shared by all.

The typical solution offered by liberal democrats is that even if people cannot at the moment agree on central principles, in the idealized state they could.[123] This means in effect that those who cannot agree are moved outside the camp and told that in a possible ideal world they would agree with the rest, but because they have some defect they cannot reach this higher knowledge at the moment. Even if this is the way modern democracy works, it sounds patronizing to many ears.

Several political philosophers from various ideological backgrounds have pointed out the problems of liberal democracy. First, it seems to place a unique burden on those whose values and actions are motivated by religion or minority ideology. Second, the epistemology on which liberal democracy is grounded gives a highly reductionistic picture of how human beliefs are formed. We do not reason like computers; our convictions are always part of the larger network of presuppositions, making it virtually impossible to draw a distinction between "religious" and "nonreligious" reasons.[124] Third, many movements and arguments now seen as part of the liberal democratic tradition were originally motivated by religion—and many of them still are, as it has been shown to be quite challenging to offer nonmetaphysical arguments for human uniqueness and dignity, for

---

122. Rawls, *Political Liberalism*, 140.

123. For an overview of these positions, see Nicholas Wolterstorff, *Understanding Liberal Democracy: Essays in Political Philosophy*, ed. Terence Cuneo (Oxford: Oxford University Press, 2012), 11–40, 76–110.

124. Eric Gregory, "Before the Original Position: The Neo-orthodox Theology of the Young John Rawls," *Journal of Religious Ethics* 35 (2007): 198. See also Jeffrey Stout, *Democracy and Tradition* (Princeton: Princeton University Press, 2005); John Perry, *The Pretenses of Loyalty: Locke, Liberal Theory, and American Political Theology* (Oxford: Oxford University Press, 2011), 17–68. Chantal Mouffe, "The Limits of John Rawls's Pluralism," *Journal of International Political Theory* 3 (2007): 109–28.

example.[125] Fourth, the exclusionist strategy may be counterproductive if it builds tension between groups and causes resentment among outsiders.[126]

This pessimistic vision is one of the factors behind the postmodern turn in political philosophy. The contemporary Western postmodern condition has made this quest for common ground more strenuous. Yet even without any influence from postmodern philosophy, it is possible to be skeptical regarding the Enlightenment project. If, for example, philosophers disagree about almost every possible detail in their own field, how can we expect them to come up with a shared concept of justice? This principle has been in the making for a long time, but consensus is nowhere in sight. This is the weak point highlighted by MacIntyrean critics. Commenting on the idea of "public reason," which is supposed to work as the basis for liberal-democratic decision-making, Nicholas Wolterstorff points out that our idea of public reason contains contradictory principles, even when religious principles are excluded.[127]

Among others, Richard Rorty has been one of the central figures in contemporary social philosophy who has employed broadly Nietzschean antifoundationalism in public life. Rorty admits that we do not have non-neutral viewpoints from which to argue our case. In his view, employing arguments that refer to culturally transcendent notions and universally shared principles smacks of fundamentalism, which can take both religious and scientistic forms.[128]

A particularly interesting feature of Rorty's thought is that religion cannot be criticized on epistemic grounds but instead must be viewed as a political phenomenon.[129] Especially in his later writings, Rorty acknowledges that religious views should be taken more seriously in the public sphere. This marks a minor shift in his views, as he had earlier defined religion as a "conversation-stopper": the discussion ends at the very moment a religiously

125. See, e.g., Raimond Gaita, *A Common Humanity: Thinking about Love and Truth and Justice* (London: Routledge 2000), 5; Jeff McMahan, "Challenges to Human Equality," *Journal of Ethics* 12 (2008): 81–104.

126. Jeffrey Stout, "Folly of Secularism," *Journal of American Academy of Religion* 76, no. 3 (2008): 533–44.

127. Wolterstorff, *Understanding Liberal Democracy*, 27–29.

128. Serge Grigoriev, "Rorty, Religion and Humanism," *International Journal for Philosophy of Religion* 70 (2011): 189.

129. Richard Rorty, "Religion in the Public Square: A Reconsideration," *Journal of Religious Ethics* 31, no. 1 (2003): 142; Stephen Louthan, "On Religion—A Discussion with Richard Rorty, Alvin Plantinga and Nicholas Wolterstorff," *Christian Scholar's Review* 27, no. 2 (1996): 177–83.

warranted opinion is offered. In his mature vision he slightly rescinds his earlier views and seems to offer a new hope for extending the conversation among both secularists and religious:

> Instead of saying that religion was a conversation-stopper, I should have simply said that citizens of a democracy should try to put off invoking conversation-stoppers as long as possible. We should do our best to keep the conversation going without citing unarguable first principles, either philosophical or religious. If we are sometimes driven to such citation, we should see ourselves as having failed, not as having triumphed.[130]

This passage reflects perfectly Rorty's general epistemic stance: disagreements should not be approached from the viewpoint of objective reasons and arguments but from the idea of solidarity. But Rorty is not an uncritical friend of religion. In fact, his relation to religion is highly selective and ultimately not far removed from aggressive secularism. Even if he cannot be included in the New Atheist canon, he wants to limit religion completely to the private sphere. Rorty thinks that in the private sphere religion (to be precise: liberal Protestantism) may have a positive role for human flourishing, but he perceives ecclesial institutions as illegitimate users of political power, which should be done away with. At most, religions should be tolerated while we await the moment when they finally die away and secularism prevails. The goal is secular, but the means of secularization are only slightly more humane than those of Lenin and Mao.[131]

The most interesting feature in Rorty's theory regarding the problem of religious arguments in the public sphere is not that religion is epistemically suspect but that it is not generally shared. This puts Rorty in a strange position, which has not escaped his critics. Rorty, who is known for his Enlightenment criticism, adopts public reason policy when he deals with religion.[132]

Wolterstorff, as one of these critics, locates the disagreement between himself and Rorty (and public reason theorists) in their conflicting ideas on how to frame the ideal of liberal democracy. Wolterstorff believes "it is the genius of liberal democracy to guarantee certain basic rights and liberties to its citizens and resident aliens, and to assure access by all normal adults to fair voting procedures. Given that basic framework, it accepts all 'com-

130. Rorty, "Religion in the Public Square: A Reconsideration," 148–49.
131. Thus Stout, "Folly," 534–36.
132. See, e.g., Grigoriev, "Rorty," 194–95; Wolterstorff, *Understanding Liberal Democracy*, 44.

prehensive perspectives'—to use Rawls' term—as they come."[133] This "equal voice" model does not enforce any *a priori* rules of reasonability: "It doesn't tell anybody that they have to shape up."[134] When, after discussions, we vote, the results will naturally make some people happy and others unhappy, and sometimes the roles are reversed. This may cause frustration, but "a liberal democracy survives as long as those who lose the vote think it's better to lose the vote than destroy the system."[135] We simply cannot do any better.

In comparison, Rorty's idea is not only a method but also an ideology. For Rorty, the raison d'être of democratic institutions is "making possible the invention of new forms of human freedom, taking liberties never taken before."[136] In other words, Rortian democracy is not about ensuring the conviviality of different viewpoints but the emancipation of individual freedoms. How is this supposed to take place? The solution resembles that which has been offered by public-reason liberals: exclusion. In his writings, Rorty often adopts a condescending tone when dealing with those with whom he disagrees. But this flows smoothly from his philosophy, where disagreements are not epistemic but political. If opponents cannot be rebutted, they can only be ridiculed.[137] So much for solidarity.

Wolterstorff has a different tone. Letting all have their say and use the arguments they wish can be taxing, but it manifests "requisite virtues." Eventually it will teach people to understand what they can say and how they should form arguments to convince others. Wolterstorff quotes Rorty against Rorty to underline his basic attitude toward other voices: "Moral decisions that are to be enforced by a pluralist and democratic state's monopoly of

133. Wolterstorff, *Understanding Liberal Democracy*, 50.

134. Wolterstorff, *Understanding Liberal Democracy*, 50.

135. Wolterstorff, *Understanding Liberal Democracy*, 50–51.

136. Richard Rorty, *Philosophy and Social Hope* (London: Penguin, 2000), 126. See also David Bentley Hart, *The Experience of God: Being, Consciousness, Bliss* (New Haven: Yale University Press, 2014), 312–13.

137. See, e.g., the famous passage in Robert B. Brandom, ed., *Rorty and His Critics* (Oxford: Blackwell, 2000), 22: "So we are going to go right on trying to discredit you in the eyes of your children, trying to strip your fundamentalist religious community of dignity, trying to make your views seem silly rather than discussable. We are not so inclusivist as to tolerate intolerance such as yours. . . . I don't see anything *herrschaftsfrei* [domination free] about my handling of my fundamentalist students. Rather, I think those students are lucky to find themselves under the benevolent *Herrschaft* [domination] of people like me, and to have escaped the grip of their frightening, vicious, dangerous parents. . . . I am just as provincial and contextualist as the Nazi teachers who made their students read *Der Stürmer*; the only difference is that I serve a better cause."

violence are best made by public discussion in which voices claiming to be God's, or reason's, or science's, are put on a par with everybody's else's."[138]

To summarize some essential aspects of this glance at the history of philosophy, I wish to emphasize the reasons people give to the reality of disagreement and the respective cures offered. At the very least, we can identify the causes and cures listed in table 1.

Table 1. Theological and philosophical reasons for disagreement and suggested cures

Reason for disagreement	Suggested cure
will: corrupted love (sin)	spiritual renewal
will: weakness of will	the better exercise of mental faculties
reason: wrong metaphysical views	adopting a better philosophy
reason: wrong order of goods	spiritual renewal
reason: lack of method	adopting a better method
world: the truth is not readily available to us	acknowledging the inevitability of disagreement
God's action: purposeful creation of ambiguous state	humility

Several thinkers can be linked with more than one of the aforementioned cause-cure pairs, and not all of them are mutually exclusive. The greatest difference among the philosophers lies in their belief in the possibility of overcoming our disagreement: some are more optimistic, while others are more pessimistic. At this point, the list merely illustrates the variety of views and the lack of consensus. Next, we change our perspective from history to the human mind and our lived reality.

138. Wolterstorff, *Understanding Liberal Democracy*, 48.

45

CHAPTER 2

Programmed to Disagree?

The fundamental cause of the trouble is that in the modern world the stupid are cocksure while the intelligent are full of doubt.

Bertrand Russell, "The Triumph of Stupidity"

We don't think rationally for very long at a time—it's too tiring.

C. S. Lewis, "Answers to Questions on Christianity"

To disagree is human. But what is it about our humanity that makes us disagree? The previous chapter charted the analyses of philosophers who have tried to explain our condition and have sought remedies for it. Next we turn to contemporary psychology and examine what insights emerge from this particular discipline. Disagreement is typically discussed within the psychology of decision-making and the theory of self-formation. In this chapter, I will present an overview of some contemporary theories that focus on human belief formation and especially on why we so often disagree. The purpose is to provide a parallel to the historical overview, emphasizing the local and perspectival nature of our beliefs.

I will briefly discuss dual-process theories of cognition, cognitive biases, neurological studies on hemisphere symmetry, and moral psychology. Although our knowledge of the human mind is tentative at best, our contemporary knowledge helps us to see how human minds are structured such that disagreement is inevitable. In this way, I hope to enable further discussion on religious disagreement, especially on what we can reasonably expect from people and how belief formation might be improved.

2.1. Constrained and Confused Minds

Like philosophers, psychologists readily acknowledge the limits of human perspective. From a cognitive standpoint, our mind has several features that make disagreement not only possible but also highly likely. Starting from the basic constituents of the human mind, we possess an ability called "theory of mind," which enables us to read the mental states of other beings or attribute to other beings similar states of mind that we perceive in ourselves. The way human minds function enables us to study the world in a manner that no other known species is capable of. Specifically, humans are by nature deeply social.[1] This gives us an evolutionary advantage, but it comes with a price. First, it leads to the possibility of deliberate deception, as we are able not only to tell a lie but also to consider whether it might benefit us somehow.[2] Second, it opens up a modal reality where things can have different outlooks and interpretations. This is helpful for problem solving, but it also creates the possibility for disagreement.

We are equipped with an efficient problem-solving cognitive machinery that enables us to form properly human relations, but our cognitive machinery does not offer perfect, nonperspectival knowledge.[3] We do not enjoy immediate knowledge of the world. Instead, we need to use the skills of judgment to understand the world around us. But reasoning, as a human phenomenon, is always constrained. These constraints are multifaceted and result from a number of factors. Offering a further specification, we can distinguish between external and internal limitations as follows:

1. Justin Barrett, *Cognitive Science, Religion, and Theology: From Human Minds to Divine Minds* (West Conshohocken, PA: Templeton Press, 2011), 73–95.

2. Admittedly, even without theory of mind we could still have disagreements, but they would look rather different. Autistic persons have underdeveloped theory of mind, and it is incomprehensible for them to say things that are not true as they perceive them. Of course, it is possible for two persons suffering from severe autism to disagree, but that would probably be more like two mathematicians disagreeing about the solution of a calculation. See Simon Baron-Cohen, "I Cannot Tell a Lie," *In Character* 3 (Spring 2007): 53–55.

3. This in no way suggests absolute relativism, antirealism, or radical postmodernism, according to which we would be barred from the world by language. I do not find these notions convincing, although I cannot argue against them here. For discussion, see Paul Boghossian, *Fear of Knowledge: Against Relativism and Constructivism* (Oxford: Oxford University Press, 2007).

External

A. Time, location, networks

Internal

B. Personal: motivation, moods, intellectual capacities, intellectual virtues and vices, personal narratives, and experiences

C. Panhuman: Heuristics and biases, cognitive processes, and constraints

In this chapter, I will discuss each of these limitations in turn.

External Limitations

Class A limitations are difficult, but not impossible, to overcome. Nevertheless, having merely a will for change is not enough if external factors are against us. Class B and C limitations can be overcome to some extent by acts of will, and here our greatest enemy is our own self. In the following, I will briefly note these limitations, with which we are so familiar: gaining knowledge requires time, correct materials, helpful colleagues, and the ways of communication that ensure that we understand the dilemmas we are facing.[4]

Time is, arguably, our most valuable commodity. It takes about five years for a typical university student to gain the basic knowledge in his or her area of study.[5] At this stage, the student has mostly theoretical information with only a little amount of practical experience (depending on the discipline, of course). Gaining a PhD takes approximately five more years. The quality of newly minted PhDs varies widely, but even after the additional five years it usually takes to finish a degree, the student has knowledge about only one particular issue in the field. The student does not necessarily know how to relate this knowledge to the field as a whole or to competing theories within his or her area of specialty.[6] When it comes to complicated issues,

4. For discussion on how the natural constraints affect our view of rationality, see Mikael Stenmark, *Rationality in Science, Religion and Everyday Life* (Notre Dame: University of Notre Dame Press, 1995).

5. I am thinking here in the Finnish context. The numbers and observations reflect this educational system.

6. Examples of even higher-level clashes within a particular discipline are, for example, different quests for the historical Jesus in theology and rationality debates in psychology. So it is not surprising that the general public disagrees if even the specialists cannot make sense of what others within their own field are saying.

like arguments in philosophy, it takes great time to master the internal logic and discussion surrounding the argument. But having a lot of time does not necessarily solve our problems. If we are given more time, we may not only have time to resolve our current disputes, we may come up with new things to disagree about.

Location plays a significant role in the intellectual life. If we want to flourish intellectually, we need good books, the right people, and other relevant resources around us that support our thinking. Having online resources and search engines is a help, but we are still dependent on mundane interaction, and rightly so. I cannot take into account many arguments and angles if someone close to me does not suggest and explain them to me. Original ideas are sometimes created in surprising settings, which makes our inquiry dependent on contingent factors and even luck. Sadly, it is a natural tendency to limit our communications to those people who share our views and can enhance them while we simultaneously push away those people who could challenge us.

Recently, Randall Collins and Charles Taylor have demonstrated the relatively contingent nature of philosophical trends and their dependence on networks. This has a mediating effect on our thinking, as the ideas discussed in our contexts are set to a large extent by random processes that are not necessarily truth tracking. Disagreement naturally ensues when people fall under the influence of different currents of thought.

Collins argues that networks play a central role in how philosophical ideas spread and succeed in convincing people. He claims that the success of ideas is to a large extent dependent on contextual factors. Let's assume, for example, that John has come up with a new and interesting idea. Even if John happens to have the right understanding of a particular matter, and he engages in an attempt to communicate this to wider audiences, his endeavor is likely to fail if certain things are not in place. One's ideas can be successful only if one is surrounded by the right kind of people. According to Collins, the successful passing on of ideas requires supportive intellectual groups, master-pupil chains, and beneficial rivalries. It is not possible for John simply to propose an idea and for it to spread widely if there is no demand for such an idea in John's context. Being heard requires that John has a recognized role within the scientific community, which normally means having a degree from a credible university and holding a teaching or research position at a respected institution. This community exists in time, so that it always forms a tradition, an ongoing process of inquiry. In order for the progress to take place, John needs to be connected with that tradition he seeks to develop.

Additionally, it helps if he has a relation to a "master," whose work John develops or critiques.[7]

The intellectuals who have a central role in their respective communities are more often than not those who publish frequently. If John wishes to be successful, he needs to have the skill to rapidly produce material that engages with past knowledge in a creative way.[8] Being creative, of course, can also sometimes mean simply being obnoxious. One obvious option is to pick a fight. The louder and more outrageous the quarrel, the more attention it gets, which consequently helps spread John's ideas.

To make matters even more complex, Collins argues that these new ideas, which he calls "cultural capital," are not enough. John needs to have "emotional energy," which enables him to work with concentration and spread his ideas effectively. This includes engaging in "intellectual rituals," attending conferences, writing articles and books, and appearing in other relevant contexts. However, "emotional energy is not enough: in the absence of sufficient cultural capital and related network positioning in intellectual community, creative enthusiasm is more likely a prelude to frustrated ambitions and failure of recognition."[9]

Of course, debates may push us toward truth, but the result is never secured beforehand. Ideas sometimes fall out of fashion, not because they are refuted but simply because something else becomes available. Charles Taylor, for instance, interprets the rise of secularization in Western societies as a result of the ability to choose one's worldviews more freely. The dwindling public presence of religion in some parts of the West does not result from the maturity of the human race, as the Enlightenment narrative would have us to believe, but from the mere availability of other options. The development in late medieval philosophy and theology, especially the waning of universalism and rise of modal philosophy, enabled the possibility of different spheres of existence. Consequently, there is no single and necessary trajectory that our history must follow. (Something like this was suggested by several Enlightenment thinkers.)[10] We are not moving toward greater unity and harmony

7. Randall Collins, *Sociology of Philosophies: The Global Theory of Intellectual Change* (Cambridge, MA: Belknap Press of Harvard University Press, 1998), 6–7.

8. Collins, *Sociology of Philosophies*, 33. Our intellectual attention space is limited. The law of small numbers restricts the number of viable positions in one space. In the history of philosophy, these positions often appear in pairs so that one philosopher proposes something, which is opposed by another. With regard to particular dilemmas, six is typically the maximum number of voices that our scientific communities can handle.

9. Collins, *Sociology of Philosophies*, 34.

10. G. E. Lessing wrote in his *Die Erziehung des Menschengeschlechts* (1780) that the

as we move from childhood to maturity, or from a religious era to a scientific one. Instead, we are being pushed around by contingent factors, sometimes bringing us closer to truth and sometimes making our thinking muddled.[11]

To summarize, the effects of external limitations on our thinking are enormous. Perhaps one of the greatest dangers is not to realize this, and interpret the trends and ideological movements as somehow inevitable and ultimately progressive. This easily leads to "chronological snobbery," which was defined by C. S. Lewis thus: "the uncritical acceptance of the intellectual climate common to our own age and the assumption that whatever has gone out of date is on that account discredited."[12] Instead of blindly accepting the spirit of the times, Lewis argues for the following stance:

> You must find why it went out of date. Was it ever refuted (and if so by whom, where, and how conclusively) or did it merely die away as fashions do? If the latter, this tells us nothing about its truth or falsehood. From seeing this, one passes to the realization that our own age is also 'a period,' and certainly has, like all periods, its own characteristic illusions. They are likeliest to lurk in those widespread assumptions which are so ingrained in the age that no one dares to attack or feels it necessary to defend them.[13]

Lewis's remarks lead to an uncomfortable idea: maybe our current disagreements lack some angles; perhaps the things we thought were settled are not.

Personal Limitations

In addition to external limitations, we are bound by our internal and personal limitations.

---

human race will develop through the following stages: First, people behave morally in the fear of immediate punishment (Old Testament model); this is followed by obedience in the fear of punishment after this life (New Testament model); and, finally, people reach the mature stage, in which people do good to others for the good itself. Kant picked up this same idea in his *What Is Enlightenment?*, as did later thinkers like Auguste Comte and John Dewey.

11. Charles Taylor, *A Secular Age* (Cambridge, MA: Belknap Press of Harvard University Press, 2008).

12. C. S. Lewis, *Surprised by Joy: The Shape of My Early Life* (New York: Harcourt, Brace, 1955), 207.

13. Lewis, *Surprised by Joy*, 207–8.

Internal

B. Personal: motivation, moods, intellectual capacities, intellectual virtues and vices, personal narratives, and experiences.

Admittedly, the line between external and personal factors can be blurred at times. By emphasizing the *personal* aspect, I wish to set these limitations against *panhuman* limitations, which do not show great variation between individuals. Instead, personal limitations are such that they affect the belief formation of a person differently depending on personal features, such as skills, virtues, experiences, and evaluations at a certain point in time.

Our physical condition affects our mind's capacity and performance. This should not come as a surprise. The amount of sleep and the type of food we have consumed can affect our mental processes. For example, judges tend to pass harsher sentences before dinnertime, when they are hungry.[14]

Obviously, we are affected by our environment in various ways. A related issue is known as *priming*: when subjected to stimuli that relate to our subsequent choices, it is purportedly possible to steer our actions to a desired direction. Or when we have been exposed to certain stimuli, some actions can be performed more easily. However, priming studies have recently been subjected to increasing criticism.[15] In many cases, psychologists have not been able to replicate the results of previous priming studies. Additionally, ruling out other possible influences and factors is incredibly challenging, and often the difference between control groups can be minute.[16] And yet our

14. See, e.g., Shai Danziger, Jonathan Levav, and Liora Avnaim-Pesso, "Extraneous Factors in Judicial Decisions," *Proceedings of the National Academy of Sciences* 108, no. 17 (2011): 6889–92.

15. Ed Yong, "Replication Studies: Bad Copy," *Nature* 485 (2012), 298–300.

16. To take an example where priming seems to be hard to prove, consider video games. There is an ongoing debate on the effects of videogame violence. Some studies point toward the conclusion that playing aggressive games makes some people slightly more aggressive, but only in the short term. Another study suggests that playing violent games had a calming effect on people with depression and ADHD. Obviously, long-term effects are virtually impossible to measure because longer time spans enable the influence of other causes. Nevertheless, video games clearly have an effect, though not the same for everyone. They influence our short-term behavior and judgment in both positive and negative ways, depending on the person. This leads us to conclude, somewhat uninterestingly, that our surroundings may influence us or they may not. There is no easy way to prove the causal link. Teena Willoughby, Paul J. C. Adachi, and Marie Good, "A Longitudinal Study of the Association between Violent Video Game Play and Aggression Among Adolescents," *Developmental Psychology* 48, no. 4 (2011): 1044–57; Christopher J. Ferguson and Cheryl K. Olson, "Video Game Violence among 'Vulnerable' Populations: The Impact of Violent Games on Delinquency and Bullying among

environment undeniably affects us in many ways, even if it is not possible to know exactly how certain stimuli will affect *this* particular individual.

Individual capacities vary a great deal, and we react to our environments based on our own personal features. Some of us are more easily affected by certain manipulation than others. Some of us are better at performing probability calculations, while others are better suited for fast knowledge acquisition and so on. Moreover, some of these personal features are easier to change than others. Concentrating on a single issue: Is it possible to learn to think more carefully? There are studies which suggest that it is possible to enhance one's intelligence and problem-solving skills, at least to some extent.[17] Psychologists call the type of intelligence in question "fluid intelligence." Fluid intelligence is vital for solving problems that require the use of logic and deduction. It helps us to identify patterns, spot relations between different factors, and come up with efficient solutions. Fluid intelligence can be improved by tests that stress our working memory, like N-back tasks. However, some scientists are more skeptical of the long-lasting results of cognitive training.[18] Even if we could improve our thinking to some measure, the average person will not reach Einstein's IQ, even if he or she trains rigorously for years. Although our intelligence is not entirely determined by genes, a relatively large part is. Some of us are better than others at certain tasks; there are no easy ways to change that.

Nevertheless, even if fluid intelligence can be improved, this seldom suffices, as the solutions to our problems often require experience ("crystallized intelligence"). The person who has the kind of experience that enables him or her to act in optimal ways in new situations is called virtuous, or to use Aristotle's concept, "practically wise" (*phronimos*). Like fluid intelligence, moral and intellectual virtues can be developed but not very easily, as they require, among other things, time, motivation, and experience. I will return to this theme in the last chapter.

Children with Clinically Elevated Depression or Attention Deficit Symptoms," *Journal of Youth and Adolescence* 43 (2014): 127–36.

17. Susanne M. Jaeggi et al., "Improving Fluid Intelligence with Training on Working Memory," *Proceedings of the National Academy of Sciences* 28 (2008): 6829–33; Susanne M. Jaeggi, "Short- and Long-Term Benefits of Cognitive Training," *Proceedings of the National Academy of Sciences* 108, no. 25 (2011): 10081–86.

18. Monica Melby-Lervåg and Charles Hulme, "Is Working Memory Training Effective? A Meta-analytic Review," *Developmental Psychology* 49 (2012): 270–91.

The Enemy Inside: The Self and Inner Disagreement

The concept of self is typically employed when we aim to answer questions like, what are we? and, who am I? A minimalist response would be to say that a self is anything that is able to have first-person thoughts. In order to have this kind of self-experience (such as, "It is I who is looking back at myself in the mirror") in the sense that humans and some animals do, symbolic language and self-consciousness are required, although this does not yet give us an answer to what the self *is*. The question about the nature of the self is one of the most complex issues in contemporary philosophy of mind, and often the discussion is rather cluttered because philosophy, theology, and the sciences are trying to answer different questions.[19] For example, scientists are looking for the neurological and biological basis for the sense of self, while sociologists observe the social processes that shape our sense of self. Philosophers and theologians are often interested in the metaphysical and ontological questions, such as, is there a thing we can call "the self"? They may also look at the bigger picture and try to find ways to tie together these different levels of understanding.

All of these inquiries are interesting in their own right. For the sake of my theme, I will concentrate on *the sense of self*, and not on the ontological question about what the self is. Sociology is, among other things, interested in those mechanisms that shape our self-image. More deterministic theories see individual selves as mere reflections of the environment they happen to dwell in; this view is sometimes called "environmentalism." In order to confront this kind of determinism, it is common to use different concepts to speak about a person's own desires and actions in contrast to the self, as it exists as a product of society. This "unsocial" self brings in the element of indeterminacy. The question of *how much* we are actually able to control how our self-image is formed and how much we can actually decide our actual forms of behavior is open for debate.[20]

19. See, e.g., Nancey Murphy and Christopher C. Knight, eds., *Human Identity at the Intersection of Science, Technology and Religion* (Farnham, UK: Ashgate, 2010); Wentzel van Hyussteen and Erik Wiebe, eds., *In Search of the Self: Interdisciplinary Perspectives in Personhood* (Grand Rapids: Eerdmans, 2011).

20. For a sociological point of view, see Anthony Elliot, *Concepts of the Self*, 2nd ed. (Cambridge: Polity, 2009). Postmodernists usually speak about "subject" instead of self as it draws attention to being subjected to something, being influenced from the outside. Postmodern theory of the subject attacks stereotypical and frozen definitions of the self, in favor of more fluid and plural identities. The apparent paradox is that, in its radical forms, this

Contemporary psychology and sociology readily acknowledge the plural nature of human self-conceptions. We can inhabit multiple self-understandings in our lives, even simultaneously. From the sociological perspective, the self appears as the place where conflicting powers meet and clash with each other. Therefore, we have disagreements not only between individuals and larger groups but also within our very selves.

Here I make use of Hubert Hermans's account of the self, known as the dialogical self theory (DST), as it gives a fairly accurate overview of how contemporary Westerners feel about their world and convictions. According to DST, selves are born and constantly shaped by social and historical processes. In a word, we, as individual and social beings, are not fixed, immutable entities, but more like currents of thought that are expanded in time and space. We have histories that have brought us to this point, and our histories have shaped our sensibilities, intellectual habits, and cognitive aptitude. DST sees the contemporary self as a kind of microcosm of the larger society: while the society is an amalgam of various stories, stances, arguments, and traditions, so is the individual self, which reflects the surrounding reality. What is typical for our time is that there are many different building materials available for our worldviews and values. Hetty Zock explains this background of DST as follows:

> Although the self is by nature "multivoiced," the cultural heterogeneity and the pace of cultural and technological change in our era have led to the extension of this process and the increase of the number of cultural voices. As self and society are mutually inclusive, the societal diversity will lead to a greater diversity in the self, which will get more "multivoiced." This has pros (the opening up of new horizons) as well as cons: the development of the self is becoming more complex, uncertainty increases, and inner and outer crises are getting more intertwined.[21]

Consequently, Hermans defines our time through the experience of uncertainty.

---

politically motivated ideological strategy seems to make any sustained and public political action ultimately vacuous or even more subject to the abuse of power.

21. Hetty Zock, "Voicing the Self in Postsecular Society: A Psychological Perspective on Meaning-Making and Collective Identities," in *Exploring the Postsecular: The Religious, the Political and the Urban*, ed. Arie Molendijk, Justin Beaumont, and Christoph Jedan (Leiden: Brill, 2010), 136.

We see the experience of uncertainty as composed of four aspects: (i) *complexity*, referring to a great number of parts (of self and society) that have a variety of interconnections; (ii) *ambiguity*, referring to a suspension of clarity, as the meaning of one part is determined by the flux and variation of the other parts; (iii) *deficit knowledge*, referring to the absence of a superordinate knowledge structure that is able to resolve the contradictions between the parts; and (iv) *unpredictability*, implying a lack of control of future developments. We assume that the experience of uncertainty reflects a global situation of multi-voicedness (complexity) that does not allow a fixation of meaning (ambiguity), that has no super-ordinate voice for resolving contradictions and conflicting information (deficit knowledge), and that is to a large extent unpredictable.[22]

Our projects of self-building take different forms depending on our historical contexts. Dealing with the uncertainty that the postmodern situation creates can take various forms. One may retreat from the world to silence the different voices, surrender to just one voice and obey it, make the boundary between the self and others clearer and more visible by declaring others somehow suspect, or increase the number of voices and adopt a broadly understood relativistic attitude. These survival methods are all likely to create problems of their own.

Hermans distinguishes these three models of self: The *traditional self* is characterized by hierarchies and clear uniformity and is usually rooted in a Platonist worldview. This is contrasted with the *modern self*, which is autonomous and relies on individual judgment and reason. Modern selves still believe in universal truth, but getting there requires a dualism between faith and reason, theory and practice, and fact and value. The *postmodern self* transcends these by a skeptical attitude toward universal rules, values, and hierarchies; it embraces diversity and fragmentation instead of unity. The gist of DST is that all these three models of self exist simultaneously in our Western culture. The constructive point of DST is that it hopes to demonstrate how all three of these models of the self are somehow deficient and that a dialogical understanding of the self would be able to circumvent these problems. Namely, these models are not able to capture all the essential features but only limited yet important aspects. On the other

22. Hubert Hermans and Agnieszka Hermans-Konopka, *Dialogical Self Theory: Positioning and Counter-Positioning in a Global Society* (Cambridge: Cambridge University Press, 2012), 3.

hand, we are not isolated entities, but we are not totally dispersed across the environment either; hence the name "dialogical self," which seeks to keep together these two notions without denying either one. In the best-case scenario, this should lead to a more relaxed identity. Since we know that we are located in time and space and our current identities are constructed as a series of our past events and we do not yet know what is to become of us, we should not hold on too tightly to our current beliefs but understand our selves as unfinished processes. In short, understanding ourselves as inherently dialectical should make us more capable of dealing with the sense of uncertainty.[23]

In this context, it is customary to speak about narrative identity. Among others, Alasdair MacIntyre, Charles Taylor, and Paul Ricoeur have stressed the role of narratives in our understanding of the self.[24] Narrative identity theories claim that the self is not an unchanging entity but comes into being when our life is presented in the form of a narrative.[25] The narrative reading of our identities has multiple purposes. First, it attempts to offer a way to maintain a unified self without resorting to metaphysical notions like souls, which are not universally acknowledged as suitable philosophical concepts. Second, narrative identity theory often takes a prescriptive stance according to which the good life is the one that is lived narratively, that is to say, coherently. Third, the narrative reading of identity underscores the role of our histories in our thinking and consequent need for critical inquiry. This is particularly true of Alasdair MacIntyre's readings of Western philosophy: our values and norms are inextricably tied to the stories that we tell about the nature of the world and our place in it.

Nevertheless, even if narrative identity describes our nonideal state well, it does not solve all our problems. For example, Richard Kearney notes that "storytelling can also be a breeding ground of illusions, distortions and

23. Hermans and Hermans-Konopka, *Dialogical Self Theory*, 4–5. A similar argument is made in Taylor, *Sources of the Self: The Making of Modern Identity* (Cambridge: Cambridge University Press, 1989), 495–99. Hubert Hermans, "The Dialogical Self," in *The Oxford Handbook of the Self*, ed. Shaun Gallagher (Oxford: Oxford University Press, 2011), 671–77.

24. Taylor, *Sources of the Self*; Richard Kearney, *On Paul Ricoeur: The Owl of Minerva* (Aldershot: Ashgate, 2004), 108–10, 157–60.

25. The narrative self is sometimes contrasted with the episodic self. Perhaps the best artistic portrayal of an episodic self is the representation of singer-songwriter Bob Dylan in the movie *I'm Not There* (2008), where Dylan is portrayed by different actors in a way that does not seem to form a coherent story. See also Leon Turner, *Theology, Psychology and Plural Self* (Farnham, UK: Ashgate, 2008); Christian Smith, *What Is a Person?* (Chicago: University of Chicago Press, 2010).

ideological falsehoods. In configuring heterogeneous elements of our experience, narrative emplotment can easily serve as a cover-up. Narrative concordance can mask discordance, its drive for order and unity displacing difference."[26] Of course, one may add to Kearney's list the opposite: difference can be attributed to things that are unified and ordered, and stories can be used to counter all kinds of arguments. In the end, we are often untrustworthy narrators of our own stories.[27]

To confront these problems, narrative identity theorists typically underscore the need for critical self-questioning. Since narratives often are tools of power, counternarratives that unmask the power structures must be told to challenge them. Kearney insists that narrative identities are grounded in narrative imagination; this requires "critical fluidity and openness," which enables one to realize that identities are always made and remade. Embracing this kind of corrective process guards against self-righteousness and fundamentalism.[28] Yet here one is reminded again of the limits of narrative theories as comprehensive metaphysical models where the world and self are what they are subjectively perceived to be. The demand to be "critical" presupposes an ontological structure to reality in which one can have more or less correct beliefs about the world. Without this ontological scaffolding, it would not be reasonable to say that critical questioning is any better than fundamentalism.

In sum, narrative and dialogical theories can serve as a descriptive and analytical tool for analyzing internal and external dialogues against a specific cultural background and structures of power. They offer a descriptive account of the subjective states of the inhabitants of our world: people live their lives according to mutually conflicting stories (both internally and externally). In conclusion, these limitations that pertain to our identities are personal in the sense that they depend on our current

26. Kearney, *On Paul Ricoeur*, 109.

27. This is stressed by, e.g., Edith Stein, who argues that we often need others to correct our perceptions of ourselves. See Stein, *On the Problem of Empathy*, trans. Waltrau Stein (Washington, DC: ICS Publications, 1989), 89. James William McClendon, *Biography as Theology* (Eugene, OR: Wipf and Stock, 1974), vi: "Autobiography runs an extreme risk of self-deception. The ordinary biographer can of course be mistaken, but only the *auto*biographer is virtually sure to produce a self-deceived account." Stanley Hauerwas, *Hannah's Child: A Theologian's Memoir* (Grand Rapids: Eerdmans, 2010), 159: "I do not get to determine the truthfulness of my story. Rather, those who live according to the gospel will be the ones to determine where I have been truthful and where I have deceived myself." See also Kristján Kristjánsson, *Virtues and Vices in Positive Psychology* (Cambridge: Cambridge University Press, 2013), 57.

28. Kearney, *On Paul Ricoeur*, 110.

state of mind as individuals. Based on our experiences and narratives, we are set into a certain interpretative framework, which, on the one hand, offers a connection with the world but, on the other hand, restricts and, in the worst-case scenario, distorts our thinking. Next, I will move on to panhuman features that tend to have effects similar to narrative theories: they open a new window to reality while simultaneously running the risk of distorting what we perceive.

2.2. The Nature of Human Rationality and Decision-Making

In our survey through the history of philosophy, we noticed a pervasive trend to solve disagreements by way of reason alone. However, these accounts had to be immediately supplemented by explaining why reasoning often goes wrong. Interestingly, recent studies in cognitive psychology have suggested that humans are not that rational after all. These claims have sparked the so-called rationality war.[29] How rational or irrational is human thinking? Does the fact that our decision-making is very much like that of other animals and, to a large extent, subconscious explain why humans make consistently poor choices? The stakes are high because our notion of rationality grounds scientific and interpretative endeavors that have enormous influence on human social reality, such as economics, moral philosophy, and behavioral sciences. Further, our metalevel understanding of rationality functions in the background when we think about what counts as rational in philosophy and theology, for instance.

However, many claims about human irrationality have created unnecessary confusion due to poor choice of words. Keith Stanovich clarifies that rationality can be described in both a weak, categorical sense and in a strong, normative sense.[30] Categorical claims about human rationality are meant to set humans against other creatures. Humans have certain cognitive capabilities that are lacking in, for example, bears and bees. Humans are culpable for their actions, therefore, because humans are always "rational," while animal behavior is "a-rational." When cognitive scientists speak about rationality, they do not use it in the categorical sense. Instead, their normative use refers

29. Richard Samuels, Stephen Stich, and Michael Bishop, "Ending the Rationality Wars: How to Make Disputes about Human Rationality Disappear," in *Common Sense, Reasoning, and Rationality*, ed. Renee Elio (New York: Oxford University Press, 2002), 236–68.

30. Keith Stanovich, *Rationality and the Reflective Mind* (Oxford: Oxford University Press, 2010), 3–4.

to the fact that human behavior is less than optimal. Irrationality in this sense does not imply that the action is performed without consulting the cognitive machinery that makes us human. Rather, their claims about purported lack of rationality refer to our habit of making suboptimal choices, despite the availability of uniquely human reason.

To simplify the nature of the debate, the field is customarily split between two factions: meliorists and Panglossians.[31] Due to the available methods that we use to observe human judgment, it is easier and safer to focus on errors rather than optimal performance. When Daniel Kahneman and Amos Tversky initiated their now-famous research program on heuristics and biases of human decision-making, it was natural to concentrate on cases where individuals perform in suboptimal ways. At the center of the heuristics-and-biases paradigm is the common habit of taking the easy way out, commonly known as "cognitive ease."[32] Heuristics refer to the simple rules that people use to make their thinking and decision-making faster. Sometimes this leads to biases, for example, when instead of reaching informed conclusions we rely on default presentations and even prejudices. Our thinking is based on these mechanisms and heuristics that help us to think fast and truthfully about everyday situations. However, these "fast and frugal" systems might not track the truth in all matters, especially when abstract thinking and reflection are needed.

Meliorists, like Kahneman, think that human decision-making is in desperate need of debiasing. We need to become more conscientious and knowledgeable about our mental life. By training, we can become more rational in the strong sense of the word. Meliorists typically offer two solutions to the sad state of human reason. First, we should adopt better reasoning strategies and learn to spot the errors before they happen. Second, we should create better environments for thinking that effectively support debiasing and lessen the influence of harmful biases. However, meliorists recognize that this is incredibly challenging, and that it is much easier for us to spot irrationality in others than in ourselves.[33]

On the other hand, Panglossians like Gerd Gigerenzer have opposed the meliorists' pessimistic conclusions about the human mind. In their view, the focus of the heuristics-and-biases program is wrongly directed. If we

---

31. Stanovich, *Rationality and the Reflective Mind*, 7–9.

32. Daniel Kahneman, *Thinking, Fast and Slow* (London: Allen Lane, 2011), 59–70.

33. Every chapter in Kahneman, *Thinking, Fast and Slow*, contains some simple rules and examples on how to alleviate potentially harmful biases.

observe human judgment as a whole, people get to the truth and get the job done—at least most of the time. Taking computers as the norm for human thinking is wrong for several reasons. The environment of human decisions includes so many variables that human decisions cannot be made simply through calculating expected utility values. Meliorists, of course, admit that humans do not always perform optimally, but that is something that we cannot necessarily deduce from the studies carried out in the heuristics-and-biases paradigm. In many of these tests, the situation is presented to the test subjects in a form that is not natural for us from an evolutionary perspective. If the formulation of the task is changed to reflect our actual life conditions, we perform significantly better.[34]

Dual-Process Accounts

One of the basic theories in contemporary psychology is the dual-process account of reasoning and information processing. Dual-process accounts have been discussed, analyzed, developed, and criticized by theorists in this field for some time, but its basic structure has remained more or less the same:[35] our decisions are, very roughly, the outcome of two information-processing types, called type 1 and type 2.[36] These types are like two detectives who have

34. Gerd Gigerenzer, *Rationality for Mortals: How People Cope with Uncertainty* (Oxford: Oxford University Press, 2010), 3–19.
35. See, e.g., Jonathan Evans, "In Two Minds: Dual-Process Accounts of Reasoning," *Trends in Cognitive Science* 10 (2003): 454–59; Evans, "Dual-Processing Accounts of Reasoning," *Annual Review of Psychology* 58 (2008): 255–78; Kahneman, *Thinking, Fast and Slow*; Stanovich, *Rationality and the Reflective Mind.* For criticisms of DPAs, see, e.g., Gideon Keren and Yaachoc Schul, "Two Is Not Always Better Than One," *Perspectives on Psychological Science* 4 (2009): 533–50; Arie W. Kruglanski and Gerd Gigerenzer, "Intuitive and Deliberative Judgments Are Based on Common Principles," *Psychological Review* 118 (2011): 97–109. Some responses are offered in Jonathan Evans and Keith E. Stanovich, "Dual-Process Theories of Higher Cognition: Advancing the Debate," *Perspectives on Psychological Science* 8 (2013): 223–41. It is not my intent in this paper to evaluate the merits and demerits of the critiques and responses.
36. Stanovich, *Rationality and the Reflective Mind*, 18. Evans and Stanovich ("Dual-Process Theories of Higher Cognition," 224–27) state that they now use "type" instead of "system." This differs from the general practice that has been adopted by many. For example, Kahneman (*Thinking, Fast and Slow*) speaks of "systems," but this can have unwanted consequences if it leads people to think that there are exactly two systems of information processing or that they refer to clear-cut entities, which are located in specific neurological systems. Also, Kahneman admits that when he is speaking about "systems" he is referring to fictional entities. The idea of two systems appears, of course, already in ancient Greek philosophy and more recently in

their own special skills. When the problems are simple, detective 1 takes the case. When we are dealing not with a simple case of shoplifting, for example, but with a serial killer, detective 2 steps in. Detective 1 is good at catching shoplifters because he runs fast, but he is not particularly clever. Detective 2 cannot run, but he can think.

From an evolutionary viewpoint, type 1 developed first, in order to ensure survival in an environment that required quick decisions. This is a feature common to both humans and other animals, whereas type 2 is considered to be a genuinely human feature, as it requires high-level computational skills.

Type 1 is fast and automatic. When we perceive something, it starts to function without conscious effort. If the object of experience is familiar, type 1 takes care of it without calling for help from type 2. Only in cases where one perceives something surprising, strange, or difficult does type 2 engage. Type 2 is slow and under conscious control; instead of quick, often emotional reactions, it follows rules to reach neutral and well-argued conclusions.

Type 1 contains several mechanisms that are designed to perform certain tasks. When a module detects certain triggering events, it turns on automatically. Think, for example, of a situation in which you hear a loud "bang" from behind you. Your physical reaction is immediate; you do not consult your slower system to determine your preferred mode of conduct. You turn, crouch, and cover yourself before you are able to think about doing so.

These two types have the following neurological basis. When we experience something, the thalamus relays the stimuli to the part of the brain that it judges the best to handle the case. The cases that end up in the amygdala are met with a fast, emotional response. If a deeper investigation is needed and there is no apparent threat in the vicinity, the case is moved to the neocortex, also known as "the thinking brain," where it is processed slowly and with less emotional interference. Even though the thalamus's functions are beyond our conscious control, they are not immutable. It performs selections based on habitual patterns, which can be transformed through other habits. The characteristics of type 1 and type 2 are listed in table 2.

William James. Sometimes they are referred to as "implicit" and "explicit" or "intuitive" and "reflexive" systems. For a list of other studies and different ways of referring to these systems, see Stanovich, *Rationality and the Reflective Mind*, 18.

Table 2. Two types of cognitive processing

Type 1*	Type 2
Evolutionarily old	Evolutionarily new
Shared with animals	Uniquely human
Generates impressions, feelings, and inclinations; when endorsed by type 2 these become beliefs, attitudes, and intentions	Engages in conscious reflection and assessing of arguments
Operates automatically and quickly	Slow
Low effort	Energy consuming
Nonvoluntary, unconscious (preconscious)	Voluntary, conscious
Independent of general intelligence	Independent of general intelligence
Can be programmed by type 2 to mobilize attention when a particular pattern is detected	Follows general rules of logic
Executes skilled responses and generates skilled intuitions, after adequate training	Type 1 can override type 2 if type 2 is "lazy"
Links sense of cognitive ease to illusions of truth, pleasant feelings, and reduced vigilance	Can learn new things and adjust itself faster than type 1
Distinguishes surprises from the normal	In proper contexts, can exercise control over type 1
Neglects ambiguity and suppresses doubt	
Is biased to believe and confirm	
Exaggerates emotional consistency	
Focuses on existing evidence and ignores absent evidence	
Generates a limited set of basic assessments	
Sometimes substitutes an easier question for a difficult one	
Overweights low probabilities	
Frames decision problems narrowly, in isolation from one another	

*Quoted selectively from Kahneman, *Thinking, Fast and Slow*, 105; Evans, "Dual-Processing Accounts of Reasoning," 257.

Meliorists argue that humans are more rational when type 2 corrects type 1 whenever needed. "Rational override" happens when type 2 sets type 1 straight. "Dysrational override" takes place when type 1 thwarts type 2. In these cases our emotions, prejudices, and biases affect our decision-making in a harmful way.

Kahneman thinks that a great deal of human misery results from dysrational override, which effectively tanks our thinking to suboptimal levels. Our brains were not evolved to deal with complex situations, which require accurate knowledge processing. To make matters worse, modern communication technology (e.g., Twitter, Facebook, tabloid journalism, and infotainment) almost solely employs type 1.

An example of how type 1 harms social life when joined with modern technology involves an incident that took place in a Finnish school in 2013. A teacher removed an ill-behaving student from the cafeteria, and was later accused of illegitimate use of force and therefore was discharged. Tabloids publicized the incident as an example of how schools have eliminated all means of discipline and are therefore becoming war zones due to "soft" values that prevent any punishment. Within two days, an Internet petition in favor of the teacher spread quickly via social media and was signed by over 200,000 concerned citizens, an astonishing 4 percent of the Finnish population. At this point no one knew what had really happened; signatories based their opinions on tabloids and rumors. After an extended investigation, it was found that the teacher's use of force had indeed been inconsiderate in that context, although firing him had been illegal as well. In the end, there was nothing in the incident that deserved nationwide interest and news coverage.

To offer a second example, *Wired* magazine reported a story in 2013 concerning Chicago gangs' use of social media to facilitate violent confrontations. According to the Chicago Police Department, 80 percent of all school disturbances result from social media exchanges.[37] These examples show how significant numbers of people can become violent in support of a cause they do not really understand when somebody no more than snaps their fingers, and how modern technology takes advantage of this weakness.

Recently, Keith Stanovich has redefined some aspects of the dual-process theory. He splits type 2 into two parts: the algorithmic mind and

37. Ben Austen, "Public Enemies: Social Media Is Fueling Gang Wars in Chicago," *Wired*, September 17, 2013, http://www.wired.com/underwire/2013/09/gangs-of-social-media/all/.

the reflective mind. The algorithmic mind is in charge of calculations, while the reflective mind controls various dispositions employed in knowledge acquisition. There are several reasons for making this distinction. One is that there are several biases that hinder type 2 thinking in cases where the intelligence of the test subjects is equal.[38] Hence there has to be something else in type 2 that produces the result. These cognitive propensities can vary from subject to subject, and include, among others, the following characteristics:

> [the] tendency to collect information before making up one's mind, the tendency to seek various points of view before coming to a conclusion, the disposition to think extensively about a problem before responding, the tendency to calibrate the degree of strength of one's opinion to the degree of evidence available, the tendency to think about the future consequences before taking action, the tendency to explicitly weigh pluses and minuses of situations before making a decision, and the tendency to seek nuance and avoid absolutism. In short, individual differences in thinking dispositions are assessing variation on people's goal management, epistemic values, and epistemic self-regulation—differences in the operation of the reflective mind.[39]

Stanovich points out that current intelligence tests solely measure the algorithmic mind's effectiveness, leaving more holistic thinking dispositions out of the picture of rationality.[40] This has far-reaching consequences for how we think about human rationality and judgment. Interestingly, there seems to be only a very weak correlation between the algorithmic mind and the reflective mind. In other words, a person can be good in math but make very poor life choices and lack the abilities to use his or her skills for good. Or one may have excellent thinking dispositions and be conscientious and thorough while lacking high-level computational skills. Fortuitously, Stanovich offers a word of consolation to those of us who did not excel in math: "A longitudinal analysis showed that self-discipline was a better predictor of changes in grade point average across the school year than intelligence. A converging finding is that the personality variable of conscientiousness—which taps the higher-level regulatory properties of the reflective mind—has been shown to

38. Stanovich, *Rationality and the Reflective Mind*, 34.
39. Stanovich, *Rationality and the Reflective Mind*, 36.
40. For an overview of algorithmic reasoning, see Philip Johnson-Laird, *How We Reason* (Oxford: Oxford University Press, 2006).

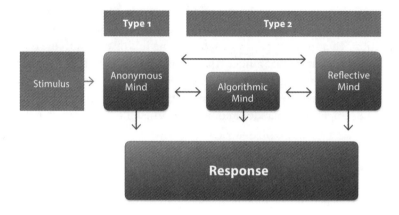

Figure 2. Stanovich's model of the dual-process account

predict (independent of intelligence) academic performance and measures of performance in the workplace."[41]

The dual-process theory, especially the tripartite version of it, can help us come to terms with the thinking processes that create situations in which people disagree. Mere intelligence is not going to offer much help, as rationality is to a large extent governed by thinking dispositions, or as I prefer to call them, *virtues*. This is important, and I will return to this theme in the last chapter, where virtues will be discussed at length.

Ecological Rationality

Gerd Gigerenzer agrees with Kahneman to a certain extent, as he also subscribes to the dual-process theory. However, he disagrees with Kahneman regarding the best form of rationality for humans. From his viewpoint, Kahneman's normative experiments are too tied to situations where factors are known and controllable. In normal environments, this is not the case. In everyday life, type 1 is able to perform relatively well by relying on its "gut feelings."[42]

41. Stanovich, *Rationality and the Reflective Mind*, 43–45.
42. Gerd Gigerenzer, *Gut Feelings: The Intelligence of the Unconscious* (London: Penguin, 2007).

Gigerenzer has argued that the picture of human rationality that has been influential since the Enlightenment is actually unfit for humans.[43] The ideal of "unbounded" rationality was based on concepts such as omniscience, unlimited computational power, and a fully determined and predictable universe. Gigerenzer claims that this idea was borrowed from the Christian notion of God, and humans as earthly images of God. This alleged similarity to God was transformed into a secularized version of deity, Laplace's demon (who is able to predict every future state of the universe because it knows every physical law and past states of affairs). This Laplacean vision of human rationality has dominated the social imagination of Western sciences for centuries, and it manifested itself especially in the Enlightenment dream of absolute certainty, which was supposed to drive away disagreement.[44]

Gigerenzer, however, thinks that this Laplacean notion is fundamentally flawed. Actual human minds have not developed to act in the way Laplace's demon is supposed to act: we are not omniscient, we have only limited amounts of time and energy, and we are quite poor at predicting the future. Therefore, defining the norm of human rationality using the demon as a yardstick is bound to recommend a strongly antihuman notion of rationality.

From the viewpoint of evolution, human reason developed to solve particular tasks in particular environments. The guiding norm of this process was not universal logic but cost-effective decision-making. In humanity's primitive stages, we had to be able to come to correct conclusions quickly and with little information. Decisions we make are based, on the one hand, on our evolved abilities that come to us naturally without the need for time- and energy-consuming reflection. On the other hand, our abilities and skills of judgment are to a large extent context sensitive. Some abilities work in certain contexts but are totally useless in some others. In Gigerenzer's view, human rationality needs to be approached, not from the ideal situation, but from the perspective of the actual, experienced world. In order to act rationally, we need to apply correct measures in right environments; this does not happen by following an abstract, universal rule or norm.[45]

Naturally, this complicates things. Gigerenzer's view of rationality makes decision-making highly contextual and opaque, as "ecological ratio-

43. Gerd Gigerenzer, "Bounded and Rational," in *Contemporary Debates in Cognitive Science*, ed. Robert J. Stainton (Oxford: Blackwell, 2006), 115–33. See also David Matheson, "Bounded Rationality and the Enlightenment Picture of Cognitive Virtue," in Stainton, *Contemporary Debates in Cognitive Science*, 143–44.

44. Gigerenzer, "Bounded and Rational," 116.

45. Gigerenzer, "Bounded and Rational," 120–21, 129.

nality . . . defines the rationality of heuristics independently of optimization and content-blind norms, by the degree to which they are adapted to environments."[46] Gigerenzer merely describes how humans perform in their real-life settings. Oftentimes we do not consult laws of logic, and doing so is unnecessary since several everyday choices are not computable in the first place (45).

This leads Gigerenzer to make a normative claim: we should not think computer-like reasoning is available to us or that such reasoning would somehow guarantee a more risk-free world. Resorting to content-blind norms as arbiters has led us astray in our search for an accurate account of human reasoning. It has resulted in an overtly positive picture of human decision-making, which is unable to take into account the complexities of human life and which reduces our choices to mere utilitarian calculations. Moreover, various virtues fall outside this sphere because they are supposed to transcend such things as personal utility. The ideal of human flourishing has often led us to ask the wrong questions and resulted in more confusion regarding human decision-making (75).

Gigerenzer's ecological rationality will lead to acknowledging substantial disagreements in human reasoning. Although he eschews Enlightenment ideals, he does side with Kant in giving description to what living in an uncertain world requires: the ability to think for oneself (151). He realizes that it requires quite a lot of effort for us to come to terms with our true nature and the inevitable constraints of human societies after the long rule of the ideal of certainty and absoluteness. He hopes that this will eventually lead humans to become more tolerant toward diversity and enable us to monitor our reactions better, although he does not really say how we are to achieve that goal. Gigerenzer does, however, suggest that "factual information will not change everyone's behavior, but by knowing the facts, people can understand their immediate emotional reactions and better control them" (97).

Ecological rationality acknowledges the possibility of error. In fact, it sees some errors as inevitable and even good. "The characteristic of a good error is that a person is better off making it than not making it—for reaching a goal more quickly or for attaining it at all. In this view, every intelligent system has to make errors; making none would destroy the intelligence of the system" (66). Making errors makes us more experienced and increases knowledge that would be otherwise unattainable.

In Gigerenzer's view we should expect disagreements in human soci-

---

46. Gigerenzer, *Rationality for Mortals*, 19. In-text references through the end of this section are to this work.

eties. The realistic goal is not the elimination of disagreement by imposing some methods or constraints that would create more uniform and consensual thinking, because, with brains like ours, such a possibility is not realistic. Humans are not machines, and certainly not demons. Our reasoning is bounded, certainly, but it is also effective in the proper contexts. The crucial problem is how to recognize the correct modes of reasoning and employ them in the right context. This is a messy question, but according to Gigerenzer we cannot really hope for anything better.

Summing up the discussion on rationality: no matter which side of the debate we land on, it is clear that human reasoning has its limits and is constrained by various factors. The fault line between Panglossians and meliorists runs along the notion of ideal rationality, but everyone agrees that human cognitive performance is often suboptimal, especially when it functions in a foreign environment. Nevertheless, by changing the contours of the decision-making environment and paying more attention to the processes, we may improve our thinking. Therefore, even if human thinking is not perfect, we may exercise a precarious optimism. In order to fully understand the weak points of human thinking, we turn to cognitive biases next.

2.3. Cognitive Biases

At this point, the concept of "bias" has already come up several times, but its nature has not yet been adequately explained. To use a simple but reductive metaphor (given the discussion in the previous section), our brains are like computers, which need operating systems to function. The operating system consists of simple applications (biases) that perform different tasks and make it easy and economical to lead our daily lives. It is, however, important to note that biases are not necessarily harmful. Instead, they are essential tools that we need to survive. Herein lies the problem. Biases are not automatically interested in truth, but in survival.

It is not possible to go through all biases because they are so numerous.[47] I will concentrate on those that are relevant for our theme. A short list of our most common biases looks as follows.

---

47. Just as an example, the current *Wikipedia* article ("List of Cognitive Biases") mentions well over one hundred different biases. For a helpful guide to biases with an emphasis on Christian settings, see Christena Cleveland, *Disunity in Christ: Uncovering the Hidden Forces That Keep Us Apart* (Downers Grove, IL: IVP Books, 2013).

Self-serving-my-side bias: We are harsher toward out-group than in-group individuals. Linda Babcock and George Loewenstein performed a study where they gave the same court case to two groups for investigation and judgment.[48] The first group was divided between plaintiffs and defendants, the second was not. Both groups received the same evidence. The first group interpreted the evidence favoring their randomly selected side, while the second group showed more variation in their judgments. If we currently inhabit a clearly defined identity and have well-argued convictions, it is harder for us to take into account the opposing arguments and see their rationale.

Simplicity bias: We favor simple solutions. Sometimes "Ockham's razor" is thought to mean that the simplest solution is the correct one, but this is not true. Ockham's razor means only that we should accept the simplest of all the possible explanations, if everything else is equal. But nothing here means that mere simplicity is an indication of truth. Nevertheless, we automatically favor simple solutions because they save time and energy. It is easy to see how propaganda can utilize this cognitive feature. Blaming the Jews for the misfortunes of Germany worked in the 1930s because it conveniently offered a simple solution to a highly complicated matter.

Coherency bias (rationalization effect): We aim to maintain equilibrium in our belief system, so we explain phenomena that create internal conflict in ways that balance with our previous beliefs with minimal changes. This can mean turning a blind eye to evidence that conflicts with our beliefs, or interpreting it in a way that supports our cause.

Confirmation bias: We automatically seek to confirm our current beliefs and neglect conflicting evidence. We read books that confirm our current views and spend more time in activities that strengthen our current commitments than in activities that could potentially challenge them.[49] We also detect fallacies more easily in material that presents views we do not like, whereas we tend to be blind to the same fallacies in literature that supports our own views.[50]

Belief perseverance bias: We cling to our beliefs even when it is demonstrated that the grounds we based our beliefs on were fabricated in order to fool us. In a study, two groups were given opposite claims, according to

48. Linda Babcock and George Loewenstein, "Explaining Bargaining Impasse: The Role of Self-Serving Biases," *Journal of Economic Perspectives* 11 (1997): 109–26.

49. For simplicity, confirmation, and coherence biases, see Gilbert Harman, "Practical Aspects of Theoretical Reasoning," in *The Oxford Handbook of Rationality*, ed. Alfred E. Mele and Piers Rawling (Oxford: Oxford University Press, 2004), 45–56.

50. Thomas Kelly, "Disagreement, Dogmatism, and Belief Polarization," *Journal of Philosophy* 105 (2008): 618.

which risk-taking fire fighters are better or worse in their job. These claims were presented with faux data that supported the given view. Naturally, people adopted the view that was supported by their evidence. But later, when they were told that the evidence was false, they maintained their view.[51] As Nietzsche wrote, "For this is how man is: an article of faith could be refuted before him a thousand times—if he needed it, he would consider it true again and again."[52]

Availability/recognition heuristic: When faced with a choice of multiple options, we typically choose the one most familiar to us. If some idea comes to us easily, we automatically consider it more probable.[53] As an example, I was walking in London one day when I saw a banner with a picture of a nun hanging above a church entrance. There was no name on the banner, but I made a guess that the nun was St. Edith Stein; my guess was correct. When reverse engineering my rationalization, I saw how I had made the choice. I know only two famous nuns, and the nun in the picture was not Mother Teresa; it *had* to be St. Edith Stein. Of course, the recognition heuristic does not guarantee that the face of an unknown nun always belongs to St. Edith Stein. Recognition heuristics can help us make efficient choices in some situations, but they can also lead us astray, preventing us from critical and fresh thinking because we favor the familiar.

Overconfidence effect/blind-spot bias: Approximately 70 percent of human beings think they are smarter than average. Obviously, something is wrong here. But from a strict evolutionary perspective, overconfidence actually helps us. The chances of Admiral Nelson's fleet at Trafalgar would have probably been slimmer if their ships' names had been *Mainstream*, *Middling*, *Run of the Mill*, *Ephialtes*, and *Vanilla*, instead of *Victory*, *Leviathan*, *Conqueror*, *Minotaur*, and *Defiance*, and so on.

Sadly, people tend to be overconfident when they are unsure. Furthermore, experts are also often prone to overconfidence.[54] Moreover, if someone

51. Craig A. Anderson, Mark R. Lepper, and Lee Ross, "Perseverance of Social Theories: The Role of Explanation in the Persistence of Discredited Information," *Journal of Personality and Social Psychology* 39 (1980): 1037–49.

52. Friedrich Nietzsche, *The Gay Science*, trans. Walter Kaufmann (New York: Vintage, 1969), 347.

53. Leslie Paul Thiele, *The Heart of Judgment: Practical Wisdom, Neuroscience, and Narrative* (Cambridge: Cambridge University Press, 2006), 64. More generally, about the effect of "cognitive ease" to our thinking, see Kahneman, *Thinking, Fast and Slow*, 59–62.

54. Thiele, *Heart of Judgment*, 67. See also Scott Plous, *Psychology of Judgment and Decision-Making* (Philadelphia: Temple University Press, 1993), 219.

thinks they are immune to biases, this is called "blind-spot bias." Recently, a study demonstrated that higher cognitive skills and intelligence do not help in avoiding blind spots. "We found that none of these bias blind spots were attenuated by measures of cognitive sophistication, such as cognitive ability or thinking dispositions related to bias," researchers note. "If anything, a larger bias blind spot was associated with higher cognitive ability." In this particular study, the researchers found no evidence suggesting that knowing one's biases actually makes it easier to overcome them.[55]

Even more troubling is the finding that even when one is given a chance to reflect on different angles and make supposedly ethical choices, this actually increases the likelihood of making unethical judgments later. This phenomenon is known as "moral self-licensing." Researchers claim, "Past good deeds can liberate individuals to engage in behaviors that are immoral, unethical, or otherwise problematic, behaviors that they would otherwise avoid for fear of feeling or appearing immoral."[56] Again the reason behind this odd behavior might have to do with evolutionary fitness. Self-licensing might help us overcome situations that would otherwise lead to indecision while relieving the anxiety that is connected with morally ambiguous decisions.

Contrast effect (framing): The context of our perception tends to distort our judgments. For example, an average-height person looks small when pictured next to a basketball player. A breeze can be warm or cold depending on the temperature to which we were exposed before experiencing the breeze. If an option is presented to us as a "moderate" choice between two "extremes," it is easy to respond to it positively compared to a situation where the choice would have been presented without the same context. Obviously, by choosing the extremes intentionally, one can influence decision-making.

Out-group homogeneity and actor/observer effect: We tend to think that "they" are more homogenous than "us." It is easier for us to allow more diversity when thinking about the in-group, but we need to picture the out-group as somehow more unified and unitary than our in-group. We think that whenever one of "them" makes a choice, they are always acting out their "nature," because "that is just the way they are." On the other hand, *we* never make choices due to our characteristic features. We merely make informed judgments based on careful assessment of the evidence. One rather comical

55. R. F. West, J. Meserve, and K. E. Stanovich, "Cognitive Sophistication Does Not Attenuate the Bias Blind Spot," *Journal of Personality and Social Psychology* 4 (2012): 506–19 (quotations are from the abstract).

56. Ann C. Merritt, Daniel A. Effron, and Benoît Monin, "Moral Self-Licensing: When Being Good Frees Us to Be Bad," *Social and Personality Psychology Compass* 4, no. 5 (2010): 344–57.

result of this is that we think others are always more biased than we are (and others think similarly about us). Recent studies have found that these features do not apply generally to human groups, but the actor/observer effect is strengthened in cases when the groups are hostile to each other.[57]

Groupthink: Biases can also affect groups. If a significant majority of the group favors a particular solution, it is increasingly difficult for individual members to oppose the majority. A typical characteristic of groupthink is the inability to take into account possible hazards or counterarguments. Groupthink can easily take hold of homogenous groups whose members share similar backgrounds and convictions.[58]

Let us draw some conclusions on what has been said so far. If we are typical human beings, we can recognize the above biases in our own past behavior. Yet it is always easier to spot biases in other people, and often very hard to spot them in our own behavior, in the moment. However, biases are not always harmful. They are evolutionarily developed cognitive shortcuts that allow us to process information efficiently, and, as Gigerenzer argues, they help us most of the time. The problem, however, is that we do not automatically know when we are in the appropriate context to rely on them, or when we need to be wary of our biases. The attempt to control biases is called *debiasing*, a theme I will return to later.

On the question of disagreement, the effects of biased thinking are obvious. Biases tend to stagnate our judgment to what we already know and what we deem familiar. In addition, they create opposition between "them" and "us," enforcing this opposition by creating simplistic images of the other and painting our own view in an excessively positive light.

2.4. Two Hemispheres, Two Ways of Thinking

Recent developments in neuroscience have enabled us to observe how our brains and minds are linked: our states of mind are profoundly dependent on the state of our bodies. Psychiatrist Ian McGilchrist, in his ambitious project to interpret the intellectual history of the world in light of the results of neuroscience, offers a parallel view to dual-process theories. According to

---

57. Mark Rubin and Constantina Badea, "They're All the Same! . . . But for Several Different Reasons: A Review of the Multicausal Nature of Perceived Group Variability," *Current Directions in Psychological Science* 21 (2012): 367–72. See also Thiele, *Heart of Judgment*, 66.

58. Paul T. Hart, *Groupthink in Government: A Study of Small Groups and Policy Failure* (Baltimore: Johns Hopkins University Press, 1994).

McGilchrist, human brains have two ways of processing information. These are more or less linked to two hemispheres, as suggested by the title of his book *The Master and His Emissary*, the master being the right hemisphere and the emissary the left.[59] Not only do the two hemispheres have structural differences (33), but they also perform different intellectual functions, as has been demonstrated by studies on split-brain patients (32–94). In optimal conditions, our brain works as a whole, but it is constantly changing and re-acting to its environment. This is commonly known as the brain's "plasticity" (240–56). Therefore, culture can affect how we use our brains and which ways of thinking are promoted and which are not.

The so-called left and right brain are to a large extent metaphors of two different models of thinking, which have physical and neurological bases. They are not, however, prescribed, and we can train ourselves to adopt a more left- or right-brain approach to the world. Some central features of the two hemispheres are outlined in table 3.

Table 3. McGilchrist's model of cognition: the master and the emissary

Left Brain (Emissary)	Right Brain (Master)
"Rational"	"Intuitive"
Objective, measurable data	Subjective experiences
Explanation	Wonder
Utility	Enjoyment
Propositions	Metaphors
Sees the world in the form of separate objects	Sees the world as a network of relationships
Impersonal knowledge	Personal knowledge
Static worldview	Dynamic worldview
Desire to control	Accepts that the world is uncontrollable
Overconfident	Critical and self-reflective
Excludes right brain	Includes left brain

59. Ian McGilchrist, *The Master and His Emissary: The Divided Brain and the Making of the Western World* (New Haven: Yale University Press, 2009). In-text references through the end of this section are to this work. In relation to Stanovich's tripartite model, McGilchrist's hemisphere theory could be seen as depicting functions of algorithmic (left hemisphere) and reflective (right hemisphere) minds.

Now, it is possible to direct ourselves toward either of these ways of thinking.[60] McGilchrist's thesis is that we need both hemispheres to function properly.[61] However, the two hemispheres are constantly in potential conflict, which is caused by the asymmetrical relations between them. "In reality we are a composite of the two hemispheres," McGilchrist notes, "and despite the interesting results of experiments designed artificially to separate their functioning, they work together most of the time at the everyday level. But that does not at all exclude that they may have radically different agendas, and over long time periods and large numbers of individuals it becomes apparent that they each instantiate a way of being in the world that is at conflict with the other" (91).

In the optimal state, the left hemisphere will act as an emissary of the right hemisphere, performing the tasks and solving the problems as the master commands. But we do not live in an ideal world. The left hemisphere has a feature that makes it very hard for it to remain a mere emissary; it wants to become the master. As it is designed to focus on details, it is natural for it to forget that there is something beyond the details. This sets it on a collision course with the right hemisphere.

How then are the different mind-sets made visible in action? McGilchrist follows Max Scheler's distinction between different kinds of values: holiness, intellectual values, values of vitality, and values of use and pleasure. It is typical for the right hemisphere to value these strata in this particular order, so that lower levels receive their inherent value from previous strata. The left hemisphere moves in the *opposite* direction. It maximizes utility value and regards abstract things, such as holiness, as unworthy (160–61).

To give an example, let us consider how "belief" is depicted within these two frameworks (170–71). The left regards belief as the absence of certainty. If one does not have proof, one does not have knowledge, and if one still wants to cling to the conviction in question, it is an irrational belief. This is the critique New Atheist authors continuously repeat.[62] From the right hemisphere's perspective, belief is about something more complex than mere evaluation of the available evidence. Belief is seen as the relationship

60. Everyone with substantive enough experience of different kinds of people is able to bring into mind persons who fit either of these categories, though this model is not meant to be used to categorize people but to recognize different thinking patterns.

61. See also Stanovich, *Rationality and the Reflective Mind*, 37–38.

62. For example, a quote commonly attributed to Richard Dawkins states, "Faith is the great cop-out, the great excuse to evade the need to think and evaluate evidence. Faith is belief in spite of, even perhaps because of, the lack of evidence."

between two living things, which requires trust. Here we have two radically, but not totally, different approaches to the same issue.

> Thus if I say that "I believe you," it does not mean that I think that such-and-such things are the case about you, but can't be certain that I am right. It means that I stand in a certain sort of relation of care towards you, that entails me in certain kinds of ways of behaving (acting and being) towards you, that entails on you the responsibility of certain ways of acting and being as well. (170)

McGilchrist claims that human life flourishes when the hemispheres work in harmony, so that the left hemisphere works under the auspices of the right hemisphere. But if the emissary controls everything, this will cause serious harm. The world and its inhabitants will be seen more and more as machines and their parts, and treated as such.

Kahneman, Gigerenzer, and McGilchrist all point to the fact that human thinking is divided and therefore fragile.[63] The greatest threats to the life of the mind are internal. This is a unique feature of human nature: through a failure to handle its own internal conflicts and reach harmony, it can bring about its own destruction. It is therefore the structure of human rationality that makes us unique, personal, morally responsible for our actions, and in the end capable of forming, and ruining, relations.

2.5. On Being Right(eous)

Typical disagreements in Western societies concern morals. Is the war we are fighting justified? Should government fund abortions? Where is the line between legitimate criticism and hate speech? What is the best way to fight drug abuse? These and many other topics cause people to rise against each other in anger. There is an irony in the fact that moral concerns so easily give rise to immoral words and actions. However, if we look at how human moral deliberation takes place, this is not surprising.

---

63. Diagnoses of different dual-process theorists and McGilchrist differ to some extent. Kahneman thinks that human life goes wrong when there is too little control by type 2. Mc-Gilchrist could be taken to side with Stanovich, as they both seek to balance the functions of calculative and holistic thinking patterns. Even if their diagnoses are emphasized differently, the proposed cure is more or less the same. We need to be able to apply correct means in right environments and avoid monomaniac tendencies.

Here I will follow the so-called moral foundations theory (MFT), developed by psychologist Jonathan Haidt. According to the MFT, moral sense is innate, which means that some forms of moral behaviors are easy to learn and more compelling than others. We are born with tendencies that help us to recognize wanted and unwanted behavior and react to them accordingly.[64] These moral foundations can be developed to become actual virtues through practice and repetition. Despite the innateness of certain moral tendencies, personal histories and life narratives, and even education and indoctrination, can all shape our moral outlook.

This view, held by many intuitionist moral philosophers, has recently been supported in both the cognitive sciences and in the neurosciences. However, it goes beyond older theories, which have located moral reasoning to some particular area in the brain or presupposed some single system that is in charge of morals. Instead, it seems to be that our minds have several moral modules that govern our thinking. Instead of straightforward conscious calculation, we react to moral challenges intuitively with our individual set of moral modules.[65]

On this view, moral decision-making is to a large extent intuitive, employing type 1 cognitive processes. Only later, when pressed, can we give reasons for our moral judgments, but as everything with type 2, this is challenging and time consuming. Already this gives a hint as to why moral disagreements are so hard to solve. If moral judgments are intuitive and unconscious, we lack the immediate capacity to discuss our moral differences.

Determining the factors that shape our intuitions is a matter of debate. Haidt stresses the role of emotions and subconscious intuitions. Recently, he has been criticized for not paying enough attention to the role of social con-

64. Jonathan Haidt, *The Righteous Mind: Why Good People Are Divided by Politics and Religion* (London: Allen Lane, 2012), 278.

65. MFT is meant to replace Kohlberg's moral development theory, where different moral outlooks are depicted as developing from punishment- and obedience-oriented stages toward moral autonomy. Haidt's (*The Righteous Mind*, 6–25) criticism is focused, first, on Kohlberg's neglecting the role of emotions and overemphasizing rationality in moral deliberation. Second, Kohlberg tends to favor unwarrantedly certain values (which are from a global perspective contingent), setting them as the basis from which everything else is judged as underdeveloped. Consequently, the basis, which happens to coincide with liberal values, does not need explanation, whereas nonliberal values do. This eventually turns the theory into a normative proposal instead of a descriptive account of moral deliberation, which it claims to be. Haidt's theory is to a great extent influenced by the theories of anthropologist Richard Schweder, who in his work has focused on cultural variability of moral norms while seeking common, unified features among them.

ventions.[66] Furthermore, some studies suggest that rational consideration in moral matters plays a stronger role than Haidt suggests.[67] Fortunately, this is a debate we do not have to solve here. It appears that our social setting and our rational deliberation will influence our moral compass and shape our intuitions, even though they cannot be totally reprogrammed.

Some studies suggest that we have a shared universal moral sense, which is common to all human cultures, although it gives us only a rough outline for behavior.[68] The differences between various cultures are not about *totally* different moral norms, it is suggested, but about different interpretations—say, what is considered to be fair or how we should define the human person. To give an example: American Republicans define fairness as proportionality; if someone gets something he or she does not deserve or has not strived for, this is considered to be unfair. Democrats have a different interpretation: fairness means equality. This is why it is proper that the rich have higher taxes than the poor. In similar fashion, liberals favor reaching toward more universal and abstract communities (such as "humanity") at the cost of neglecting local, traditional communities (such as family and religion), while conservatives go the opposite direction.[69]

The ordering of cognitive modules that ground our moral reasoning varies from person to person, which consequently produces different moral outlooks. In his recent work, Haidt has distinguished five basic modules, which are connected to particular emotions.[70]

1. Care/harm   compassion
2. Fairness/cheating   anger, gratitude, guilt
3. Loyalty/betrayal   group pride, rage at traitors
4. Authority/subversion   respect, fear
5. Sanctity/degradation   disgust

66. Recently Jordan Kiper and Richard Sosis ("Moral Intuitions and the Religious System: An Adaptationist Account," *Philosophy, Theology and the Sciences* 2 [2014]: 172–99) have argued for a stronger role of social conventions as a slight corrective to Haidt's proposal.

67. Steve Clarke, *The Justification of Religious Violence* (Malden, MA: Wiley-Blackwell, 2014), 77–79.

68. E.g., Jesse Graham, Jonathan Haidt, and Brian A. Nosek, "Liberals and Conservatives Rely on Different Sets of Moral Foundations," *Journal of Personality and Social Psychology* 96 (2009): 1029–46.

69. Haidt, *Righteous Mind*, 137–38.

70. Haidt, *Righteous Mind*, 124.

In a series of studies, Haidt and his colleagues found interesting correlations. More liberal individuals typically use only modules 1 and 2, while conservatives employ all five of them. Haidt goes on to argue that we in fact have three different major moral clusters that are based on different ideas of what humans are.[71] Within "the ethics of autonomy," the person is perceived as a free individual. The "ethics of community" brings in extra-personal entities, such as family, sports team, military unit, or nation. Last, "the ethics of divinity" enables persons and their communities to see themselves as transcending their immediate material existence. Human beings are "children of God" and are therefore holy. The aforementioned modules are divided between different ethics in the way depicted in figure 3 (p. 80).

The conservative outlook helps people cultivate communities that consequently help their members improve their characters. It is natural for us to emphasize intragroup fairness, because this tends to strengthen our chances of survival. The same applies to empathy and care, which resonate with our attachment system. Our moral modules also work on a communal level. Loyalty, self sacrifice, subordination, respect for authority, and sanctity enhance group cohesion, demarcate the boundaries of communities, and suppress selfish behavior. Furthermore, Haidt suggests that the ethics of divinity offers tools for both understanding and criticizing ethically problematic developments in society.[72]

When basic moral sentiments and the interpretation of virtues clash, it often creates puzzling confrontations. One group will likely conclude that the other group is not acting morally, and the confrontation is colored by the emotions related to given modules. If a person who identifies as a "liberal" confronts views that manifest values of other moral clusters, it is natural to respond with anger, because there are only two basic moral emotions, and compassion is not something reserved for opponents. From the "conservative" side, liberal views are typically seen as leading to choices that harm the community. These observations are joined together with rage. And so we have the basic ingredients of a culture war. As Gigerenzer interprets the situation: "Because moral feelings are anchored in different roots, conflicts will be the rule rather than the exception."[73] Haidt's constructive proposal

71. Haidt, *Righteous Mind*, 98–100.

72. Haidt, *Righteous Mind*, 106.

73. Gigerenzer, *Gut Feelings*, 188. Earlier I mentioned how our selves are fractured and we often feel drawn in multiple directions. Robert Kurzban, among others, has pointed out how our moral views are often incoherent. Moreover, when asked, we are often unable to produce reasons for our moral views. According to Kurzban, the modularity of our mind makes it easy

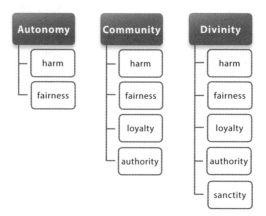

Figure 3. Haidt's three ways of ethical deliberation

in this situation is that we need to better understand how our moral deliberation works. Typically, we judge the other side as evil, but this is often a
visceral, nonreflective reaction. If we were more conscious about the way our
minds work, we could be more effective in resolving our disputes. Of course,
reaching a high reflective state of moral reasoning is not necessarily possible
for everyone, but this does not do away with the moral obligation to strive
for better understanding of how to reason about morals.

2.6. Human Cognition and Religious Disagreement

So far we have examined human belief formation in general and how it produces beliefs that help us survive but that are not necessarily true (although
sometimes these may, and will, coincide). In this section, I will point out two
further psychological factors that are relevant for religious disagreements.
The first type arises from our dual-process mode of thinking and creates
the theological correctness effect. The second type involves our personality
traits and how they make us susceptible to certain philosophical positions.

---

for us to form moral beliefs in a way that correlates more with our subconscious intuitions
and emotions, rather than reflective judgment. Consistency and the transparency of reasons
is not the default state of the mind. Instead, we naturally contradict our own principles and
disagree with people without really knowing why. Like Haidt, Kurzban stresses unconscious
more than conscious and reflective decision-making. Robert Kurzban, *Why Everyone (Else)
Is a Hypocrite: Evolution and the Modular Mind* (Princeton: Princeton University Press, 2010),
186–205. See also Haidt, *Righteous Mind*, 69–70.

The theological correctness effect marks the two-level phenomenon that takes place in every religious community.[74] According to dual-process accounts, we have two levels of religious information processing. The fast, subconscious, and automatic type 1 processing is related to folk religion, which is contrasted with theology, a product of slow, conscious, and reflective type 2 processing. As there is often a tension between our folk beliefs about the natural world and the scientific worldview, our cognitive faculties easily create discrepancies between our natural religious intuitions and more refined, theological views. Along these lines, Robert McCauley argues,

> Ordinary participants in religious systems may dutifully learn and even memorize theologians' radically counterintuitive formulations that their leaders codify and insist upon. My claim, however, is that those formulations will prove unstable in participants' online religious thinking, including their understandings of their day-to-day religious activities. No matter how much effort religious authorities put into standardizing, inculcating, and regulating religious representations, participants will re-construe them, mostly unconsciously, in their online cognition in ways that are theologically incorrect.[75]

As McCauley notes, popular religion and academic theology are distinct endeavors. Theologians may and will try to systematize the belief structure of a religion, but the members of religious communities will continue to express their beliefs in ways that are not necessarily in line with the official theology. Religion tends to morph itself according to natural biases. Theologians and religious authorities sometimes attempt to limit these biases and bring about a more uniform belief system; sometimes they are successful. Nevertheless, humans have an innate tendency to degrade sophisticated accounts of philosophical theology toward less counterintuitive forms.

For example, even if the religious elite tell their lay congregants that God is omnipresent and all-powerful, the congregants still think about God using anthropomorphic categories, for example, that God is in one place, or

---

74. Barrett, *Cognitive Science*, 138–39; Robert McCauley, *Why Religion Is Natural and Science Is Not* (Oxford: Oxford University Press, 2013), 237–44; D. Jason Slone, *Theological Incorrectness: Why Religious People Believe What They Shouldn't* (New York: Oxford University Press, 2004). While Barrett uses the term "theological correctness effect," Slone speaks about "theological incorrectness." I will follow Barrett's usage.

75. McCauley, *Why Religion Is Natural*, 242; See also Slone, *Theological Incorrectness*, 64–67, 91–97.

does things in sequential order instead of doing two things at the same time. It is challenging for us to cognize about God with omni-attributes. Consequently, we naturally resort to categories more in line with type 1 thinking.[76] The cognitive science of religion helps us to see one possible focal point of religious disagreement: that between academic elite or religious authorities and lay members. These disagreements typically concern matters of intracommunal debate, though in some cases intracommunal debates may have wider public effect. A supermajority of lay members may have different ethical convictions than the magisterium (or similar governing body) of a church. Contraception in the Catholic Church is just one example.

Our second case is based on research that demonstrates how we are able to predict the philosophical stances persons tend to take based on their personality traits. For example, people who are extroverts are very likely compatibilists, and those who are more open to new experiences are likely to think that there are no objective moral facts. Adam Feltz and Edward Cokely stress how close this tie between our personalities and beliefs is: "The link between personality and philosophical intuitions is about 100 times stronger than the benefit of using aspirin to reduce heart attacks, 20 times larger than the relation of chemotherapy to breast cancer survival, and six times larger than the effect of Ibuprofen on pain relief. . . . The link between personality and philosophical intuitions is about the same as the strength of the relation between gender and body weight (i.e., men tend to weigh more)."[77] Since several theological disputes are closely related to philosophical stances and intuitions, it is easy to see how our personality affects our theological deliberation.

First, it needs to be acknowledged that the above studies do not show that one's personality *totally* determines one's philosophical beliefs. Just as it is possible that Jill weighs more than Jack, we can have extrovert determinists and adventurous moral realists. Second, this correlation does not show that a link between a given belief and a certain personality type makes the belief true or false. There are several external and internal factors that have an effect on our belief formation, but nothing of this sort as such has bearing on the truth-value of these beliefs. Additionally, it is impossible to argue for the preference of a certain set of intuitions, as these intuitions seem irrelevant regarding the truth of a given philosophical position.[78]

---

76. Barrett, *Cognitive Science*, 137.

77. Adam Feltz and Edward Cokely, "Predicting Philosophical Disagreements," *Philosophy Compass* 10 (2013): 984.

78. Feltz and Cokely ("Predicting Philosophical Disagreements," 983) list among pos-

These two cases illustrate how our cognitive system pushes us, often without our conscious approval, toward stances that seem natural for us at that moment. The current state of scholarship, however, reveals a major weakness in how religious belief formation is analyzed, and also enables a critique of Slone's theological incorrectness thesis. So far the cognitive science of religion has concentrated almost solely on religion as a product of type 1 cognition. This tends to distort the religious reality the theories are trying to depict and explain. It is not clearly the case that religious believers are not engaging in higher and refined forms of cognition, or that theologians' ideas are systematically disregarded.[79] Even if some scholars acknowledge the role dual-process theory plays in religious cognition, there is much to be done in that field. For the time being, the image that a casual reader gets from the literature in the cognitive science of religion (CSR) is still that religion is almost purely a matter of type 1 cognition, and that type 2 cognition (theology and philosophy) are post hoc rationalizations of fundamentally irrational folk beliefs. However, if we investigate, we see immediately how odd and ad hoc this claim is. The same dialectic also pertains to scientific theories and philosophical arguments as they supervene on folk beliefs and try to control and refine them. In fact, Justin Barrett argues that religious people typically surround themselves with all kinds of activities that boost subjective certainty. However, at the same time, this increases the likelihood that beliefs produced by type 1 cognition are given more attention by type 2 cognition and thereby become more reflexive.[80]

Moreover, Evans and Stanovich note several fallacies that appear regularly in the literature in their own field of cognitive science. These include "the beliefs that (a) Type 1 processes are always responsible for cognitive bias and Type 2 processing is always responsible for correct responses, (b) Type 1 processing is contextualized and Type 2 processing abstract, and (c) fast

---

sible influential factors things like socioeconomic status, culture, order of presentation, and one's perspective.

79. This lack of research is pointed out by Lluis Oviedo, "Religious Cognition as a Dual-Process: Developing the Model," *Method and Theory in the Study of Religion* (2013): 2: "The first generation of cognitive studies of religion focused almost exclusively on unconscious or automatic processes, in the expectation that they might offer clues providing better explanations regarding the internal logic of religion beyond its apparent surface of supernatural beliefs and shared worldviews."

80. Justin Barrett, *Why Would Anyone Believe in God?* (Walnut Creek, CA: Altamira, 2004), 64. Olli-Pekka Vainio, "What Does Theology Have to Do with Religion? Dual-Process Accounts, Cognitive Science of Religion and a Curious Blind Spot in Contemporary Theorizing," *Open Theology* 2 (2016): 106–12.

processing is necessarily indicative of Type 1 processing." These fallacies lead one to think that type 1 processes are "nonconscious, automatic, impulsive and associative," while type 2 cognition is "conscious, controlled, reflective and rule-based."[81]

Thus the simplistic use of dual-process accounts is problematic, especially if they are employed to make claims about the epistemic nature of beliefs produced by given types of cognition.[82] Even if we are offered an interesting angle of religious belief formation, these theories are not the complete picture. It is possible to interpret types 1 and 2 as working in a hermeneutic circle, instead of viewing type 2 processing as a method of damage control. That is, type 2 cognition already influences how type 1 operates, which puts "theology" inside the fast and frugal cognition.[83]

In this chapter I have outlined several psychological factors that make disagreement likely. The view offered by psychology is somewhat different from that of philosophy, but they can be seen as complementary. Table 4 provides a summary of different factors that contribute to disagreement and how their influence might be alleviated.

Table 4. Psychological reasons for disagreement and suggested cures

Reason for disagreement	Suggested cure
Lack of material resources	better resources
Lack of mental resources	improving mental skills
The role of narratives	critical thinking
Biases and other cognitive constraints	debiasing

Much hangs on the possibility of critical thinking and debiasing. I will examine these issues in detail in the last chapter. Next, we turn to several distinct, yet important, factors that pertain specifically to religious disagreements.

81. Evans and Stanovich, "Dual-Process Theories of Higher Cognition," 226–27.

82. It is customary, yet fallacious, to think that type 2 produces correct beliefs, while type 1 produces false beliefs. It is possible for type 2 to lead us astray and type 1 to lead us to truth. Moreover, type 1 is activated when we cut down time and energy. Religion is not something that takes place only when we are in a hurry or tired.

83. See also James A. Van Slyke, "Moral Psychology, Neuroscience, and Virtue," in *Virtues and Their Vices*, ed. Kevin Timpe and Craig A. Boyd (Oxford: Oxford University Press, 2014), 473–77.

CHAPTER 3

Science, Philosophy, and Religious Disagreement

Religious faith deserves a chapter to itself in the annals of war technology, on an even footing with the longbow, the warhorse, the tank, and hydrogen bomb.

Richard Dawkins, *The Selfish Gene*

But you also charge the poor Monks and Religious with being the causes of war, while you acquit and flatter the Alexanders and Cæsars, the Louises and Fredericks, who alone are its causes and its actors. . . . The glory of Christianity is to conquer by forgiveness.

William Blake, "To the Deists"

What does science teach us about religious disagreement? If someone yearns for a simple answer, he or she will be sorely disappointed. Although there are voices that attempt to oversimplify this highly complex issue, this rabbit hole is very deep indeed. The complexities start with the definition of "religion." The contemporary state of the scientific study of religion is riddled with scholarly disputes that make an uncomplicated account virtually impossible.

In this chapter, I will first examine our current scientific knowledge on religion and what it might tell us about religious disagreements. Then I will move on to the epistemological discussion that concerns the meaning of disagreements for our beliefs and convictions. Last, I will discuss two epistemological questions: whether widespread religious disagreement undermines the truth claims of particular religions, and how we should deal with some recent proposals that endorse inclusion of doubt in the life of faith.

3.1. Scientific Perspectives on Religion

Defining religion is not an easy task. For example, Martin Marty suggest five principles that characterize religion: a focus on ultimate concerns; community building; the use of myths and symbols; performing rites and ceremonies; and demanding particular kinds of behavior. The obvious problem with this definition is that these same principles are also manifested in secular politics.[1] Consequently, it is difficult to tell whether a particular disagreement is in fact political or religious. Disagreements and conflicts are clearly not the sole property of religious institutions, as Mary Midgley puts it well: "It turns out that the evils that have infested religion are not confined to it, but are ones that can accompany any successful human institution."[2]

But let us start with the attempt to define religion. In comparative religion, we have seen several shifts in research trends within the last hundred years.[3] The first attempts to study religion from a scientific perspective employed universalist notions of the essence of religion: even though we experience religion in various forms, all religions nevertheless share a common core. What united the first scientific theories of religion was that they were more or less openly antireligious and sought to reveal the true naturalistic side of religiosity. For example, James Frazer's *The Golden Bough* described religion as a means to explain events that seemed strange for primitive minds. However, as humanity progresses, the brutal, animistic religions give way to more evolved worldviews, which are ultimately overcome by atheism, as the need for supernatural explanation becomes obsolete. Freud's psychoanalytical readings interpreted religion as a projection of human desires and needs, and Marx saw religion as a tool to keep the poor satisfied with their conditions, which at the same time gave a reason for the elite to be religious—it strengthened their power over the poor. Émile Durkheim's

1. Martin Marty, *Politics, Religion and the Common Good: Advancing a Distinctly American Conversation about Religion's Role in Our Shared Life* (San Francisco: Jossey-Bass, 2000), 10–15.

2. Mary Midgley, *Myths We Live By* (London: Routledge, 2004), 40. See also Ara Norenzayan, *Big Gods: How Religion Transformed Co-operation and Conflict* (Princeton: Princeton University Press, 2013), 155–69.

3. For the evolution of the scientific study of religion, see D. Jason Slone, *Theological Incorrectness: Why Religious People Believe What They Shouldn't* (New York: Oxford University Press, 2004), 7–47; Rodney Stark, "Atheism, Faith, and the Social Scientific Study of Religion," *Journal of Contemporary Religion* 14 (1999): 41–62; Aku Visala, *Naturalism, Theism and the Cognitive Study of Religion* (Farnham, UK: Ashgate, 2011), 17–84; Daniel Pals, *Seven Theories of Religion* (Oxford: Oxford University Press, 1996).

theories approached religion from the viewpoint of social cohesion and indoctrination: religious behavior boosts the mutual sense of belonging, making the group stronger against its competitors.

These naturalistic theories were met with suspicion by a group of "transcendentalists," who criticized naturalists for not accounting for the *religious* part of religion. According to, for example, Mircea Eliade and Rudolf Otto, religion possesses a sui generis character and is thus irreducible to sociology, psychology, or any other mechanism for survival or enjoyment. Even if we could explain some parts of religion with the help of the sciences, something would always be left out. This remainder is the essence of religion. While trying to save religion from reductionist explanations, transcendentalists nevertheless applied universal categories to religion similar to their naturalist counterparts. They focused on sacred texts and their accounts of religious experience, a search that was conducted by using such categories as "the holy." By looking behind the particular features of these accounts, these scholars were slowly reaching for the common religious experience.

This approach soon started to draw criticism as well. After the 1960s, the sciences faced an unprecedented wave of critique in Western societies. The movement later labeled "postmodernism" saw in earlier readings of culture and religion imperialistic attitudes that interpreted the world from the viewpoint of a cold, impersonal, Western mind that sought to transform everything into its own image. The postmodern reaction turned the tables on modernist social science; instead of focusing on the universal essence of religion, studies should focus on the particular instantiations of religion. To really understand religion one must perceive it as it is lived and practiced in some specific context. Clifford Geertz was a pioneering figure in this new approach. Instead of explaining religion, observers should try to understand it on its own terms. The focus shifted away from the texts and abstract notions toward a plethora of local, lived experiences and cultures. In many ways, this was a totally different approach compared to the initial ideas that gave birth to the scientific study of religion. The attempt to discern a universal religious core behind all religions and to therefore explain their true nature was discarded as ethically suspect.

The cognitive revolution and the rise of the cognitive science of religion (CSR) can be seen as a response to postmodern contextualism. CSR seeks to reinvigorate the Enlightenment idea of the science of religion: explanation and reduction are in, particularism is out. CSR suggests that cognitive psychology in fact provides us with the means to get in touch with the panhuman mechanisms that produce religious or quasi-religious beliefs. Some even argue that religion is nothing more than a product of these subconscious mechanisms. Why should we be interested in how particular groups and individuals understand their own practices and beliefs in their own environment if we can understand the essence of religion with the help of cognitive psychology? Isn't religion just our cognitive mechanisms gone haywire? This recent shift in emphasis enforces the idea that we can speak about religion in an abstract, general way. CSR explanations bracket the supernatural and observe only those mechanisms that take place in the minds of believers. In this way, it might be possible to explain at least some parts of religion as a natural, this-worldly phenomenon.[4] These naturalistic explanations typically appear in three different forms: cognitive, evolutionary, and coevolutionary explanations.[5] Here it suffices to provide only a short description of each.

Cognitive explanations assume that human thinking is rather uniform across cultures, and that modules in the human mind give rise to religious beliefs. First, human minds are prone to react strongly to claims that are minimally counterintuitive. Cognitively optimal beliefs are weird, but not too weird; they must conflict with some of our basic intuitions, but not too many. This makes them interesting, effortless to remember, and easy to pass along.[6]

Second, the human mind naturally attributes agency to various things. This mechanism is called hypersensitive agency detection device (HADD). When we walk in a forest and hear a crack behind us, we immediately think some agent has caused it, and we take necessary and automatic measures to flee or protect ourselves. The mechanism is called *hyper*sensitive because it attributes agency automatically, even in cases where there is no agent. (The crack could have been caused by the wind breaking a dry branch, for example.) But in these cases, where there is no visible agent in sight, it is natural for us to attribute the cause to a supernatural agent (a god or a spirit).[7]

---

4. CSR theorists differ on how much their methods actually explain. See Visala, *Naturalism*, 85–111.

5. The distinction is used by Jeffrey Schloss, "Introduction: Evolutionary Theories of Religion," in *The Believing Primate: Scientific, Philosophical, and Theological Reflections on the Origin of Religion*, ed. Jeffrey Schloss and Michael J. Murray (Oxford: Oxford University Press, 2009), 14–25; Aku Visala and David Leech, "Naturalistic Explanations for Religious Belief," *Philosophy Compass* 8 (2010): 552–63. For a general overview of CSR, see Justin Barrett, *Cognitive Science, Religion and Theology: From Human Minds to Divine Minds* (West Conshohocken, PA: Templeton Press, 2011); Robert McCauley, *Why Religion Is Natural and Science Is Not* (Oxford: Oxford University Press, 2013).

6. Barrett, *Cognitive Science*, 104–6. McCauley, *Why Religion Is Natural*, 167–68.

7. McCauley, *Why Religion Is Natural*, 158–59.

Third, theory of mind is a uniquely human capacity, which enables us to regard other humans as agents. This entails attributing intentional mental states, like beliefs and desires, to other beings, which eventually helps us to see them as persons. Together with minimal counterintuitiveness and HADD, theory of mind makes it natural for us to have an idea of personal deity or deities.[8]

Evolutionary explanations typically see religion either as an adaptation, produced by natural selection, because it gives an evolutionary advantage for individuals or groups, or as a by-product, which has no immediate survival benefit but follows on other mechanisms that are adaptive (like HADD and theory of mind). One possible reason why evolution would produce religion might be its power to enhance cooperation and altruistic behavior in communities. Also, belief in a supernatural Judge who sees all and knows all is a useful tool for minimizing slothfulness. In this way, the use of external force and threat is internalized in the idea of a righteous deity, who punishes the wicked and rewards the good.[9]

Coevolutionary explanations take advantage of the previously mentioned cognitive and evolutionary explanations, while acknowledging them as too reductive on their own. In addition to these forces, humans have in their possession unique cultural information that transcends mere biology. The contested notion of "meme" plays the central role here. Culture, and religion as a part of it, spreads by imitation. Religion may have had an adaptive role in the past, but it is now best viewed as a sort of virus, which serves no obvious beneficial purpose.[10]

At this point it should not come as surprise that there is no agreement as to what theory best explains the existence of religion. The problem is that the data is underdetermined, and it might ultimately be impossible to know how well our theories fully account for religion. Our current theories typically leave something unexplained, even when they are able to offer vital insights into some aspects of religiosity and human behavior in general.[11]

It is, of course, reasonable to study human cognition by any means available, but how much are these methods able to help us? Abraham Maslow's famous saying seems to be true in religious studies: if all you have is a hammer, everything looks like a nail. For example, CSR has been mostly

8. Barrett, *Cognitive Science*, 74–80.

9. Thus especially Norenzayan, *Big Gods*.

10. Schloss, "Evolutionary Theories of Religion," 22–25.

11. Christian Smith, *Moral, Believing Animals* (Oxford: Oxford University Press, 2009), 106–27; Schloss, "Introduction: Evolutionary Theories of Religion," 18.

occupied with type 1 processes in religion and has neglected more refined type 2 cognitive processes, which also affect religious judgment. Nevertheless, it is type 2 that gives to many religions their peculiar outlook and typical, local beliefs. Even after the recent cognitive turn, it does not seem warranted that we uncritically return to universalist models of depiction, because the tools employed by cognitive science point us toward particularist modes of thinking about cognition. Therefore, it seems reasonable to make a distinction between features of religiosity that are more or less universal and more local.

But what do the currently available explanations of religion contribute to our topic? Do scientific explanations of religion help us say something valuable about religious disagreements? We must tread carefully here. Not only is our knowledge of these matters limited, but there is also ample hype surrounding the new field of CSR and neuroscience.[12] I will briefly mention three issues here, returning to them at length in this and the following chapter.

First, Richard Dawkins and Daniel Dennett have claimed, for instance, that contemporary science settles the question of the (un)truth and (ir)rationality of religious belief. Thus, if we are able to tell a plausible naturalistic story about how religiosity emerged in the course of human evolution, we have provided a debunking account that reveals the true nature of religion: it is a natural phenomenon, produced by impersonal forces of evolution, not the handiwork of a supernatural force. The conclusion is that religious believers are irrational. Consequently, religious disagreements are irrational as well because they concern a topic that is itself void of truth. Let us call this the debunking question.

The second issue pertains to the negative effects of interreligious conflict and conflicts between religions and other worldviews. Some critics argue that currently available evidence concerning the adaptive and beneficial value of religion suggests that religion causes more harm than good. Even if we grant that religion has had a positive adaptive function in the past, it does not have such a function anymore, it is argued, since we can arrange human social life better without it. It might be granted that religion produces some beneficial contributions even today, but it produces so much evil, in the form of disagreements and out-group hostility, among other things, that again we are better off without it. Let us call this the bad religion question.

---

12. For an extended argument as to why empirical neuroscientific research has virtually no effect at all on our normative conceptualization, see Selim Berker, "The Normative Insignificance of Neuroscience," *Philosophy and Public Affairs* 37, no. 4 (2009): 293–329.

Third, the naturalness of religion requires us to take into account the pervasive nature of religious beliefs. Because religiosity cannot be obliterated, we must find ways to organize our public life so that it is able to accommodate both religious and nonreligious worldviews. Moreover, religious disagreements are a natural and ineradicable part of the life of religious communities, of all human communities for that matter. How then should communities accommodate their internal disagreements? Let us call this the accommodation of religious disagreement question.

In the following sections, I will discuss the first two questions; and I will answer the third question in the last chapter.

3.2. Naturalistic Accounts of Religion

Let us first examine the debunking issue. Critics claim that naturalistic accounts of religion help us to see that religions are not what they seem. Religious people generally believe that prayer is a way of communicating with a supreme being. But if religion is a purely natural phenomenon, they in fact pray because praying is adaptive (it makes us more honest, which benefits the group's survival, for instance), or because prayer seems like an adequate response to the impulses produced by HADD. Therefore, disagreeing about religious claims as if they were factual claims is a categorical mistake. There is no truth to be had in religion because it was never about truth in the first place.[13] From this perspective, it is easy to understand why certain people think that erasing religion is a good idea. Religion is a natural but fundamentally irrational and needless response to something that is not there.

This evolutionary explanation is supposed to debunk religious beliefs by laying out their real history. The discussion surrounding the so-called debunking arguments is vast and complicated. One recent debate in moral

---

13. CSR writers have different views about the religious relevance of their theories, but negative relevance is often simply assumed without further argument. For discussion, see Visala, *Naturalism*, 154–59. Often the relation between CSR and religious truth is expressed like this: "Thus, these facts about the ubiquity of religion provide no reason to believe in the truth of religion. In fact, we think that today philosophical and scientific progress has reduced the credibility of religion virtually to zero, by providing natural explanations for most of what happens in the world and raising difficulties for religious explanations." Thus Ingmar Persson and Julian Savulescu, "The Limits of Religious Tolerance. A Secular View," in *Religion, Intolerance, and Conflict: A Scientific and Conceptual Investigation*, ed. Steve Clarke, Russell Powell, and Julian Savulescu (Oxford: Oxford University Press, 2013), 236.

philosophy, for example, has focused on the evolutionary background of moral beliefs and how this affects the status of those beliefs. Interestingly, the same form of argument can also be expanded beyond the moral domain to debunk *all* human beliefs.[14] The standard form of such "evolutionary debunking arguments" can be stated as follows:[15]

> *S* has a belief *x*, which can be explained though process *z*.
> Process *z* is not truth tracking.
> *S*'s belief in *x* is not justified.

If successful, this kind of argument demonstrates that belief in absolute moral norms and obligations is not justified.[16] Therefore, moral antirealism follows. While belief in absolute moral values might be conducive to human flourishing, such a belief is false, or at least unjustified. When translated into religious contexts, the argument runs thus:

1. The existence of religious beliefs can be explained by using CSR-type naturalistic explanation of religious beliefs (NERB).
2. We have good reasons to believe that the processes described by NERBs are not truth tracking because:
   a. Cognitive explanations demonstrate how the mechanisms that produce religious beliefs were not selected for their truth conduciveness in the religious domain.

---

14. Sharon Street, "A Darwinian Dilemma for Realist Theories of Value," *Philosophical Studies* 127 (2006): 111–12.

15. Thus Guy Kahane, "Evolutionary Debunking Arguments," *Nous* 45 (2010): 103–25.

16. Because our cognitive functions have been heavily influenced by natural selection, which seeks survival rather than tracking the truth, it becomes problematic to claim that our moral evaluations are true in any objective and absolute sense. If the content of our basic evaluative tendencies (social emotions, etc.) had been different, then our evaluative judgments would have been different as well. If human society were more like that of lions, we would not find it especially disturbing if we sometimes killed and ate our offspring. If we were an insect community, we would not think much of our own individual survival, but we would always willingly sacrifice ourselves for the good of the community. So why think that our judgments about moral value are *true*, in a realist sense, if the way we have reached these evaluations is highly contextual and random? Of course, it is not random in the sense that this morality surely gives *our* species the tools of survival; if we *were* to start living like lions and ants, the story of humanity would come to an abrupt end. In other words, morality is *beneficial*, but not *true*. For discussion, see Street, "Darwinian Dilemma."

b. Cognitive explanations demonstrate that religious beliefs and their alleged targets are not properly causally connected.

3. Therefore, religious beliefs are not justified as factual statements, but they might have some aesthetic, moral, or some other noncognitive value.

There are several things that need to be discussed in relation to this argument. I start with premise 2a. The first problem is that debunking arguments, thus formulated, are too strong: almost all our beliefs, including scientific, moral, and everyday beliefs, are products of mechanisms that were not selected to produce true beliefs in such domains. For instance, our cognitive systems did not evolve to solve problems like the existence of universals, to construct theories about the nature of time, or to build fusion reactors. We can form beliefs about such things, but the systems by which we form such beliefs were not selected for such tasks. Thus most of our beliefs—not just religious beliefs—are sailing in the same leaky epistemic boat. In order to make debunking arguments work against religion and nothing else, we would need to give an account of why debunking arguments cut through religious beliefs but not, say, scientific or philosophical beliefs.

But demarcating the debunking power only to certain areas of life is challenging. So far, the best suggestion is that of Paul Griffiths and John Wilkins, who claim that it might be possible to guard scientific and everyday beliefs against debunking by linking them to commonsense thinking. More specifically, it would be very strange from an evolutionary point of view if our everyday beliefs did not track the truth. If this were not so, we would have been eaten by lions long ago. It is therefore reasonable to think that our commonsense beliefs, generally speaking, track the truth. Griffiths and Wilkins further claim that science itself is simply an extension of commonsense cognition (which is just applied more rigorously), and thus science inherits its reliability from our everyday cognition. Furthermore, they maintain that truth-trackingness and fitness-trackingness are not mutually exclusive categories.[17]

17. Paul E. Griffiths and John S. Wilkins, "Evolutionary Debunking Arguments in Three Domains: Fact, Value, and Religion," in *A New Science of Religion*, ed. Gregory Dawes and James Maclaurin (New York: Routledge, 2013), 140: "The reasons we have to think that our scientific conclusions are correct and that the methods we use to reach them are reliable are simply the data and arguments which scientists give for their conclusions, and for their methodological innovations. Ultimately, these have to stand up to the same commonsense scrutiny as any other addition to our beliefs. Thus, if evolution does not undermine our trust in our

However, as Jonathan Jong and Aku Visala have pointed out, Griffiths and Wilkins give no good reasons why religious beliefs could not be justified in the same way as scientific beliefs. That is, why could religious beliefs not inherit their reliability from commonsense cognition? Griffiths and Wilkins even acknowledge that evolutionary explanations do not affect independent reasons one may have for holding religious beliefs. These reasons can be used to strengthen, construct, and reshape our commonsense beliefs, and this moves the focus of the debate away from NERBs.[18] This relates to dual-process accounts of cognition, mentioned earlier. Although type 1 can explain some aspects of how religious cognition works, it should be acknowledged that more refined modes of cognition also shape our thinking about religion.

A related issue concerns the explanatory power of NERBs. To make the argument "you only believe p because of x" succeed, one would have to demonstrate that those things that are within the reach of NERBs are *the only and exclusive* source of the belief p. But this is something that NERBs cannot do, because CSR only looks at general tendencies in relatively large human populations. In other words, it is not possible to use NERBs to prove that *you* believe p only and exclusively because that is what humans are prone to do. Of course, it is possible to claim that my belief p is affected by x, but this does not rule out my epistemic reasons for p. Claiming that "you believe p because you are prone to do so" does not really support the antireligious conclusion. This is simply an invitation to examine one's epistemic reasons for p, which removes the discussion from the field of NERBs altogether.

Despite these caveats, we still need to acknowledge that quite a large amount of our religious cognition is channeled through type 1 cognitive processes. Even if this does not automatically cause massive suspicion, it may cause some theological problems within religious systems. CSR as such does not present anything that is in conflict with theism broadly construed, but it may give rise to a need to rethink some auxiliary beliefs in a theistic belief system.

The second problem concerns the nature of belief formation as outlined in premise 2b.

---

cognitive faculties, neither should it undermine our trust in our ability to use those faculties to debug themselves—to identify their own limitations, as in perceptual illusions or common errors in intuitive reasoning. Nor should it undermine our confidence in adopting new concepts and methods which have not themselves been shaped by the evolution of the mind, but whose introduction can be justified using our evolved cognitive faculties."

18. Jonathan Jong and Aku Visala, "Evolutionary Debunking Arguments against Theism, Reconsidered," *International Journal of Philosophy of Religion* 76 (2014): 243–58.

2b. Cognitive explanations demonstrate that religious beliefs and their alleged targets are not properly causally connected.

Should not beliefs about divine reality be caused by this reality, and not by some random process? However, in the light of the Christian theological tradition, there seems to be nothing wrong in God's choice to use natural processes or secondary causes. In response to contrary suggestions, Michael Murray has argued for "cognitive fine-tuning," according to which it is enough that God creates a capacity that is able to bring about the rise to religious faith in the right contexts. Therefore, God can act somewhere in the causal nexus, and it is not necessary for him to bring about the previous act before faith arises out of nothing.[19]

But is the issue different if we put our finger on the obvious feature of these processes—namely, do they create (from God's point of view) idolatrous belief commitments? Visala and David Leech call this "the deceiving God (*Deus deceptor*) argument."[20] The crux of the argument is that our cognitive processes produce a great deal of false positives, which potentially undercut the reliability of normal religious cognition. Additionally, this same belief-formation method manifests in the form of religious diversity. If God has enabled a method of belief formation that is properly described by NERBs, the method does not seem to be efficient, a critic might say.

This is potentially troubling from the viewpoint of classical theism, which assumes that God wishes to establish a personal relationship with individual beings. The belief-formation methods outlined by CSR appear to be poorly designed from this perspective, as they produce mostly false results. From the viewpoint of the history of the human race, the majority of humans have not been Christian. Therefore, it seems that God is responsible for creating a set of cognitive processes that, for the most part, *prevent* real knowledge of spiritual reality, while allowing multiple false conceptions to develop freely.

We can now see how the argument for noncognitive and antirealist religiosity could be made on this basis. We could still entertain a religious form of life, but it should be viewed more along the lines of enthusiasm about some composer, sports team, or painter. The benefits of religiosity would be similar to those one receives from going to a concert, play, exhibition, or ice

---

19. Michael J. Murray and Andrew Goldberg, "Evolutionary Accounts of Religion: Explaining and Explaining Away," in Schloss and Murray, *The Believing Primate*, 179–99.
20. Visala and Leech, "Cognitive Science of Religion," 309–13.

hockey game. These noncognitive versions of religion have sometimes been suggested as more developed versions of religiosity and possible tools for attenuating religious disagreements.[21]

At this point, anyone who has ever been to a hockey match or is acquainted with artists knows that if one's aim is to reduce disagreements this is not a very helpful move. More disagreement and actual violence takes place between the supporters of sports teams qua sports teams than members of different religions qua religions, and artists regularly stir a good deal of outrage, debate, and violent actions. The move toward more aesthetic understandings of religion will most likely not prevent disagreements. Instead, it will probably make religious tolerance and accommodation even harder, because it removes religious claims from the sphere of reasonable discussion altogether, creating one more reactionary religious position on top of all the already existing positions. Although I cannot argue for it here, I think these are among the reasons we need to take religious claims as cognitively and metaphysically realistic, at least prima facie.[22]

But let us move these pragmatic considerations aside for a moment and concentrate on theological problems. Particularly those religions that make claims about the nature of the world are painfully aware that their claims are met with raised eyebrows in most settings. The heretical imperative seems to be a true description of the world; no single set of religious claims is unanimously held. Still, most religions are unmoved by this and continue to make exclusivist claims. By exclusivism, I mean what Nathan King calls "open religious exclusivism," according to which "the doctrines of the home religion are true, doctrines incompatible with these are false, and there may be religious truths to be found outside the home religion." I take it that this is more or less the view taken by the practitioners of major religions.[23] Is open religious exclusivism (for the sake of clarity, I speak now within the

21. For discussion, see, e.g., James Kraft and David Basinger, eds., *Religious Tolerance through Humility: Thinking with Philip Quinn* (Farnham, UK: Ashgate, 2008).

22. For example, Don Cupitt's noncognitivist version of religion is designed to be more human and suitable for a postmodern context. The problem with various noncognitivist proposals is that the humble and tolerant attitude they wish to espouse cannot be supported by noncognitivist models. See William Lane Craig, "Is Uncertainty a Sound Foundation for Religious Tolerance?," in Kraft and Basinger, *Religious Tolerance through Humility*, 13–28.

23. Nathan King, "Religious Diversity and Its Challenges to Religious Belief," *Philosophy Compass* 4 (2008): 834. This position can be compatible with some forms of inclusivism. Sometimes it is called "moderate exclusivism." David Basinger, *Religious Diversity: A Philosophical Assessment* (Burlington, VT: Ashgate, 2002), 69–73.

Christian tradition) compatible with the results of CSR? As noted, there is nothing necessarily problematic about God's using secondary causes to bring about faith. But how about the fact that these secondary causes do not seem to reflect God's wish that everyone experience the same beatific vision?

In the history of Christian theology, there have been several attempts to answer the challenge of religious diversity. One of the central claims has been that God created humans with free will, which they can use to choose their own way. Naturally, this will result in diversity, and therefore there is nothing problematic in diversity as such.[24]

However, unbelief is highly geographically restricted (like languages), and against this background NERBs would appear to offer a parsimonious explanation for religious diversity: people do not form beliefs using their will and reflective skills; they adopt the status quo. It might seem that having correct beliefs, from a Christian point of view, is a matter of luck in the sense that your physical location on this planet dramatically restricts the beliefs available to you.

Yet it is possible to absorb NERBs to support a version of Christian exclusivism, even if the aforementioned fact is taken to be true. For example, from a Molinist perspective, it is possible to make the following claim. In order to guarantee the constraints of normal human interaction (such as the central role of testimony in belief formation), God has grouped certain individuals to certain locations according to their status. Because God has (according to Molinism) middle knowledge, he can set apart those who would not believe in any possible world. These individuals (i.e., those who are not elected) are then located in a time and place where Christian faith is nonexistent or rare.[25]

A more stern-minded response would be that of classic Calvinist theology: God wishes to save only those whom he has elected from *massa perditionis*. Because all have sinned, God is not under obligation to save anyone, and therefore he does not want to establish relationships with all human beings. The fact that God saves even a relatively few humans is a supererogatory act. Although this is a coherent answer and has been held by many central theologians in the Christian tradition, it will likely leave many dissatisfied.

24. Olli-Pekka Vainio, "Salvation and Religious Diversity: Christian Perspectives," *Religion Compass* 10 (2016): 27–34; Max Baker-Hytch, "Religious Diversity and Epistemic Luck," *International Journal of Philosophy of Religion* 76 (2014): 171–91.

25. Jason Marsh, "Do the Demographics of Theistic Belief Disconfirm Theism? A Reply to Maitzen," *Religious Studies* 44 (2006): 465–71.

On the other end of the spectrum, it is possible to argue that God, in order to guarantee equal chances to everyone, offers a chance for those who lived without contact with the Christian religion to accept his love postmortem. Additionally, one can adopt universalism: the belief that everyone will be saved in the end. Even in this case, however, it would still be possible to be an exclusivist, as salvation (of all) takes place solely through Christ's sacrifice.

Therefore, NERBs do not seem to pose any serious threat to theism as such, but they do require some accommodation. Yet this is not something that theistic religions have never encountered before. Throughout their history, theistic religions have formulated answers that take into account the diversity of religions in a way that reflects their core beliefs. NERBs do not bring anything new that would dramatically change the situation. We already knew that diversity existed; suggesting a cognitive mechanism that brings about diversity does not alter the basic premises of the solutions that Christian theologians have already suggested in the course of history.

In relation to the diversity issue, cognitive scientist Justin Barrett has pointed out that religious diversity actually helps counter skeptical conclusions that could be drawn from CSR. Barrett argues that

> beliefs about gods, souls, and the rest would likewise be more suspect if it were discovered that no matter the information available, the mind used it to arrive deterministically at such beliefs. If 100 percent of humans believed in the existence of an immortal human soul, for instance, and cognitive science was able to demonstrate that we have cognitive systems that unswervingly make us believe in immortal souls, then we might have reason to doubt their actual existence. . . . Ironically, then, the fact that no religious belief is completely universal and uncontroversial affords religious belief some protection from being "explained away" by cognitive science.[26]

For Barrett, NERBs combined with the *unity* of religions and worldviews would count against theological realism. In order for NERBs to acquire their debunking power, we would need a uniform belief-formation process that produces demonstrably false beliefs, not supported by epistemic arguments. So if NERBs plus uniformity would be more problematic for exclusivists, we can conclude that NERBs plus diversity does not have an immediate effect

26. Barrett, *Cognitive Science*, 150–51.

on the evidential force of the exclusivist's claims. Therefore, the debunking thesis fails. Contemporary CSR provides nothing that would make religious noncognitivism or antirealism more plausible than they were before.

3.3. Religion and Violence

In many ways, the 9/11 terrorist attacks changed the world as we know it. Besides the expected political consequences, it had surprising outcomes that only a few could have foreseen. Among these was the interest in religion and its relation to violence. It is not an exaggeration to claim that 9/11 created the New Atheism, since the main motivator behind the movement appears to be anti-Islamic culture war. Other religions also receive their due share, as collateral damage.[27] Ironically, academics gained from this sad event. Many projects and individual scholarships have been funded to study the "dark side of religion," and scholars have not been timid to use alarming language to underline their projects' importance. For example, D. Jason Slone describes his study on the cognitive science of religion thus: "The events of September 11, 2001, reveal that our very lives might depend on us getting [religion] right."[28] These kinds of claims form the background of the *bad religion question*.

Putting the doom-laden rhetoric aside, the actual results of empirical studies on religion and violence have hardly been earth shattering. Anthropologist Scott Atran notes that, even in the case of Islamic terrorism, actual, lived religion plays a minor, almost nonexistent role. Atran points out that the major source of antiterrorist activity in Islamic countries is their religious leaders, and that those Muslims who engage in violent acts are not typically religiously active.[29] More generally, according to the *Encyclopedia of Wars*,

27. The New Atheist evangelists, especially Sam Harris, Richard Dawkins, and the late Christopher Hitchens, have expressed openly anti-Islamic and politically right-wing views. See, e.g., Kelly James Clark, "Calling Abraham's Children," in *Abraham's Children: Liberty and Tolerance in an Age of Religious Conflict*, ed. Kelly James Clark (New Haven: Yale University Press, 2012), 3–5.

28. Slone, *Theological Incorrectness*, 11.

29. Scott Atran, *Talking to the Enemy: Violent Extremism, Sacred Values and What It Means to Be Human* (London: Allen Lane, 2010), Kindle ed. loc. 6109 of 10127. Thus also Robert Pape, *Dying to Win: The Strategic Logic of Suicide Terrorism* (Carlton North, Australia: Scribe, 2005), 4–5. Before 2001, the most active group that endorsed suicide bombing was the Tamil Tigers of Sri Lanka, a nonreligious and thoroughly secular organization. Even in the Middle East, suicide bombings have not traditionally been of a religious nature. It is only after 2001

only 7 percent of human wars had significant religious influence. According to a BBC audit, "God and War," religion was some kind of factor in 40 percent of 3,500 conflicts, though hardly ever the major cause.[30]

In the religion-and-violence literature, the same, well-known events appear as examples in every book: Jonestown, killings of abortionists, Aum Shinrikyo, Heaven's Gate, and Al-Qaeda.[31] These serve as examples of the dark side of religion. No one denies that these are deeply problematic instances; at the same time, one cannot help but notice their isolated nature. If religion is prone to give rise to these kinds of acts, and since the supermajority of humans are religious, why do we not see these horrific events happen more often? Of all the violence that takes place in the world, why should we be especially worried about religious violence, based on these incidents?[32] Monica Duffy Toft, however, points out that of the civil wars during the last one hundred years, we have seen a recent increase in conflicts with religious elements. Of these, 80 percent have taken place between Islamic groups or have involved an Islamic group as one side of the conflict.[33] This finding does give a reason for concern, yet it does not warrant a general labeling of religion as a major source of conflict.

---

that Islamic jihadists have adopted these measures; there is no antecedent for such behavior in Islamic tradition. Pape argues that people resort to suicide bombings typically only in cases when one's homeland is being occupied. Even in such cases, religion does not appear to be a motivating factor for the killings, though it might be used for recruiting purposes.

30. Norenzayan, *Big Gods*, 157; Charles Phillips and Alan Axelrod, eds., *Encyclopedia of Wars* (New York: Facts on File, 2004); Greg Austin, Todd Kranock, and Thom Oommen, "God and War: An Audit and an Exploration," BBC, 2003, http://news.bbc.co.uk/2/shared/spl/hi/world/04/war_audit_pdf/pdf/war_audit.pdf.

31. See, e.g., Mark Juergensmeyer, *Terror in the Mind of God: The Global Rise of Religious Violence* (Berkeley: University of California Press, 2000), 19–118; Clarke, *Justification of Religious Violence*, 153–82.

32. Religion is a good target for criticism for two reasons. First, religions are groups that are "labeling friendly." They are usually clearly defined with their public creeds. Second, religions typically have high ethical ideals. This forms a contrast with violent acts, which effectively draws our attention to the contradiction. When the Catholic sexual abuse scandal became public, for example, it was pointed out that it is in fact more probable that a person would be subjected to abuse everywhere else than in the church. This did nothing to alleviate the negative stigma, however, mainly because the glaring difference between lived reality and the Catholic Church's ideals. Philip Jenkins, *The New Anti-Catholicism: The Last Acceptable Prejudice* (New York: Oxford University Press, 2003), 142.

33. Monica Duffy Toft, "Religion, Terrorism, and Civil Wars," in *Rethinking Religion and World Affairs*, ed. Timothy Shah, Alfred Stepan, and Monica Duffy Toft (Oxford: Oxford University Press, 2011), 127–48.

We should not let the lack of frequent extreme examples trick us. As noted in the introduction, there are several different forms of religious conflict, even if religious wars are rare. We may ask more generally: Is religion a force for good or a force for evil? Some critics claim that the effects of religion in modern society are predominantly negative. If religion has some positive value, it is suggested, that could be secured through other, nonreligious and secular means. However, religions in our contemporary context are volatile and therefore not suitable agents for sustainable modern society. Others acknowledge that religion still has some real benefits for human societies, but they hurry to emphasize that these same features that make religion "good" are also the ones that make it "evil." For example, Russell Powell and Steve Clarke claim: "Religion has two faces when it comes to social behavior: one that produces a sense of compassion, brotherhood, and concern for others, and a dark side that leads to intolerance, bigotry, and violence."[34]

There are a number of studies that list religion's prosocial benefits. Religious people tend to be more happy, for example, suffer less from mental illnesses, recover faster after suffering from diseases, more altruistic and honest, and so on.[35] Many of these benefits are correlates of a strong sense of communal belonging, which creates a paradoxical situation: in order to get certain goods that promote human flourishing, you also enter into a social state that easily generates in-group/out-group distinctions. If there is a dark side of religion, this seems to be the mechanism that creates it.

But how should we think about claims according to which "religion *causes* harm"? Merely acknowledging the existence of this dialectic mechanism of communal well-being and out-group derogation does not as such allow us to make very strong general claims about religion. The problem concerns the meaning of the words *religion*, *harm*, and *cause*. Let us take a look at each of them in turn.

34. Russell Powell and Steve Clarke, "Religion, Tolerance, and Intolerance: Views from across the Disciplines," in Clarke, Powell, and Savulescu, *Religion, Intolerance, and Conflict*, 11.

35. For a review of studies on covariation of religiosity and various benefits, see Harold G. Koenig, Dana E. King, and Verna Benner Carson, *Handbook of Religion and Health: A Century of Research Reviewed* (New York: Oxford University Press, 2001); B. Aukst-Margetić and B. Margetić, "Religiosity and Health Outcomes: Review of Literature," *Collective Anthropology* 29 (2005): 365–71.

Defining the Word Religion

We have three problems regarding the meaning of *religion*:

1. The problem of defining *religion*.
2. The problem of different individual religious outlooks.
3. The problem of locating the properly "religious" part in religion.

The previous section demonstrated to some extent the problems of finding reasonable ways of approaching religion. The central problem is how to find out and balance, on the one hand, universal characteristics of religion and, on the other hand, local instantiations of a particular religion. For example, William Cavanaugh argues that there is no "religion" as such, but only particular religions, which are essentially different. Others defend the idea of having a universal concept of religion but disagree about the particular features that should define it.[36]

While some theorists argue that all definitions of religion are almost equally bad, I tend to think that all definitions are almost equally good: they capture some features of religiosity in a certain context. It does not really matter that sometimes we can count Marxism, football, or even New Atheism as a religion and sometimes use more strict criteria as long as we make clear what kind of definition we are using and why. For our purposes, the following definition should capture most of the communities that interest us when talking about religious disagreement or conflict.[37]

Religion$_{def}$ =

1. The ideology provides us with the problem, which relates to the fundamental problems of human existence, and the cure.
2. The cure involves implicit or explicit metaphysical views, which are vital for truly understanding both the problem and the cure.
3. The ideology contains some rules regarding how to behave and act in order to realize the potential of the cure.

36. For example, William T. Cavanaugh (*The Myth of Religious Violence* [Oxford: Oxford University Press, 2009], 57–122) resists the use of "religion" in this context because he thinks that there is no shared essence in religions. Among others, C. A. J. Coady and Joshua Thurow regard this conclusion as unnecessarily strict. See Coady, "Violence and Religion," *Revue International de Philosophie* 265 (2013): 237–57; Thurow, "Religion, 'Religion,' and Tolerance," in Clarke, Powell, and Savulescu, *Religion, Intolerance, and Conflict*, 155.

37. I am modifying here the account of Thurow ("Religion," 157).

4. These rules have public and visible forms of communal practice.

When I now speak about "religion," I refer to a group or ideology that reflects tenets 1–4.[38] Tenet 4 is of special importance here because the critics typically underline the group-forming feature as the most problematic element in religion, mainly because it imposes debiasing and makes compromise harder.[39] But even if we could land on a definition like this, what can we achieve with it? Not much. Let us translate this definition to the context of "game," to use the Wittgensteinian concept. There is no real and clear essence of game, although we can define a set of properties that some known games have and that we use to identify them as games. In this way we could have a definition of "board game" (which differs from the set of games that involve, for example, a spherical object and teams). But does someone play this "board game," this abstract set of game-related properties? Of course not. People play *particular* games, not "board games" as such. On the one hand, it is useful to have a concept of "board game" or "religion" in order to identify some things as board games or religions, and others as not.

Things get more complicated if we use an abstract concept to indicate something that "board game" *does* because "board game" cannot be a genuine subject. Therefore, the definite (or something close to it) definition of religion will be so broad that it is of no practical value. On the other hand, stricter definitions leave out some movements that should be included. For our purposes, it is enough to have a working definition, like the one above that captures those aspects of religiosity that are important to potential conflicts. As a critical point, it suffices to say that using the word *religion* in a sentence without being aware of these conceptual difficulties is going to cause confusion.

In sociology of religion studies, it is customary to point out that there are different religious outlooks.[40] Since the 1950s there has been a series of studies focusing on how religious people relate to other groups. The initial results indicated that religiosity covaried with out-group prejudice. A

---

38. I admit that there can be religions that have only one practitioner or religions that have no public or communal forms of practice. But in this context, these examples do not have any reasonable weight that should be taken into account. My definition is able to include Buddhist or atheist spirituality, which do not involve belief in supernatural beings yet have metaphysical commitments.

39. Thus, e.g., Powell and Clarke, "Religion, Tolerance, and Intolerance," 1–35.

40. A good overview of these studies is Powell and Clarke, "Religion, Tolerance, and Intolerance." References to multiple studies charting this area of debate can be found there.

natural move at this point was to pay closer attention to different types of religious lifestyle; thus the well-known characterization between *extrinsic* and *intrinsic* forms of religiosity was born. In 1967 Gordon Allport and J. M. Ross suggested that there were two distinct religious orientations that had differing correlation with those aspects of religion that had been seen as problematic. Extrinsic religious orientation (ER) was characterized as more occupied with the external benefits of belonging to a religious community, such as personal advancement and comfort. ER was shown to perceive religious life as a way of beneficial networking, with only minimal adherence to the actual teachings of a given religion. According to Allport and Ross, in ER "the embraced creed is lightly held or else selectively shaped to fit more primary needs."[41] It was found that this type of instrumental view of religiosity correlated more with out-group prejudice than intrinsic religious orientation (IR), which showed less hostility toward out-groups and more internalized and conscious relationship to one's creed. Nevertheless, when more studies were conducted it became apparent that ER and IR were not clearly distinguishable. IR often appeared differently in self-reporting than in actual life, when people made value choices.

The next phase in the social study of religious forms of life was C. Daniel Batson's introduction of a third type of orientation: "religion as Quest" (QR).[42] QR is characterized by a less rigid "grasp" of religious beliefs. This religious orientation welcomes doubt and tentative attitudes, and is generally more open to disagreement and cognitive dissonance.

The varied nature of religious conviction, or the "grasp" people apply to their beliefs, complicates this conversation significantly, making any simplistic and general comments regarding the harmfulness of religiosity impossible. Ironically, it seems that superficial "civil religion," which is often used for openly political purposes (by the religious Left as well as the Right) covaries more with out-group hostility than deep and active religiosity.[43]

---

41. G. W. Allport and J. M. Ross, "Personal Religious Orientation and Prejudice," *Journal of Personality and Social Psychology* 5 (1967): 434.

42. C. Daniel Batson, *Religion and the Individual: A Social-Psychological Perspective* (Oxford: Oxford University Press, 1993), 166–68; Batson, "Individual Religion, Tolerance and Universal Compassion," in Clarke, Powell, and Savulescu, *Religion, Intolerance, and Conflict*, 88–106.

43. The religious Right is often accused of using religion to advance political agendas, but the religious Left is active in this approach as well. See James Davison Hunter, *To Change the World: The Irony, Tragedy, and Possibility of Christianity in the Late Modern World* (New York: Oxford University Press, 2010), 132–50.

The third problem identified at the beginning of this section concerns scientific interpretations of the elements that give religions their visible features, which overlaps with the universal-particular distinction mentioned earlier. Is it the beliefs or the communal practices that make religion what it is? Of course, this is a false juxtaposition, as beliefs influence practices and vice versa. The question is, should we look at the creeds, which are universal and often abstract, or should we focus on how the religion is lived out and practiced?[44] When commenting on the bad religion question, it is customary for many to draw attention to sacred texts or creedal statements. Often in the case of Islam, people cite passages in the Qur'an to prove that Islam permits and even praises the use of violence to further religious ends.[45] On the other hand, when the relation of religion and violence is discussed from a scientific perspective, it is more typical to refer to panhuman, communal features of human behavior that are enhanced by religion.

The latter is a stronger tactic because it attempts to connect violence to features common to all religions. Merely citing potentially dangerous texts of different religions' sacred books, however, leaves out a vast number of religious traditions and groups that have either less problematic passages or creedal statements or that perhaps do not have a clear creed at all. Furthermore, text- or creed-based approaches easily lead to an endless loop, where violent texts are countered with texts that underline compassion, virtue, and love of enemies, or where violent passages are interpreted metaphorically.[46]

If religion is taken to be an evolutionary adaption, this naturally entails that the essence of religion is its ability to help people form competitive groups.[47] But group-formation and mutual competition happens in politics all the time, and vast research exists on how groupishness plays out in partisan politics and nationalism.[48] Moreover, team sports are obviously good group-forming prac-

44. In CSR, it has been more typical to concentrate on belief formation, whereas evolutionary anthropologists have been more interested in religions' group-forming capabilities.

45. E.g., Qur'an 8:12: "I will cast terror into the hearts of those who disbelieve. Therefore strike off their heads and strike off every fingertip of them." Qur'an 2:191: "And kill them wherever you overtake them and expel them from wherever they have expelled you, and *fitnah* [disbelief] is worse than killing. . . . Such is the recompense of the disbelievers."

46. For a treatment of problematic biblical themes, see, e.g., Paul Copan and Matt Flanagan, *Did God Really Command Genocide? Coming to Terms with the Justice of God* (Grand Rapids: Baker Books, 2014).

47. See, e.g., Clarke, *Justification of Religious Violence*, 45–54.

48. For example, national identification often correlates with out-group rejection. See Amélie Mummendey, Andreas Klink, and Rupert Brown, "Nationalism and Patriotism: National Identification and Out-Group Rejection," *British Journal of Social Psychology* 40 (2011):

tices, and football-related violence alone, for example, has been the source of well over two thousand annual arrests in the United Kingdom in recent years.[49]

Several studies suggest that religions are especially good at being groupish. According to Richard Sosis, religious groups typically outlast secular ones since they exhibit more cooperation and other survival-inducing values.[50] If we choose the adaptationist account of religion and agree that religious beliefs make groups better by increasing evolutionary fitness, we have some basis for claiming that religions are potentially dangerous: it is in their nature to compete with each other. However, even the practice-based approach does not allow easy generalizations; the same religion can be practiced in different ways in different contexts. For example, Roman Catholicism in Norway causes no recognizable problems, whereas the same religion had a recent violent period in Northern Ireland. And again, emphasizing groupishness extends the problematic behavior well beyond the bounds of world religions into the world of secular politics. Moreover, as this locates the core of the problem in human nature, the focus moves away from abstract religion to particular instantiations of groupishness, some of which can be religious but often is not. It may still be that religiosity is especially effective in creating groupishness, even more so than immediate secular alternatives (like football and nationalism), but current data does not allow that conclusion. In fact, it can be safely assumed that the supermajority of Westerners are willing to kill for their country, but those who are willing to kill for their religion are much harder to find.

Defining the Word Harm

The second problem concerns the word *harm*. In order to test this term, we should be able to come up with a class of actions that are harmful to

---

159–72; Shana Levin and Jim Sidanius, "Social Dominance and Social Identity in the United States and Israel: Ingroup Favoritism or Outgroup Derogation," *Political Psychology* 20 (1999): 99–126.

49. For statistics, see "Statistics on Football-Related Arrests and Football Banning Orders, Season 2012–13," Home Office of the UK Government, https://www.gov.uk /government/uploads/system/uploads/attachment_data/file/248740/Football_Arrest_BO _Statistics_2012–13.pdf (accessed October 3, 2016).

50. E.g., Richard Sosis, "Does Religion Promote Trust? The Role of Signaling, Reputation and Punishment," *Interdisciplinary Journal of Research on Religion* 1 (2005): 1–30; Richard Sosis and Eric Bressler, "Cooperation and Commune Longevity: A Test of the Costly Signaling Theory of Religion," *Cross-Cultural Research* 37 (2003): 211–39.

human flourishing. Yet here we face an apparent problem because harmfulness is subjective. Discussing whether some action is, for example, discriminatory toward some people is often beside the point.[51] In many Scandinavian countries, it is forbidden to smoke in restaurants, which is a rule that discriminates against smokers and therefore might be classified by smokers as a negative action since smoking is regarded as conducive for their flourishing. Societies have ways to discriminate against some of their citizens in order to promote some public goods, but this is not usually seen as a problem. A policeman may be permitted to harm a criminal in some circumstances, and a mother can force her child to swallow bad-tasting medicine.

People sometimes intentionally engage in actions that have known negative consequences to a group of people, but mitigating conditions permit these actions. It is not enough to merely point out that some people are discriminated against or suffer due to some actions. Also, it is unrealistic to expect that everyone will agree on when discrimination or suffering is allowed. Instead, we would need objective criteria of sorts to locate real harm as effectively as possible.[52] Clarke restricts his inquiry only to physical harm, for the aforementioned reasons. Including other kinds of harms would complicate the discussion significantly. This restriction is understandable if one desires to avoid vacuous claims. But as I noted in the introduction, there are several levels of religious disagreement:

1. Religious disagreements in the public sphere
   a. Violent clashes between religions and worldviews (ideologically motivated violence and war)
   b. Clashes between ideologically motivated values (arguments about abortion, euthanasia, marriage, etc.)

51. See John Perry and Nigel Biggar, "Religion and Intolerance: A Critical Commentary," in *Religion, Intolerance, and Conflict: A Scientific and Conceptual Investigation*, ed. Steve Clarke, Russell Powell, and Julian Savulescu (Oxford: Oxford University Press, 2012), 253–61.

52. Thurow suggests that the relevant definition should be such that both "religious and non-religious folk, each using their own standards, would agree about the goodness or badness of the action of tolerance or intolerance." See Thurow, "Religion," 153. Asking for agreed-on value judgments regarding harmful actions seems to be a tall order, though I do not think it should be prima facie rejected, as there might be cases where it proved beneficial. For example, focusing on physical harm or those acts that are perceived as bad by everyone makes it in principle possible to conclude that a religion actually causes a certain type of harm.

   2. Intrareligious disagreements
      a. Disagreements between members of the same community in a smaller scale (such as the Anglican Communion crisis or the Great Schism of 1054)
      b. Disagreements between the members of neighboring communities (ecumenical debates)
   3. Personal conflicts
      a. Disagreements among family members and other close peers
      b. Individual feelings of cognitive dissonance

Restricting the debate to merely physical harm means that we should discuss only those issues that exemplify tenet 1a. But 1b, 3a, and 3b also include cases that can be deeply problematic and classified as harm (though not necessarily physical). Yet the problem is, as noted, the subjective nature of our evaluations. For the purposes of this study, it is perhaps enough to note that it is possible that religious groups may cause harm in all these levels of disagreement, even when there is no disagreement.

To summarize, the problem with "harm" is that sometimes violence, intolerance, and even war are good things, in the sense of being the lesser of two or more competing evils. This complicates the simplistic claims by refocusing the debate on the grounds and arguments for the use of force, which leads naturally to the third problematic notion: causal influence.

Defining the Word Cause

If we wish to find out whether religion causes harm, we need to address at least three issues:

   1. Multiple causes for action
   2. Differing ways things can be caused
   3. Lack of control groups

How can we know whether religion has some kind of influence on human actions? Giving a simple answer is not possible because our actions are generally caused by many things at the same time.[53] For example, I have several reasons for writing this book: I want to make the world a better place; I

---

53. See also Thurow, "Religion," 150–51.

want to earn money to support my family; I enjoy the intellectual challenge that questions like these pose; and so on. In similar fashion, when people actually perform any action, they often have various reasons for doing so. These reasons are hard to distinguish from each other. In many cases, we would still act exactly the same way if some reason or reasons were absent. Let us suppose that I have reasons *z*, *x*, *c*, and *y* for act *T*. It is possible to claim that *x* was my reason for *T*, but it is also possible that I could do *T* without *x*. In what sense, then, is *x* a reason for *T*? We can easily see how these things get increasingly complicated if we acknowledge the fact we are often unaware of what causes us to act as we do. This allows some leeway to either downplay the role of religious motives or to exaggerate them, based on subjective interests.

Second, there are numerous ways things can be caused. Religion can be a cause for evil in several ways; I have listed here five of the most obvious ways:

a. Religion *a* in context *y* enables evil actions.
b. Religion *a* in context *y* enhances evil actions that would have happened anyway.
c. Religion *a* in context *y* motivates someone to perform evil actions.
d. Religion *a* in context *y* makes someone passive and unwilling to prevent evil actions.
e. Religion *a* in context *y* makes it harder for dispute participants to reach a compromise or seek resolution to the conflict.

It is necessary to add the qualifier ("in context *y*") to emphasize that religions do not always have the aforementioned consequences. If we grant that sometimes even one's own coreligionists behave badly, the crucial question to be asked is whether religions cause more damage than other forms of groupishness. To make this comparison, one needs a control group. But if, as statistics show, the known events of religious violence are both rare and contextually located, is it possible to have a control group that exemplifies all the other features of the religious group, minus the religion, and is located in a similar political context? Finding such groups is evidently hard, but not impossible. Nevertheless, we do not presently have any studies that could offer more light on this issue.[54]

54. The best we have is Richard Sosis's study on religious and secular kibbutzim, but as such this study does not offer much valuable information for understanding conflicts. See

The Recipe for Doom

Let us then take a look at a possible scenario of how religious acts of violence might take place. Based on a survey of recent literature, I have sketched out "the recipe for doom":

1. Groupishness
2. A multicultural state
3. Tension or hostilities between groups
4. Notions of
     a. cosmic war
     b. eternal life
     c. the sacred

In the following section, I will explain the contents of the recipe in more detail. Ingmar Persson and Julian Savulescu sum up ingredients 1–3 as follows:

> It might be feared, rightly as we shall suggest, that the other side of this social unification is a deprecatory and intolerant attitude to people of different religious persuasions. In a world in which there is not as much contact between people of different religions as there is in the modern world, this might not be a decisive drawback. But in the globalized world of today, this makes religion liable to create extremely dangerous conflicts, especially if there are weapons of mass destruction around. Moreover, since many contemporary societies are huge and significantly multicultural, it is most unlikely that all citizens of any one of them will accept the same religion. Rather, the citizens will belong to different religions, and, because of the progress of science, many will be secular, believing in no religion whatsoever. This suggests that today religion is more likely to cause friction than harmony within societies, as well as between them. So, it might be feared that today religion is socially more harmful than beneficial, more of a seed-bed of conflict than of harmony.[55]

Based on the fact that religiosity correlates with community building, we

---

Richard Sosis and Bradley J. Ruffle, "Religious Ritual and Cooperation: Testing for a Relationship on Israeli Religious and Secular Kibbutzim," *Current Anthropology* 44 (2003): 713–22.

55. Ingmar Persson and Julian Savulescu, "The Limits of Religious Tolerance: A Secular View," in Clarke, Powell, and Savulescu, *Religion, Intolerance, and Conflict*, 239.

could claim that strong in-group favoritism makes it harder for religious persons to be open-minded toward other viewpoints than their own, hinders epistemically humble attitudes, and prevents wide perspectives necessary for practical wisdom and conviviality in the late modern West.[56] In-group favoritism is strengthened when the group is threatened or under pressure, which, again, is a common human reaction. In these cases, we feel "pressure to opinion uniformity, encouragement of autocratic leadership, . . . rejection of deviates, resistance to change, conservatism, and perpetuation of group norms," researchers tell us.[57]

In other words, when people act in clearly defined groups and identify themselves with them, certain biases increase in-group/out-group distinction. This means that the beliefs of in-groups are constantly strengthened through exposure to data that comes from within the group. Simultaneously, out-groups are viewed with suspicion and their criticisms are not taken seriously. In a multicultural state, we will have a plethora of groups who might feel threatened in the pressure of other identities, and, in the worst-case scenario, some of them might have access to weapons of mass destruction.

In his recent analysis of the justification of religious violence, Clarke focuses on three notions that are typical to religions and that can function as justificatory notions that could lead one to perform violent acts in the name of religion.[58] First, the idea of "cosmic war" may create a state in which persons feel that they are participants in a struggle between light and darkness, where the stakes are exceptionally high. Second, the idea of eternal life may influence one's actions in several ways. For example, the law of karma may cause people to neglect the humane treatment of prisoners or enemies because they deserve to be treated badly (otherwise they would not be in the state they are). Karma may also lead one to conclude that someone is better off dead if one's current life adds more bad karma to one's account. Third, the idea of the sacred can cause several kinds of extreme reactions. For example, the controversy concerning the cartoons depicting Muhammad in Denmark

---

56. Ara Norenzayan also argues that this is the first step that leads to religious violence. It is followed by increased distrust of other communities and, further down the road, inability to compromise one's convictions because they are considered to be sacred. Norenzayan, however, adds a disclaimer by saying this should not be viewed as something that happens everywhere religion is involved. In his mind, "there is . . . the potential for religion to reduce conflict as much as to create it." Norenzayan, *Big Gods*, 160.

57. Arie W. Kruglanski et al., "Groups as Epistemic Providers: Need for Closure and the Unfolding of Group-Centrism," *Psychological Review* 113 (2006): 84–100.

58. Clarke, *Justification of Religious Violence*, 89–152.

in 2005 and the Charlie Hebdo strike in 2015 were such reactions. Similar cases are situations where sacred places are destroyed or pieces of holy land are occupied. The central idea in all three cases is that they raise the stakes so high that almost anything is allowed to protect the interest of the in-group.[59] Clarke's account is descriptively accurate. If harmful actions are performed in the name of religion, these ingredients are quite likely in the mix.

On the surface, many conditions listed in the recipe for doom are a given in our late modern Western societies. Our minds tend to make us groupish, we live in pluralistic societies, and religions employ, to use Jonathan Haidt's term, the ethics of divinity. Nevertheless, we should not interpret the recipe as a sequence that necessarily produces acts of violence. We have many cases where tenets 1–4 are in place but nothing bad happens. The recipe is best seen as a list of things that, when combined, create a volatile state, which may cause problems in some contexts. That phrase "in some contexts" is key. The environment and other contingent factors play a crucial role. But this moves the focus away from religions as such.

If we ask ourselves whether we should be especially worried about *religions* in the contemporary world, the answer is, not really. This does not mean that religions cannot be involved with evil, but that the problematic elements of religion are usually those that are shared by every human being, regardless of their worldview. If there is something that we *should* worry about, it is the dynamics that create and enforce in-group/out-group distinctions—be they religious or secular.

Finally, some critical points regarding the recipe itself. First, if the essence of religion is its ability to form in-groups, and this is the most volatile feature of religion, why do we see so little violence that bears the marks of religiosity? Again, my intention is not to brush aside the reality of those horrendous acts that are performed in the name of religion or ideology. Yet the extreme evils that are in some way caused or enabled by religion are so relatively rare that it is incredibly difficult to prevent them.

Of course, the critic may still claim that religious groupishness as such

---

59. A related interesting phenomenon is called moral self-licensing. If you are able to perform certain virtues, you easily forget that those were not the only virtues that you should pay attention to. For example, people who buy "green" products are more likely to, e.g., cheat and lie compared to nongreen consumers. Quite likely, this same effect can be manifested in religious communities, which can be very selective in the virtues they choose to espouse; yet again the problem of moral self-licensing is not related to religiosity as such. Nina Mazar and Chen-Bo Zhong, "Do Green Products Make Us Better People?," *Psychological Studies* 21 (2010): 494–98.

is dangerous because it creates intergroup hostilities and prejudices, which are less serious than actual war. Thus, even QR is not free from some level of groupishness. Powell and Clarke use these results to show that not even those who perceive religion as a search for truth show "unlimited tolerance."[60] However, one can only wonder what unlimited tolerance might look like. Do we have any examples from human history that have shown unlimited tolerance? If it were possible, is unlimited tolerance not clearly a vice, which should be denounced by any moral agent?[61]

Powell and Clarke's critical claim points to the fact that the language of tolerance easily betrays. Not all tolerance is good; sometimes being intolerant is good. There are instances in which even a (religiously motivated) war might be the lesser of two evils. Instead of discussing whether some group tolerates some other group or not, we should be more interested in *why* they are doing so. Observing the mere attitude of tolerance or the lack of it does not help us understand when tolerance is bad and when it is not. Instead, we need to look for the arguments groups produce for their actions. However, this does not fit easily into the approach that downplays the cognitive commitments of religions or regards them as secondary. If there is no reason behind the act, then the discussion about the reason is not reasonable.

My second point concerns the second ingredient in the recipe for doom: multiculturalism. The recipe suggests that multiculturalism is the worst possible state for religions to exist in. But sociologist Rodney Stark, for example, begs to differ. Stark argues that the times when religion has become a problem have coincided with the attempts to control religion by outside force or to sustain a monoreligious state. Multireligious states, in contrast, are typically rather peaceful. Stark argues that the presence of various religious groups in a shared space does not lead to chaos but to mutual recognition of other groups and to a consequent search for harmony. "Where there exist competing religions, norms of religious civility will develop to the extent that there exists a pluralistic equilibrium," Stark argues. "Norms of religious civility exist when public expressions and behavior are governed by mutual respect. A pluralistic equilibrium exists when the power is sufficiently diffused among the set of competitors so that conflict is not in anyone's interest."[62]

60. Powell and Clarke, "Religion, Tolerance, and Intolerance," 14.

61. Thus, e.g., Alasdair MacIntyre, "Toleration and Goods in Conflict," in *Selected Essays*, vol. 2, *Ethics and Politics* (Cambridge: Cambridge University Press, 2006), 223.

62. Rodney Stark, *The Triumph of Christianity: How the Jesus Movement Became the World's Largest Religion* (San Francisco: HarperOne, 2011), 366. For an argument why religious

Based on what has already been said, there are great challenges to answering the bad religion question in a simplistic way. It is not only that we have little empirical research on this point, but also that the research quickly runs into severe conceptual troubles. On the one hand, using general categories makes our claims too broad to have any reasonable content, even if we grant that the concept "religion" has some actual traction. On the other hand, concentrating on some particular case makes drawing general conclusions incredibly difficult. You can instead make local observations that might be valuable per se, but they offer little help when you want to say something about how religion in the abstract or even particular religious traditions function as such. Even if we leave aside the issue of universal definition and focus on a particular religion, say, Christianity, we are still faced with a plethora of problems. Do we have the means to distinguish between religious and nonreligious motives behind particular choices? Do we have the means to control the effect of personality, sociopolitical context, or other contingent factors? Further, "Christianity" hardly represents a monolithic entity. Christianity exists in such a vast variety of beliefs and practices that to treat it is as a uniform, shared reality is simply unrealistic.

These questions are typically acknowledged when the problem is probed in research literature—the reader is often met with dictums like "this may point to," "this might indicate," and "there is so much we do not know." The question in its current form is too big and has too many factors beyond our control. The most we can do is to say that worldview a, if it is held in political and sociological situation b, by a group having general characteristics c, may have an unwanted consequence d.[63] Instead of "religion poisons everything," a more scientifically accurate claim would be, for example, "certain factions of Islam, if feeling threatened and harassed by an outside force, and if a large enough constituency within a given faction has a character that makes it easy for them to react aggressively, may poison something." But this is not likely to make any headlines.

---

diversity is ultimately beneficial, see Victoria Harrison, "Religious Diversity," in *The Routledge Companion to Theism*, ed. Charles Taliaferro, Victoria S. Harrison, and Stewart Goetz (London: Routledge 2013), 488.

63. See, e.g., Keith Ward, *Is Religion Dangerous?* (Oxford: Lion, 2006), 56–82; David Martin, *Does Christianity Cause War?* (Oxford: Clarendon, 2002).

3.4. Philosophy of Religious Disagreement

It was demonstrated in the first chapter that disagreement is common in philosophy. In fact, for every widely held philosophical view *p* we have an argument that gives us a reason to be skeptical about *p*. By philosophical views, I mean here simply the topics that philosophers argue about. An illustrative example of this is the survey of philosophical positions, where professional philosophers all around the world were asked about their views on various philosophical questions.[64] Here are some examples of their answers.

> *Abstract objects*: Platonism (40%), nominalism (37%)
> *Free will*: compatibilism (59%), libertarianism (14%), no free will (12%)
> *Epistemic justification*: externalism (42%), internalism (26%)
> *Meta-ethics*: moral realism (56%), antirealism (28%)
> *Mind*: physicalism (56%), nonphysicalism (27%)

What should we make of this data? The problem of disagreement is old news within political philosophy, but it has only recently gained the interest of analytic philosophers and epistemologists. One of the liveliest topics in recent analytic epistemology has been the epistemology of disagreement.[65] In this section, I shall present a general outline of the state of the present discussion, examine some topics that have been raised especially in the context of religious disagreements, and in the end I will propose some ways to react to religious disagreements.

In the literature, genuine disagreement entails that epistemic peers who have shared all the relevant evidence come to different conclusions concerning which proposition the evidence confirms more strongly. By epistemic peerage I mean the relation between two or more persons who (1) share equal reasoning capabilities in the relevant domain; (2) have a sufficient degree of intellectual virtues, that is to say, when they reason, they reason conscientiously; (3) have equal access to the relevant evidence; and (4) have shared the reasons for their respective position with each other.

It might be worthwhile to add that the persons must be intelligent and well trained in the subject of debate, because disagreement between two

---

64. The survey can be found at "The PhilPapers Surveys," *PhilPapers*, 2009, www .philpapers.org/surveys. See also Helen de Cruz, "Religious Disagreement: An Empirical Study among Academic Philosophers," *Episteme* (2015): 1–17.

65. Feldman and Warfield, *Disagreement*; Christensen and Lackey, *The Epistemology of Disagreement*. See also *Episteme* 6 (2009) for a collection of articles on this theme.

untrained persons is not philosophically interesting. It is the combination of epistemic peerage and the asymmetry of beliefs that causes the philosophical problem of disagreement. If either or both are missing, the situation is not philosophically noteworthy.

Two basic solutions emerge. According to the *conciliatory view*, if persons *a* and *b* are epistemic peers holding opposing views, they will lose their epistemic rights to their respective views.[66] Their views cancel each other out, or they just might be required to move closer to one another's position. But according to the *steadfastist view*, *a* and *b* retain rights to their respective beliefs.[67] Both conciliatory and steadfastist views are general if their proponents think that there exists one rule that defines the proper way of conduct in all possible cases of disagreement. What makes the generalist position problematic is that we can easily think of particular cases when either conciliatory or steadfastist positions seem correct and rational to choose.

Think, for example, of simple perceptual beliefs. I see an animal running across the frozen lake and I say to my friend, "Look, there's a fox." He answers, "No, it is too big and gray. It must be a wolf." In this case, it seems rational for us to withhold our beliefs until we see the creature's footprints. But think of another case where *a* says, "We need to continue sentencing people to death for extreme crimes," and *b* says, "We should not sentence people to death, no matter what their crimes are." In this case, it seems rational for *a* and *b* to stick to their respective positions, because withholding would in effect lead to the automatic victory of the prevailing condition.

Thus it seems that generalism is not the ideal strategy, and we need to be more case sensitive. Recognizing this has given rise to a third option, which can be called the *dynamic view*. This position is inherently particularistic, as it does not subscribe to the generalist thesis. Because there is no

---

66. See, e.g., Hilary Kornblith, "Belief in the Face of Controversy," in Feldman and Warfield, *Disagreement*, 29–52; Richard Feldman, "Reasonable Religious Disagreements," in *Philosophers without Gods: Meditations on Atheism and the Secular Life*, ed. Louise M. Antony (New York: Oxford University Press, 2010), 194–214; Earl Conee, "Peerage," *Episteme* 6 (2009): 313–23.

67. Thus, e.g., Peter van Inwagen, "Is It Wrong Everywhere, Always, and for Everyone to Believe Anything on Insufficient Evidence?," in *Faith, Freedom, and Rationality*, ed. Jeffrey Jordan and Daniel Howard-Snyder (Lanham, MD: Rowman and Littlefield, 1996), 137–53; "We're Right. They're Wrong," in Feldman and Warfield, *Disagreement*, 10–29; Alvin Plantinga, *Warranted Christian Belief* (New York: Oxford University Press, 2000), 450; Joseph Kim, *Reformed Epistemology and the Problem of Religious Diversity* (Eugene, OR: Pickwick, 2011); Jeroen de Ridder and Mathanja Berger, "Shipwrecked or Holding Water? In Defense of Plantinga's Warranted Christian Believer," *Philo* 16 (2013): 42–61.

general rule for cases of disagreement, every case is considered unique.[68] However, it seems that both conciliatory and steadfastist views are able to appreciate some genuine intellectual virtues, such as critical thinking and persistence. But the problems of these two views are clear: the conciliatory view will make skepticism the default philosophical position; steadfastism, in the worst-case scenario, creates intellectual ghettoes and disables dialogue. Yet these problems are pragmatic, not epistemic, worries. It might well be that both skepticism and steadfastism have consequences that are not desirable, and this gives a pragmatic reason for someone to avoid them. Epistemic rationality is not the same as pragmatic rationality, even if they can both point in the same direction: this choice is both true *and* beneficial. These two types of rationality are often conflated in debates, but this should be avoided. Further, epistemic approaches should be employed also in religious matters. How, then, should we approach religious disagreements from the viewpoint of epistemic rationality?

William Alston has pointed out the conceptual problems that influence the ways to think about epistemic justification: even among epistemologists we have several criteria concerning epistemic rationality. According to Alston, different views about epistemic justification are not necessarily wrong, but, taken individually, too narrow.[69] The same issue applies to the epistemology of disagreement. Concentrating on just one particular epistemic good is likely to result in problems.

Instead of representing an attempt to find the perfect criterion for knowledge, actual knowledge acquisition involves complex processes, time, and will, which is shaped by necessary features, such as intellectual virtues. Moreover, Alston lists various epistemic desiderata, some of which are more essential than others, and which instantiate some genuine epistemic good, such as truth, understanding, reliability, and coherence. Alston's remarks about different epistemic goods are important because they can help us realize how people may have multiple goals in their knowledge acquisition. Instead of just finding out "what is the truth, plain and simple," they might want to learn new things, find ways of relating pieces of knowledge together, or in the case of disagreement, finding out which epistemic goods are instan-

---

68. For discussion, see e.g., Michael Thune, "Religious Belief and the Epistemology of Disagreement," *Philosophy Compass* 5 (2010): 712–24; Nathan L. King, "Religious Diversity and Its Challenges to Religious Belief," *Philosophy Compass* 3 (2008): 830–53; Michael Bergmann, "Rational Disagreement after Full Disclosure," *Episteme* 6, no. 3 (2009): 336–53.

69. William Alston, *Beyond "Justification": Dimensions of Epistemic Valuation* (Ithaca, NY: Cornell University Press, 2005).

tiated in the given position by each participant. Of course, these other goals cannot be ultimately divorced from truth if they are supposed to make any sense, but often the path toward greater understanding and truth proceeds through the realization of several epistemic goods.[70]

In my suggested solution, I will take my cue from Alston's account. I will argue that for religious disagreements the dynamic option is the most suitable one, and the way disagreements are handled should involve an analysis of different intellectual and moral goods. Before turning to religious disagreements, we need to say something about religious and philosophical beliefs in general.

Nature of Religious and Philosophical Beliefs

Colin McGinn and Peter van Inwagen, among others, have suggested that philosophical questions are difficult for beings who have minds like ours because of the central role of intuition in our philosophizing. In *Problems in Philosophy*, McGinn writes:

> Philosophical theses can sometimes be assented to, but often they can expect only to be taken seriously. We may hope to find sufficient reason actually to believe a philosophical proposition, but often enough the best we can do is to get ourselves into a position to regard the proposition with respect. . . . A good deal of philosophical debate consists in persuading others to take seriously a hypothesis one has come to find attractive for reasons that defy summary statement or straightforward demonstration. . . . The relation between evidence (argument) and truth is very often not close enough to permit full-blown assent.[71]

McGinn's point is that our cognitive capacities are such that they make it difficult for us to access the truth. He also claims that our philosophical inclinations are mostly driven by our intuitions. We end up appreciating and defending some particular philosophical theory because its assumptions have certain intuitive plausibility for us (examined briefly in the previous chapter). The central role of intuitions does not mean that reasons do not come into

70. Alston, *Beyond "Justification,"* 39–49. See also Rik Peels, "Epistemic Desiderata and Epistemic Pluralism," *Journal of Philosophical Research* 35 (2010): 193–207.

71. Colin McGinn, *Problems in Philosophy* (Oxford: Blackwell, 1993), 1. See also Peter van Inwagen, *The Problem of Evil* (Oxford: Oxford University Press, 2006), 37–55.

philosophy at all. Reasons can force us to abandon a view that we hold to be intuitively plausible. Often it is also the case that reasons can be used to vindicate our intuitively preferred views. McGinn is known for his "mysterianism," something of an agnostic stance toward great philosophical problems. When the available evidence equally supports several rational options, a reasonable stance is to maintain that the issue is truly mysterious to us.[72]

It is easy to see how this attitude would play out in a religious context: should we be agnostic about ultimate reality? Peter van Inwagen agrees with McGinn in that he also considers the great philosophical problems to be unsolvable. Nonetheless, van Inwagen opts for steadfastness: we are entitled to hold on to our beliefs even in the face of peer disagreement in matters that are mysterious to us if we have good reasons for doing so. The reason for steadfastness is the fact that van Inwagen finds it unimaginable that he could become agnostic about things over which he disagrees with his peers. Beliefs are not under our direct voluntary control. Is van Inwagen here making a pragmatic or epistemic point? Perhaps a bit of both. If I read him correctly, he argues that the reasons one has for one's position are epistemic. Once the person has these positions, he or she cannot annul them. Thus it is not pragmatically rational to ask people to give up their convictions because of pragmatic reason *x* if the reasons are epistemic.[73]

Before trying to find some way out of this standoff, we need to take a deeper look at those philosophically crucial factors (which resonate with what was said earlier about human cognitive processes) that generate religious disagreement. In his recent metaphilosophical work, Gary Gutting explores the nature of philosophical knowledge and the idea of progress in philosophy. He also touches on religious knowledge and the nature of the arguments that people use either to prove or disprove God's existence. At first, Gutting seems to support the skeptical or agnostic conclusion when he claims, "For any standard version of [theistic or atheistic] argument . . . there are solid philosophical reasons that show just why the argument fails." Therefore, there is "no generally compelling argumentative basis for accepting or rejecting the existence of God."[74]

72. Of course, here one faces the problem of self-defeat: if one ought to regard philosophical issues as being truly mysterious to us when there are good arguments on both sides, then shouldn't we also regard as truly mysterious the issue of whether philosophical issues are truly mysterious to us where there are good arguments on both sides?

73. Van Inwagen, "We're Right. They're Wrong," 27–28.

74. Gary Gutting, *What Philosophers Know* (Cambridge: Cambridge University Press, 2009), 232–33.

Does this then lead to holding religious convictions by faith alone, against reason and without arguments? According to Gutting, this does not follow from the aforementioned impasse. The impasse itself results from serious philosophical work; it is not evident. It is extremely hard to provide knockdown arguments to philosophically basic positions. It might be that there are abstract entities or that there are not. It might be that God exists or that God does not exist. Both are conceptually possible and, at least in some sense, rational positions to hold.[75]

But what role do the arguments themselves play in religious life if they are unable to demonstrate either of the desired conclusions? Gutting adopts a moderate steadfastist position.

> This [impasse] does not exclude the possibility that some individuals may be in epistemic situations that entitle them to the premises of valid arguments for or against religious beliefs. If, after careful reflection, it just seems overwhelmingly obvious to me that, say, the universe must have an intelligent cause or that certain sorts or amounts of evil are just incompatible with an all-good, all-powerful creator, then I have an intellectual right to accept the conclusions that follow from these premises. But I still have no basis for claiming that others, who see things differently, are not epistemically entitled to their views.[76]

Gutting thinks that it is enough for our beliefs to be justified by moderate internalist standards. If we have done our epistemic job conscientiously and still have our convictions, we are entitled to believe them, even in the face of peer disagreement.

Paul Helm defends the view according to which it is possible that two persons, a and b, who are apparent epistemic peers, hold on to exactly the same rational procedures but remain in disagreement while retaining the status of rationality for their respective beliefs.[77] The reason for this is the person-relative nature of the relevant evidence. Some of the evidence can be experiential, like memories, and therefore not completely available to others.[78] This kind of evidence is unique in the sense that it cannot be totally

---

75. However, if classical theism is true then it is not *metaphysically* possible that it be false (i.e., because if classical theism is true then God exists necessarily).

76. Gutting, *What philosophers Know*, 233n2.

77. Paul Helm, *Faith with Reason* (Oxford: Oxford University Press, 2000), 66–83.

78. Helm denies that evidence being person-relative entails subjectivism. Even if it is rational for a in t_1 to believe p, and irrational for b in t_1 to believe that not-p, these must be

communicated to others. Even if some beliefs based on experience can be eliminable so that the source of disagreement can be defined and conflict resolved, often this is not so.

Experiences of a religious or existential sort cannot but have an influence on a person's belief formation processes. Helm also points out how people may appreciate different things in religion. Subjective states, like shame, personal fulfillment, awe, fear, and guilt, can influence how one evaluates different worldviews. (Helm uses Martin Luther as an example of how feelings of guilt may increase one's propensity to adopt a certain religious option.)[79] Without actually recommending it, Helm acknowledges that some people can prioritize pragmatic issues over evidential ones in their religious reasoning. Thus two apparent epistemic peers may end up having different conclusions if their evaluative hierarchies differ due to the fact that one regards a certain piece of evidence as more important than the other.

Religious worldviews, like any other comprehensive worldview, are highly complex. They constitute thousands of individuals' beliefs and convictions, some of which are held consciously while some are not. All of them have certain histories; my Christian worldview is not 100 percent the same as your Christian worldview. These facts complicate the evaluation of the encounters between differing parties. Graham Oppy has summarized the relevant factors of religious disagreement as follows:

> It seems to me to be plausible to suppose that all of the following kinds of factors are present in at least some cases of religious disagreement between doxastic peers: (1) there are differences in starting points—i.e. differences in prior probabilities, doxastic presuppositions, worldviews, initial assumptions, doxastic frameworks, and the like; (2) there are differences in evidential bases for belief that are not amenable to full disclosure . . . ; (3) there is disagreement on a relatively wide range of topics—i.e. disagreement is not restricted to a relatively small number of related propositions—even though, of course, there is also wide agreement on a massive background of less relevant matters; (4) there is not total transparency of reasons for beliefs about religious matters—i.e. the

---

understood as cases where belief supervenes on the evidence, which might be different for *a* and *b*. See Helm, *Faith with Reason*, 77, 89–93.

79. Helm argues that religious reasoning is often concerned with complex issues like long-term life goals and personal fulfillment that are very hard to evaluate from a purely evidential perspective. Helm, *Faith with Reason*, 80–81. On this same issue, see also Jonathan Kvanvig, "Affective Theism and People of Faith," *Midwest Studies in Philosophy* 27 (2013): 109–28.

reasons that one has for holding one's beliefs about questions of religion are not fully transparent to oneself, and the reasons that others have for holding the beliefs that they do on questions about religion are not fully transparent to one either; (5) there are hard questions about the extent to which the judgments that one makes about questions of religion are independent of the judgments that other people make about questions of religion; and (6) there is mutual knowledge—prior to any particular religious disagreement between doxastic peers—that there is a very wide spectrum of peer opinion on many questions about religion.[80]

All this leads to the conclusion that it is actually incredibly difficult to know when we really are epistemic peers.[81] Although we might not be in a position to give absolute evaluations of our own or our peer's epistemic status, the recognition of *possible* peer disagreement can still have an effect on our beliefs.[82] Nathan King has proposed that one needs to be able to offer reasons why one's epistemic position is better than his or her dissenter's.[83]

To remain steadfast, one needs to demote the dissenter's epistemic status. This takes place, for example, by coming up with reasons to think that my opponent has some particular defect in their reasoning, epistemic status, or that they do not have the same evidence or value it in the same way. Absent these kinds of reasons, the belief is in danger of losing its status as a rational belief.

Yet part of the problem is that we do not know when we have reasons to believe that our demotion of a dissenter has been successful. Nevertheless, these questions are important and need to be pursued, but it might be good to recognize the difficulties that frustrate this project. Finding the answer to the question concerning the peerhood and demotion of epistemic status

80. Graham Oppy, "Disagreement," *International Journal of Philosophy of Religion* 68 (2010): 197.

81. See also Robert Audi, *Rationality and Religious Commitment* (New York: Oxford University Press, 2011), 202; Audi, "Cognitive Disparities: Dimensions of Intellectual Diversity and the Resolution of Disagreements," in Christensen and Lackey, *Epistemology of Disagreement*, 205–22.

82. For a refined argument against overly strict criteria for epistemic peerhood, see Jennifer Lackey, "Taking Religious Disagreements Seriously," in *Religious Faith and Intellectual Virtue*, ed. Laura Frances Callahan and Timothy O'Connor (Oxford: Oxford University Press, 2014), 312.

83. See, e.g., Nathan L. King, "Disagreement: What's the Problem? Or A Good Peer Is Hard to Find," *Philosophy and Phenomenological Research* 85 (2012): 269.

is often not a starting point, but a result of extended discussion, which may take years or even a lifetime.

Doubting My Religion

Merely granting that both relativism and absolutism are unwanted positions does not take us very far; we should be able to say something that goes beyond platitudes and address the question of how we should actually regulate our beliefs. Everyone agrees that we should be able to avoid both overt laxity and rigid unassailability, but how?

In what follows, I will look at how doubt has been suggested as a way of avoiding these horns, especially in the work of Peter Berger and Robert McKim. The central concern in their work is finding ways to regulate doubt. Later, I will use the work of Robert Audi and some other philosophers of religion to illumine the issue. I will be arguing that a doubt-oriented religious belief policy is deficient compared to more evidence- and virtue-based approaches.

In his recent work on doubt, Peter Berger begins with an analysis of modernity.[84] First, modernity does not secularize (contra the so-called secularization thesis); it pluralizes. Urbanization creates spaces where people with radically different moral, political, and religious outlooks are in contact with each other. This interaction is extended beyond physical communities to virtual realities through communication technology.

The second stage in this movement of modernity is that plurality relativizes. It becomes harder and harder to believe that my way is the only correct option when we are faced with other apparently rational and compelling alternatives. Granted, this might sometimes be a benefit, but Berger argues that what we are experiencing is a pendulum swing. Relativism creates as its evil twin (in fact, both twins are evil in this story) reactive fundamentalism, which abhors uncertainty and doubt.[85]

While relativism is in effect a metatheory about the possibility of knowledge in general, fundamentalism always takes a particular form; it is *this* story, and no other, that is true. Fundamentalism can take both religious

84. Peter L. Berger and Anton J. Zijverfeld, *In Praise of Doubt: How to Have Convictions without Becoming a Fanatic* (San Francisco: HarperOne, 2009), 1–48.

85. See also Peter Berger, "Introduction: Between Relativism and Fundamentalism," in *Between Relativism and Fundamentalism: Religious Resources for a Middle Position*, ed. Peter Berger (Grand Rapids: Eerdmans, 2009), 3–6.

and secular/atheistic forms.[86] Berger targets both and makes a plea for a more civilized culture of conversation. This is allegedly in our reach if we apply to our belief policies of what he calls "consistent and sincere doubt."[87]

Berger regards doubt as the heart of modern democracy and an indispensable element of mature and rational religious faith. Doubt is opposed to all "isms" because embracing an ism entails that one has (too) securely landed somewhere. Although Berger's emphasis on the importance of doubt can seem to equal mere agnosticism, he denies this by resorting to the idea of verisimilitude, truth-likeness: we can approach the truth while being skeptical about our current convictions.[88]

All of this would be merely abstract talk without some ways of enacting these ideas in public. For Berger, doubt is located in the core of belief formation, as a sort of ever-present interlocutor. The aim of this is to join belief commitments together with a critical element, which enables constant reflection and keeps the system from stagnating.[89] Berger goes on to argue that faith communities should accept doubt's positive role in religious life. For example, faith communities should be able to distinguish between core beliefs and more marginal components of their belief systems, and be open to historical scholarship, which helps to bring out the historical roots and contingencies of one's own tradition. Simultaneously, one's community needs to reject relativism, build empathic relations to the "others," participate in peace building and conflict resolution, and finally, accept that in contemporary Western society, choosing one's belief system is morally desirable.[90]

All these are probably good things to do, but are we actually talking about doubt? Berger's proposal contains an interesting mix of proposed uncertainty and praise of attitudes that do not square well with uncertainty. Despite many wise suggestions, detailed analysis of what doubt is and how it appears in relation to stronger convictions is needed.

Robert McKim thinks along the same lines as Berger but provides a

---

86. For an evaluation of epistemic attitudes in the New Atheism debate, see Ian J. Kidd, "Epistemic Vices in Public Debate: The Case of 'New Atheism,'" in *New Atheism's Legacy: Critical Perspectives from Philosophy and the Social Sciences*, ed. Christopher Cotter and Philip Quadrio (Dordrecht: Springer, forthcoming).

87. Berger and Zijverfeld, *In Praise of Doubt*, 112–13.

88. This notion is used in the philosophy of science, especially in relation to critical realism. See, e.g., Ilkka Niiniluoto, *Scientific Critical Realism* (Oxford: Clarendon, 1999).

89. See also James Davison Hunter, "Fundamentalism and Relativism Together: Reflections on a Genealogy," in Berger, *Between Relativism and Fundamentalism*, 33.

90. Berger and Zijverfeld, *In Praise of Doubt*, 116–18.

more detailed thesis. McKim argues that all religions should adopt what he calls the "Critical Stance" (CT). CT is based on the following two principles:

> *E-principle*: Disagreement about an issue or area of inquiry provides reason to think that each side has an obligation to *examine* beliefs about the issue.
> *T-principle*: Disagreement about an issue or area of inquiry provides reason for whatever beliefs we hold about that issue or area of inquiry to be tentative.[91]

According to McKim, tentativeness means, among others things, exposing oneself to other perspectives, trying to get a sense of their appeal and the concerns of those who advocate them, exploring strategies that attempt to solve the conflict, recognizing that one may be wrong, remaining open to revise one's beliefs, and last, being willing to abandon those beliefs if it becomes important or reasonable to do so. McKim's argument for E- and T-principles is as follows:

1. Disagreement about an issue or area of inquiry provides reason to think that that issue or area is an ambiguous one.
2. If an issue or area is ambiguous, it is more likely than it otherwise would be that our views on it are mistaken.
3. The more likely it is that our views on an issue are mistaken, the more likely it is that we have an obligation to examine our own beliefs and the beliefs of the other groups with whom there is disagreement about that issue.
4. If an issue or area of inquiry is ambiguous, it is more likely than it otherwise would be that we have an obligation to examine our own beliefs and the beliefs of other groups about that issue.
5. Disagreement about an issue or area of inquiry provides reason to think that each side has an obligation to examine beliefs about that issue.[92]

There is much to commend in McKim's careful analysis. In fact, I think that the E-principle is a rational principle to hold, while I am a bit skeptical

91. Robert McKim, *Religious Ambiguity and Religious Diversity* (Oxford: Oxford University Press, 2000), 140–41. See also McKim, *On Religious Diversity* (Oxford: Oxford University Press, 2012), 131–70.
92. McKim, *Religious Ambiguity*, 182–83.

about the T-principle. But let us now take a closer look at the underlying principles. CT seems to presuppose at least five fundamental claims, which are not included in the definition, though they are presupposed.

> *Realism*: Religious truth claims have cognitive content and truth value. Noncognitivism about religious truth is not a plausible option.
>
> *No closure*: on this side of the grave, it is not possible to know with absolute certainty which religious truth claims are true.
>
> *Ambiguity*: Widespread disagreement is evidence for no closure.
>
> *Peerage*: Religious experts in different traditions are genuine epistemic peers, and their respective views should be given equal weight.
>
> *Tolerance*: The best way to guarantee mutual conviviality is to adopt CT.

I agree with McKim on realism: religious language should be taken as asserting an objective state of affairs regarding the mind-independent transcendental reality, at least prima facie. Of course, not everything in religious language refers to an objective state of affairs, but in the case of Christianity, the claim that, for example, "God exists" is typically understood in the framework of metaphysical realism. Trying to solve disagreements by saying that you just do not mean what you think you mean is not convincing.[93]

Regarding no closure, quite a lot hangs on how we understand the role of knowledge. If we raise the bar of knowledge quite high, as some Kantians do, then we do not have religious knowledge. Kantians would also likely subscribe to ambiguity in the list above. For Kant, the fact that people come to hold opposing views about some matter (these are called "antinomies") is taken to be evidence for the view that we are trying to understand something that we cannot understand with our current faculties. However, ambiguity as such does not take us all the way to no closure.[94]

---

93. See also Roger Trigg, *Religious Diversity: Philosophical and Political Dimensions* (Cambridge: Cambridge University Press, 2014), 23–41. For the opposing view, see Peter Byrne, *God and Realism* (Aldershot: Ashgate, 2003).

94. On Kant, see Andrew Chignell, "'As Kant Has Shown . . .': Analytic Theology and the Critical Philosophy," in *Analytic Theology*, ed. Oliver Crisp and Michael Rea (Oxford: Oxford University Press, 2009), 117–35. On other responses to Kantian skepticism, see Richard Swinburne, "Why Hume and Kant Were Mistaken in Rejecting Natural Theology," in *Knowledge, Action, Pluralism: Contemporary Perspectives in Philosophy of Religion*, ed. Sebastian T. Kołodziejczyk (Frankfurt: Lang, 2013), 31–48; Nicholas Wolterstorff, "Is It Possible and Desirable for Theologians to Recover from Kant?," *Modern Theology* 14 (January 1, 1998): 1–18.

The demands and criteria for knowledge are often relative to context. As Alston has claimed, I do not think it is reasonable to adopt very strict criteria. Of course, our knowledge acquisition should always aim for the truth, but it cannot do so without paying attention to various epistemic desiderata. Moreover, as I pointed out in the introduction, there are areas of inquiry where we expect to achieve closure more easily compared to others. In these areas—such as ethics, aesthetics, politics, philosophy, and religion—we need to pay attention to the subject matter. But if we grant that it is hard to achieve consensus on these areas, it still does not follow that people cannot have good epistemic reasons for having beliefs in these areas—that is, beliefs that are in conflict with beliefs of other people. I think that, for example, moral realists can make a good case for their view (although they would also deny that the moral knowledge we have is obvious or self-evident). In philosophy and religion, I think people can have good, public reasons for their views that give them sturdy epistemic ground to hold certain views—and to oppose others.

To follow van Inwagen, if I have fulfilled all the epistemic duties I have, but have failed to convince my dialogue partner, I still cannot do anything else but hold on to my views. Granted, disagreement gives me a reason to hold on to the E-principle, but not necessarily the T-principle. For example, Martin Luther King Jr. acted in an ambiguous context, but he surely did not hold his beliefs tentatively. In moral and political cases people would hardly embrace ambiguity, and McKim recognizes that. Sometimes in moral, political, and public policy issues, the case can be solved by adopting relativism, and sometimes one of the views is "manifestly mistaken," he suggests.[95] But how can we tell when this is so?

Let's think of cases like the bailing out of failed banks after the recent financial crisis in the United States and Europe, the surveillance of US citizens by the NSA, and same-sex marriage. In all these cases, there are reasonable people on both sides who think that the other side is "manifestly mistaken" and do not therefore form a serious challenge for their own view. As naive as it may sound, I still think that the better way in all of these disputes is to continue pursuing the epistemic path, which means that we need to offer public reasons for our views. The epistemic way treats persons with dignity, as holders of reasoning skills and capabilities who can use their skills to argue for their views—although this also entails that their views can be defeated in public argument. Again, given our biases, we might not end up giving up

95. McKim, *Religious Ambiguity*, 200–201.

our beliefs even if they are proved wrong, but that is not a reason to discard the epistemic standards. Nevertheless, the T-principle is a reasonable principle to hold in cases that have no immediate effect on our behavior, but this makes it somewhat unfit to be used in the context of worldviews.

The problems of peerage have already been mentioned. It seems that we are not in a position to know when we are dealing with genuine religious epistemic peers. At best, we may recognize that someone is likely very close to being a peer, though we can never tell whether the person in fact is. But to do its supposed task, peerage needs to be coupled with the "equal weight view," according to which every proposition expressed by every epistemic peer is given similar value. In effect, this creates a state where agnosticism follows. The equal weight view is defensible in some cases, but those are the kinds of situations where it is easy to recognize peerhood, and as I have argued, in the case of religion this does not apply that easily.[96] Nevertheless, if I have good reasons to think someone challenges my views on good grounds, and I remain uncertain regarding my epistemic credentials in relation to his or hers, it is reasonable to follow the E-principle. The T-principle would come into question if, after I have followed the E-principle, I cannot offer good epistemic reasons that would confirm my view or disconfirm the opposing view.

I also have some minor hesitations concerning tolerance. McKim introduces his own concept, "deep tolerance," which means not only preservation and protection of the other view but also respect. "Weak tolerance" entails only "mere willingness not to attack it."[97] McKim argues that adopting deep tolerance is the best way to ensure peaceful coexistence of different worldviews. Deep tolerance can be recommended in many cases, but in some cases employing it effectively transforms tolerance into mere acceptance. Let us compare this situation to our democratic ideals. In democratic countries, the parliament consists of groups who hold very different beliefs and support different policies. In order to participate in the democratic process, they need to subscribe to democracy as a method of governing. After that, the agreement ends, and in the best case people follow the advice of (apocryphal) Voltaire: "I disapprove of what you say, but I will defend to the death your right to say it."

In keeping with this, do we really need to require that the disagreeing

96. McKim, *Religious Ambiguity*, 197–98; McKim, *On Religious Diversity*, 146. See also Tomas Bogardus, "The Vindication of Equal Weight View," *Episteme* 6 (2009): 324–35; Kim, *Reformed Epistemology*, 63–65.

97. McKim, *Religious Ambiguity*, 177–80.

parties respect each other's views? It might be that parties should respect each other as parties and as individual human beings, but why should party *a* protect and respect the view *x* held by party *b*, which party *a* is explicitly trying to strike down? Although I sympathize with McKim's concerns for tolerance, I do not think that we should require this much. Of course, we could define more clearly what respect here means. If we take respect as a general attitude of treating the opposing views fairly and as worthy of rational judgment and rebuttal, then there seems to be nothing to object to. I will return to the question of tolerance in the last chapter.

Summing up my concerns, the common problem in Berger and McKim is that they do not enable one to have robust convictions that could be supported by public arguments. They argue for this using a combination of pragmatic and epistemic arguments: because religious disagreements cannot be solved using epistemic criteria, they should be solved by revising the hold we have on our beliefs, as this will result in better chances of conviviality.

I have a few worries concerning this last pragmatic move. What if someone sincerely thinks we can solve these problems using epistemic criteria? What kind of reasons could this person have to adopt the T-principle? The T-principle works well when all disagreeing parties decide to adopt it, but this is seldom the case. Often disagreements involve asymmetrical power relations that strengthen, not lessen, one's hold on his or her identity.[98]

Moreover, we revere certainty and hate uncertainty. These issues were already discussed in the last chapter, but tentativeness does have an additional pragmatic problem. If we come to hold beliefs or convictions in a way that leaves us doubtful, we feel less satisfied and more stressed as our working memory continually checks for other alternatives.[99] Choosing an identity that is unstable makes us dissatisfied and regretful. This leads to a reversal of our choices and a search for a new identity, which may lead to cynicism and relativism in the end. Berger and McKim wish to avoid this. So how should we proceed instead?

---

98. See also Christian Smith, *American Evangelicalism: Embattled and Thriving* (Chicago: University of Chicago Press, 1998), 7.

99. Lottie Bullens, Frenk van Harreveld, and Jens Förster, "Keeping One's Options Open: The Detrimental Consequences of Decision Reversibility," *Journal of Experimental Social Psychology* 47 (2011): 804: "We believe that people's minds remain occupied with a changeable decision and that the cognitive processes activated by decision reversibility eventually result in lower levels of satisfaction and stronger feelings of regret."

Faith, Doubt, and Evidence

Audi has analyzed the concept of religious faith in many of his writings. Most recently, he offers a summary and refined version of his views in *Rationality and Religious Commitment*.[100] Audi starts off by rejecting the idea that doubt is a "structural feature of a healthy, mature religious faith."[101] He relates this view with influential twentieth-century theologian and existentialist Paul Tillich, who famously stated, "Doubt isn't the opposite of faith; it is an element of faith." Tillich's way of relating faith and doubt is peculiar. On the one hand, Tillich's "absolute faith," which he takes to be the authentic Christian form of being, is free from all propositional content.[102] However, the act of faith that Tillich describes seems content-full. Even saying that faith is "being grasped by God above God" does not escape some literal truths that seem to have a truth value. Tillichian faith is a balancing act, which tries to say so many things at the same time while denying everything that has been said that it is almost impossible to make any sense of it.[103]

Audi's analysis helps us to see how a more reasonable relationship between faith and doubt could be defined. Audi's basic vocabulary includes several nuanced distinctions, of which I will mention only a few. First, it is useful to distinguish between propositional faith and attitudinal faith. Propositional faith indicates believing that a certain state of affairs is true. For example, I have propositional faith that the carpenter, whom I hired to build me a sauna, follows all regulations about insulation, ventilation, and other relevant details.

Attitudinal faith means trusting some being, typically a human person. Again, I have attitudinal faith that the carpenter is a conscientious person, trustworthy, and that he will keep his promise to do his work according to the highest standards. Attitudinal faith implies that at least some propositions are believed with certainty, although it is hard to say how high the certainty must be.[104] It is important to note that one cannot have attitudinal faith without propositional faith. To be precise, attitudinal faith requires

---

100. Audi, *Rationality and Religious Commitment*.

101. Audi, *Rationality and Religious Commitment*, 54.

102. Paul Tillich, *The Courage to Be* (Glasgow: Collins, 1986), 177.

103. For a profound treatment of themes of ineffability in both recent and historical theology, see Timothy D. Knepper, *Negating Negation: Against the Apophatic Abandonment of the Dionysian Corpus* (Eugene, OR: Cascade, 2014).

104. For a more detailed treatment, see Lara Buchak, "Rational Faith and Justified Belief," in Callahan and O'Connor, *Religious Faith and Intellectual Virtue*, 49–73.

some propositional faith that the case really is so. The example above illustrates this. I cannot have a trusting attitude (faith *in*) toward the carpenter if I do not have faith *that* he is trustworthy in this given task.

The proposition in question must be adequately grounded. It would not be rational for me to trust the carpenter if I knew him to be lazy, cut corners, and generally have a bad reputation. Thus propositional faith is incompatible with dominating and pervasive (but not momentary) doubt. I may have short moments of uncertainty (for example, if I see him injuring himself with a power tool), but if uncertainty is a structural feature of my faith, it really does not make sense to speak about having faith in this person.

However, I may hope that the carpenter succeeds this time. In this case, I may have known this man for a long time, including the fact that he occasionally drinks too much, but I still decide to give him a chance. As a result, my expectations are low and I think it more likely that I will do some repairs afterward myself. Yet I entertain a positive possibility, however small, that things will turn out fine. Hope always has a specific content, but it does not need strong evidence (however, the object of hope cannot be impossible).

A stronger mode of faith is fiducial faith, which, according to Audi can be nondoxastic; that is, it does not entail belief that p. Consequently, a person who has fiducial faith does not know that p, but she trusts that p. In order to trust that p, she needs some grounding for her trust. Exemplary attitudes that do not satisfy unqualified belief that p includes attitudes like believing p to be probable or certain, half-believing that p, accepting that p is true, being disposed to believe that p, and implicitly believing that p.[105] So Audi raises the bar of belief, or doxastic faith, quite high. Believing something with doxastic faith means having a positive attitude toward p, which wasn't exhausted by previous examples of other belief attitudes.

In keeping with this, doubt is compatible with fiducial faith, but not if doubt is very strong. Audi writes, "Grave doubt that p, even combined with believing it highly improbable, is compatible with hoping that p, but not with having fiducial faith that p. Granted, it is also true of belief that it does not preclude *some* degree of doubt; but typically, if one believes p, one does not doubt it; and one may have fiducial faith that p when one's degree of doubt is high enough to prevent unqualifiedly believing it."[106]

Audi develops his notion of fiducial faith in order to draw attention to the obvious fact that religious faith does not boil down to having just dox-

---

105. Audi, *Rationality and Religious Commitment*, 69.
106. Audi, *Rationality and Religious Commitment*, 72.

astic faith. During their lives, people may entertain different faith attitudes, from hope, through fiducial faith, to full-blown doxastic faith, and they are best seen as stages people inhabit in different moments of their lives. It is possible that a "person of faith" wants to proceed from hope through trust to belief, and this seems both recommendable and natural regarding both religious and other value convictions. It is beneficial to maximize the degree of one's level of confidence. Additionally, worldviews consist of several tenets. One typically subscribes to these tenets in various ways, and the way a person holds these tenets can go through changes in the course of one's life.

Audi explains, "To object that if people lose confidence in certain propositions in a way that precludes unqualified belief of the tenets of their religion, they cannot remain religious is to exaggerate the importance of the doxastic side of religious commitment. For people in this plight, fiducial faith may be thought to be a position of retreat; but it is not a position of surrender. And if it does not represent an ideal for faith, it is nevertheless a position from which ideal faith can develop."[107]

Audi admits that there are cases when it is not irrational (or it is practically rational) to settle with lesser evidence, but as a general belief policy, he maintains that our beliefs are justified only if they have sufficient grounds. It is rationally preferable to always seek stronger grounding for one's convictions. Audi makes a basic distinction between rationality, reasonableness, justification, and knowledge. He clarifies: "My strategy . . . is to consider whether religious commitment can be rational, particularly in the sense in which rationality is consonant with reason, and then to pursue the question whether, given the grounds on which it may be rational, it is also reasonable."[108] Being rational basically means having the capacity to reason, and being able to give adequate responses to experiences in both theoretical and practical senses. Rationality is more permissive than justification, which entails some public grounds that point toward truth. Being rational thus means merely being consonant with reason. Reasonable acts do not necessarily require explicit justification, and sometimes things that have only minimal justification can be reasonable. Audi, however, defines reasonability as something that is rational and at least minimally justified. However, he argues against the demand to raise the bar of reasonability too high. A strong evidentialist view that requires "the raw materials to mount a justifying argument" is in Audi's view too demanding and practically un-

---

107. Audi, *Rationality and Religious Commitment*, 80.
108. Audi, *Rationality and Religious Commitment*, 44.

workable. Instead, he opts for weak evidentialism which holds that belief needs adequate grounds but also allows noninferential, experiential justification, which enables using experiences as evidence.[109]

We now have two slightly different ways of dealing with doubt. The first one argues that all our convictions should be accompanied with doubt. The second draws our attention to the amount of evidence that supports our belief. All that has been said above leads us to define two slightly different belief policies.

BP1 We should hold all our convictions tentatively.
BP2 We should have a maximal number of well-argued and correct beliefs that are held self-reflectively.

The reason for promoting BP1 is to battle fundamentalism and intolerance. However, BP1 as a belief policy too easily leads to performative contradiction. Of course, doubting is sometimes wise, but as a general attitude, doubt is counterproductive. Instead, we should not hold our convictions in a way that does not correlate with the grounds that we have for our convictions. It is naturally possible that we have misjudged our evidence or fallen prey to some other epistemic vice. But our only way to realize our mistake is to assess our evidential situation better.

Instead of insisting that doubt should accompany all our convictions, we should merely make sure that the degree of our certitude matches the evidence and the nature of the issue at hand. Therefore, I suggest that BP2 succeeds better than BP1 in taking into account both the lived reality and worries related to fundamentalism and relativism.

3.5. Reacting to Disagreement: A Dynamic View

Let's recapitulate what has been stated so far.

- Disagreement is ubiquitous (both in a historical and contemporary sense).

109. Audi, *Rationality and Religious Commitment*, 34–47. Paul Helm thinks along similar lines (*Faith with Reason*, 157). He also acknowledges the practical element in religious faith, when it is not irrational for someone to have a momentarily stronger belief than the evidence warrants, but insists that "in faith, over the long term, belief ought to be proportioned to evidence, and desire to belief."

- Our cognitive limitations make rational reflection often hard for us.
- Philosophical and religious matters are very complex and therefore, to a great extent, "mysterious."
- We have no easy method of recognizing epistemic peers in religious contexts.
- Doubting as a general epistemic stance is not a viable option.

In effect, we are in a state where we need to balance two axioms.

> *Humility*: We have good reason to think that our belief system is not perfect.
>
> *Antiskepticism*: Doubting as a general stance is not a viable option.

Forgetting humility leads to dogmatism, while removing antiskepticism leads to, well, skepticism. It is worth noting that it is not only disagreement that makes believing in humility reasonable. Our general condition as humans already gives us good reasons for believing it. Disagreement as such does not add much to it since consensus is not a guarantee of truth. Nevertheless, peer disagreement does increase the likelihood that we might be in need of some kind of belief revision if we have other good reasons to think so.

In saying that our beliefs are "not perfect," I mean the following. If we currently hold to belief p, we need not think that we grasp the issue perfectly; we just need to assign a positive credence to it. It is possible that we may have a correct picture in general but miss some details; or we may get some details exactly right but miss the big picture; or we may just have a vaguely correct, but still distorted, understanding.

If we grant all this, how then should we go about holding our beliefs while avoiding both dogmatism and skepticism? Earl Conee has suggested that it is possible to hold views that are subject to disagreement in an "instrumental" way. One can "argue for it, . . . seek further reasons for it, [and] . . . object to its rivals."[110] However, one cannot consider one's contested beliefs as justified. This works well within scientific inquiry, where we can expect resolution in due time. But in philosophy and religion, this may not be so simple. This is because religion, or any worldview, is an action-guiding principle, and religious convictions are manifested in action. The questions and problems of life do not grant us unlimited amounts of time. And in many cases of disagreement, there seems to be no neutral ground where we can

110. Conee, "Peerage," 322.

withdraw if we withhold our beliefs. Nonetheless, there are cases where the matter is not urgent, and in these cases Conee's suggestion seems wise. But in the case of more central beliefs, we are forced to act. On such points, we can no longer stay at the level of instrumentality. We either act reflectively after weighing the options, or we act nonreflectively. We should, of course, aim at the reflective action (even while acknowledging that our judgment may later prove to be wrong).

If we need to act while disagreeing with peers, or at least someone very close to being a peer, what should we do? A part of the "dynamic view" is that our convictions can be "partially defeated." In this case our level of confidence suffers some kind of damage and we cannot go about our business as if nothing has happened, as some versions of steadfastism seem to suggest. However, one issue in the discussion has been the lack of a precise formulation of what "the reducing of confidence" or beliefs "having less justification than before" actually means.[111]

Catherine Elgin and Michael Bergmann approach this question from the viewpoint of mutual recognition of rationality.[112] Simply put, it is possible that the parties think the rival view is wrong but still rational. Elgin thinks that the best way to make progress in disagreement situations is for both parties to hold to their positions, each side trying to demonstrate its superiority. But what does the mutual recognition of rationality mean in practice? I think the best way to illustrate this would look something like this: both parties acknowledge that all involved are able to realize some genuine epistemic good through their beliefs and actions; and, likewise, both parties should be able to point out those goods that their own beliefs are not able to realize. Moreover, Audi has proposed that investigating whether our partners in dispute really are our epistemic peers is one thing that disagreement entails because this helps to demonstrate the reasons for belief, and it may increase or lower credence attributed to the beliefs.[113]

Alston argues that trying to find one way to settle once and for all the nature of epistemic justification will only multiply our problems. In addition to disagreeing about particular claims, we end up disagreeing about the criteria for how to evaluate those claims. Of course, it would be very nice indeed to have one general criterion for knowledge, but it seems that philosophers

111. Michael Thune, "Partial Defeaters and the Epistemology of Disagreement," *Philosophical Quarterly* 60 (2010): 358–59.

112. Catherine Elgin, "Persistent Disagreement," in Feldman and Warfield, *Disagreement*; Bergmann, "Rational Disagreement," 336–53.

113. Audi, *Rationality and Religious Commitment*, 203.

disagree so widely about these criteria that it takes an incredible amount of optimism to think that a consensus will ever be reached.

Alston advises epistemologists (and humans in general): "We human beings are thrust into a matrix of uncertainty and fallibility, and the better part of wisdom is to recognize that and make the best we can of it, without wasting time yearning for absolute guarantees outside the activity of human inquiry."[114] This leaves us with "irreducible plurality of epistemic desiderata and forces us to undertake the baffling task of integrating them somehow into a comprehensive epistemology of belief."[115] The epistemic desiderata Alston has in mind include things like having adequate evidence for a belief p, p being formed by a reliable belief-forming process and cognitive faculties, p being formed by the exercise of an intellectual virtue, the epistemic subject s having high-grade access to the evidence, s being able to defend p against defeaters, and believing p without violating intellectual obligations, explanation, understanding, coherence, and systematicity.[116] Alston readily admits that allowing the existence of partial defeaters and mutual recognition of rationality of opposing positions will inevitably result in pluralism. However, could it be that Alston's multiple-desiderata approach might give us grounds for assessing which flowers are worth nurturing?

Recognizing this plurality of values and worldviews, and meeting it with multiple relevant criteria of evaluation, could be a fruitful way to evaluate, communicate, and criticize beliefs. This would prevent the slide to simplistic standoffs and enable the possibility of transcommunal discourse, when competing parties have multiple epistemic desiderata from which to choose and which they recognize as their own. This will not do away with disagreement, and from this perspective disagreement is not necessarily a bad thing. Disagreement can be seen as an enhancing factor in knowledge acquisition, a necessary means of criticism, and a boundary against intellectual and political absolutism.

To summarize: in cases where we have peer disagreement, or something very close to it, we are under obligation to do the following:

- Investigate more properly whether we really are epistemic peers.
- Explore how different epistemic desiderata are manifested in our beliefs.

114. Alston, Beyond "Justification," 239.
115. Alston, Beyond "Justification," 176.
116. Alston, Beyond "Justification," 43.

- Openly reveal the problems that our own beliefs have.
- Locate the points where we agree and disagree.
- Give answer to defeaters.
- Offer defeaters to the other positions.

As I stated, the actions that we are to undertake in the case of disagreement can be expressed as balancing humility and antiskepticism.[117] The afore-mentioned obligations offer some practices that help to illustrate what that would entail in practice. The next question to be considered concerns the virtuous nature of this effort.

117. On this from the viewpoint of theological method, see Olli-Pekka Vainio, *Beyond Fideism: Negotiable Religious Identities* (Aldershot: Ashgate, 2010).

CHAPTER 4

Disagreeing Virtuously

Socialism as a social or moral philosophy was based on the ideal of human brotherhood, which can never be implemented by institutional means. There has never been, and there will never be, an institutional means of making people brothers. Fraternity under compulsion is the most malignant idea devised in modern times; it is a perfect path to totalitarian tyranny.

Leszek Kołakowski, "What Is Left of Socialism?"
(in *My Correct Views on Everything*)

When I was a teenager I wished for world peace, but now I yearn for a world in which competing ideologies are kept in balance, systems of accountability keep us all from getting away with too much, and fewer people believe that righteous ends justify violent means. Not a romantic wish, but one that we might actually achieve.

Jonathan Haidt, *The Righteous Mind*

In the final chapter of this book I examine the real-life possibilities and ways of reacting to disagreement so that human flourishing is enabled to the highest possible degree. A natural element in reaching this goal is virtue. I begin with a short discussion on the theory of virtue in general, how it is relevant for our topic, and what the expected difficulties and criticisms of this approach might be. Second, I examine the possibility of debiasing and growth in virtues in order to secure the viability of virtue discourse. The third section contains discussion of particular virtues that pertain to our topic. Last, I will consider some ways in which the virtues can be of help in religious disagreements. In effect, this final chapter seeks to answer the *accommodation of religious disagreement question*.

4.1. The Nature of Virtue

Virtue usually refers to some kind of perfection or excellence, as its opposite, vice, refers to the lack or the excess of the valued qualities. The central property of virtue is that it is a golden mean between excess and deficit.[1] For example, courage is a mean between cowardice and foolhardiness; humility is a mean between pride and lack of self-respect; an open-minded person strikes a balance between dogmatic absolutism and intellectual carelessness; and so on. In many cases, however, the golden mean cannot be defined invariably.[2] For example, what is courageous for one person can be foolhardiness for another. In Western tradition, the fundamental virtue that is supposed to control reflection and help one find the proper way of conduct is called prudence, or practical wisdom (*phronēsis*).[3] There cannot be excess in wisdom, which makes it sui generis among the virtues. You cannot be too good at finding the golden mean.

Both virtues and vices equip their holders with a potency to act toward some determined end. In Christian theology, especially in the Thomistic tradition, virtues have been understood as "good operative habits" that are in accord with reason and human nature. From the viewpoint of actions, being virtuous means not necessarily always succeeding to produce desired ends and simply "being good" (while this is always hoped for), but rather "being for the good" through loving, respecting, protecting, and acting to promote, wishing for, and speaking in favor of good things.[4]

---

1. The classical definition comes from Aristotle, *Nicomachean Ethics* 1106a–b.

2. For discussion on practical problems on finding the golden mean, see Harry Clor, *On Moderation: Defending an Ancient Virtue in a Modern World* (Waco: Baylor University Press, 2008).

3. Aristotle, *Nicomachean Ethics* 1142a.

4. This is the view of Robert Merrihew Adams, *A Theory of Virtue: Excellence in Being for the Good* (Oxford: Oxford University Press, 2006). The traditional account of virtues contains a so-called success component, according to which in order to be genuinely virtuous you should be able to succeed in bringing about the state of affairs that portrays virtue. Although there are cases when this success component seems reasonable, it faces significant problems if held as a general requirement. For example, a soldier who sets out to save a friend in a battle without succeeding would not count as virtuous. Therefore, it is helpful to distinguish between

Some virtues are virtues absolutely, like love or wisdom, while others are so only in a restricted sense, which means that possession of such a virtue does not make the person good even if the person's actions may display excellence. For example, it is possible for a criminal to be loyal and courageous, but the criminal is not good in an absolute sense because they lack the more fundamental virtues of justice and love. Some virtues, such as benevolence, are motivating: they aim a person's actions toward good ends and thus enable the flourishing of one's neighbors as well. Some virtues, such as courage and temperance, are structural: they are not defined in relation to some external good or aim. Instead they are ideal ways of conducting one's actions.[5]

Virtuous action (or the process of habituation) is usually illustrated with the help of the triad of norm, act, and nature. Norms help us to understand the difference between good and bad. If we choose to follow the norms, we act according to them. This action shapes our nature so that we become more accustomed to do the good the norms require of us. Consequently, good nature helps us to understand and appreciate the norms better, including how they should be applied in practice. This is practical wisdom.

Habituation should affect us in three different ways: helping us to perform good actions; stabilizing our acquired traits of character; and reforming our more deeply ingrained, or given, features of our character, such as when a timid person slowly grows more confident.[6] This last feature is sometimes called temperament, and it is harder to change than habits that we have learned later in our life. A timid person is not likely to become a charismatic public speaker, but may learn to fight against excessive lack of self-confidence.

As virtues deal with the excellence of human conduct, they are not restricted to the religious sphere. Ancient Greek and Roman philosophers such as Plato, Aristotle, Seneca, and Cicero offered accounts of virtue, which were later discussed by religious thinkers. The ancient Greek and Roman cultures were known for their interest in virtues; the concept itself originated from the Latin word *vir* (man), and the meaning of virtue was initially associated

---

general and immediate virtuous aims. The soldier aims to virtuous action in general, even if the immediate aims are sometimes frustrated. This is enough to count the soldier among the virtuous, although the fulfillment of more immediate aims is also desired. For discussion, see Wayne D. Riggs, "Understanding 'Virtue' and the Virtue of Understanding," in *Intellectual Virtue: Perspectives from Ethics and Epistemology*, ed. Michael DePaul and Linda Zagzebski (Oxford: Oxford University Press, 2003), 208–13.

5. Adams, *A Theory of Virtue*, 31–35.
6. See, e.g., *ST* I-II.49–56.

with manliness. Later, the meaning was expanded to include general good behavior, not only on the battlefield but in everyday life as well. The first Christian philosophers saw in virtue theories something they could resonate with, and the virtues were to some extent redefined and absorbed as a part of Christian theology. Sometimes the pagan virtues were referred as "excellent vices," that is, good in themselves, but not worthy of heaven. Since Augustine, there has existed a basic criticism of virtue in Christian theology.[7] In *De civitate Dei*, Augustine compares Christian and Roman virtues in order to point out the deficiency of pagan notions of virtue. Augustine thinks that the Romans can represent various virtues, like courage, but their understanding of virtue as a whole is thwarted because the virtues are not in balance and they lack proper understanding of the metaphysical ordering of the universe, which transforms their love into concupiscence. Augustinianism represents the critical element in the Christian tradition that approaches human actions from the viewpoint of perfection. Thus the emphasis lies not in the actual status of the works themselves but in the deficient nature of those works: how much they fall short of perfection.

If Augustine is the critical voice, Thomas Aquinas attempts to make room for a different view, allowing the appreciation of human, non-Christian good works. Aquinas makes a distinction between acquired and infused virtues. It is possible for anyone to have acquired virtues through one's natural powers, but infused virtues are given by God as a gift. The difference between these two classes is that one can lose infused virtue through one action (mortal sin), but still retain the acquired virtues. Consequently, it is possible for one to have all acquired virtues but still be in a sinful state.

The ebb and flow of virtue's role in Christian theology has taken place mostly in relation to soteriological discussions. If we put too much weight on human performance, something goes wrong with the doctrine of grace. This is the worry behind Augustine's and Luther's critiques of virtue. Here it is sufficient to note that there is a theological debate on virtues and their role in the Christian life, but this discussion is not directly linked with the thesis of this book. Even Luther, who is perhaps the most vehement anti-Aristotelian in the history of theology, admits that Aristotle's theories work well in society, even if their use in theology is often harmful.[8]

After this short introduction, we can move to more vital issues. In what

7. For a historical overview, see Jennifer Herdt, *Putting on Virtue: The Legacy of the Splendid Vices* (Chicago: University of Chicago Press, 2008).
8. WA 40 I, 410, 24–411, 19. See also WA 21, 510, 26–511, 6; WA 25, 33, 29–34, 5.

ways, exactly, are virtues supposed to help in the case of disagreement? Can we teach virtues?

How Are Virtues Relevant to Disagreement?

I argue that virtues can be helpful to our present topic in at least the following two senses:

1. Virtue discourse provides a universal mode of communication.
2. Virtues offer a recognizable ideal for our performance in knowledge acquisition and intercommunal dialogue.

Let us take a look at each of these in turn. First, all religions and cultures have more or less similar virtue vocabulary, consisting of six main classes: courage, justice, humanity, temperance, transcendence, and wisdom, which can then be divided into various subclasses. Different religions, however, stress some virtues more than others, which gives the religions some of their unique features. Some religious virtue theories are dependent on metaphysical views. In Thomism, for example, *phronēsis* presupposes knowledge of final causes, namely, God. In Confucianism, the virtuous actions of humans should reflect the balance of *Tian* (heaven). The central virtue in Islam is obedience or submission to Allah, from which all other virtues follow.[9]

Despite these metaphysical underpinnings, it has been suggested that because virtue vocabulary is common to all cultures, virtue language can function as a common feature that can join together different worldviews and help communities to communicate their values in an understandable manner, even when there is no consensus (e.g., on deontological rules of action). I agree that the language of virtue could provide the tools for dealing with disagreement situations since this provides ways of paraphrasing what is wrong in a given situation. According to Rosalind Hursthouse:

> It is a noteworthy feature of our virtue and vice vocabulary that, although our list of generally recognized virtue terms is comparatively short, our

9. Christopher Peterson and Martin Seligman, *Character Strengths and Virtues: A Handbook and Classification* (Oxford: Oxford University Press, 2004), 33–55. Transcendence as such does not appear in classical lists of virtues. Peterson and Seligman use it as an umbrella term for virtues like gratitude, hope, and the appreciation of beauty.

list of vice terms is remarkably, and usefully, long, far exceeding anything that anyone who thinks in terms of standard deontological rules has ever come up with. Much invaluable action guidance comes from avoiding courses of action that would be irresponsible, feckless, lazy, inconsiderate, uncooperative, harsh . . . , selfish, mercenary, indiscreet, tactless, arrogant, unsympathetic, cold, incautious, . . . feeble, presumptuous, rude, hypocritical, self-indulgent, materialistic, grasping, short-sighted, vindictive, calculating, ungrateful, grudging, brutal, profligate, disloyal, and on and on.[10]

The conceptual range of virtues and vices provides tools to relate both constructively and critically to all sorts of behavior. Of course, mere use of virtues and vices to classify various actions does not take us all the way to agreement; we may disagree whether a certain action does in fact portray practical wisdom. Yet in cases like this, we can get a few steps further by locating those values different parties cherish and why they value certain things more than others. A practical example of this is Jonathan Haidt's moral psychology, which was discussed in section 2.5 above.

Second, virtues should offer us the ideal of perfection when acquiring knowledge and assessing different alternatives. Let us assume that I am a person who has become aware of my lack of knowledge and who wants to maximize my correct beliefs about the world. What should I do? Virtue theorists are likely to say that I need to develop habits that are able to boost my knowledge acquisition.[11] There are several habits that are likely to increase our ability to get it right, such as wisdom, good judgment, intellectual conscientiousness, flexibility, thoroughness, intellectual candor, courage, apt doubt, appropriate trust, perseverance, understanding, humility, open-mindedness, studiousness, and the like. What this means is that the person who exhibits these characteristics is likely to be more efficient in knowledge acquisition than the person who lacks these virtues and who exhibits prejudice, narrow-mindedness, stubbornness, carelessness, and dishonesty. Paying attention to these characteristics and evaluating our own performance in their light can guide our knowledge acquisition. As I have already stated, merely

---

10. Rosalind Hursthouse, "Virtue Ethics," in *Stanford Encyclopedia of Philosophy*, ed. Edward N. Zalta, fall 2013 ed., http://plato.stanford.edu/archives/fall2013/entries/ethics-virtue/.

11. See, e.g., Robert C. Roberts and W. Jay Wood, *Intellectual Virtues: An Essay on Regulative Epistemology* (Oxford: Clarendon, 2008); Riggs, "Understanding 'Virtue,'" 215; Jason Baehr, *Inquiring Mind: On Intellectual Virtues and Virtue Epistemology* (Oxford: Oxford University Press, 2011).

invoking virtues will not secure agreement, but if movement toward reconciliation and understanding takes place, it quite likely happens due to the good practical judgment of the parties.

Approaching the question from the negative side, Miranda Fricker offers an analysis of what can go wrong in our knowledge acquisition when intellectual virtues are not cherished.[12] Fricker names two different forms of epistemic injustice that inhibit the virtue of understanding. First, *testimonial injustice* happens when prejudice, stereotypes, or similar attitudes limit our access to truth. As an example, Fricker offers the impossibility of a black man appearing as a credible witness in a US court, as depicted in the novel *To Kill a Mockingbird*. Testimonial injustice hampers the flow of information by placing some of us outside the community of legitimate knowers and offers to the opinions of powers that be a "cognitive sanctuary."[13] Testimonial injustice can become systemic if the skewed categories of interpretation are given privileged status. Fricker defines *hermeneutical injustice* thus: "the injustice of having some significant area of one's social experience obscured from collective understanding owing to a structural identity prejudice in the collective hermeneutical resource."[14] In order to fight against epistemic injustice, one needs to "neutralize the impact of prejudice in her credibility judgments."[15] Ultimately, the epistemic virtues are supposed to create an environment that mitigates the influence of harmful prejudices and reduces the marginalization of unpopular opinions. This, according to Fricker, requires not just individual conversion, but renewal of institutions as well, which can also be subjects of both epistemic vices and virtues.

It is not always easy to see clear fault lines between subjects and objects of prejudice because everyone can be subject to different prejudices. The picture can get distorted from both directions. Especially in the case of culture war or religious disagreements, it is not always clear who in fact is privileged and who is not. Or it might be that two parties are privileged in different ways. Furthermore, as Fricker acknowledges, being an object of prejudice or other form of injustice does not guarantee that you are right.[16] Nonetheless, in these kinds of cases it is ethically important that the assessment of various claims takes place so that harmful biases are kept at bay and the claims are treated fairly.

12. Miranda Fricker, *Epistemic Injustice* (Oxford: Oxford University Press, 2007).
13. Fricker, *Epistemic Injustice*, 38.
14. Fricker, *Epistemic Injustice*, 155.
15. Fricker, *Epistemic Injustice*, 92.
16. Fricker, *Epistemic Injustice*, 170.

Is It Possible to Learn Virtues?

It is a central part of traditional virtue theories that achieving virtues is considered to be difficult. Moreover, various religions contain theorization that seems to denigrate the feasibility of the virtuous life. For example, Confucius says: "I have never seen one who loves virtue as much as he loves sex" (*Analects* 9.17). In the Protestant Reformation, it was customary to depict human nature in grimmer, more pessimistic tones than in the Eastern or Catholic traditions. Therefore, it is worth asking, what are our prospects for learning virtues?

In addition to problems pointed out by religious traditions, virtue theories have drawn criticism from several other sources. The most important philosophical set of criticisms is known as "situationism."[17] The situationist critique is best depicted through its opposition to central theses of traditional virtue theory, which argues for robustness, stability, and interconnectedness/unity of virtues.

Robustness means that the virtuous person will act virtuously regardless of the context. For example, courageous soldiers will display the virtue of courage in the battlefield but also in their mundane lives. Stability underlines the pervasive character of virtues: soldiers will not lose their courage overnight or by simple fiat. They may lose their courage after several traumatic events, but this takes time. Interconnectedness means the dependence of one virtue on another, so that an action can be considered genuinely virtuous only if it is connected with other virtues. Thus a person who is courageous and loyal but unjust (like a contract killer) is not truly virtuous.

Situationism rejects robustness and interconnectedness claims, offering a modified version of the stability claim. Situationists claim that we are not so robust in our behavior as the traditional theory suggests. Further, it seems problematic to argue that we possess stable dispositions, which are consistent in all relevant contexts for this particular virtue. In some contexts, it is easier to be, for example, honest or tempered, when things are all right. But when the context changes, our performance changes as well. Therefore,

---

17. A well-known substantial critique is John Doris, *Lack of Character: Personality and Moral Behavior* (Cambridge: Cambridge University Press, 2002). See also Gilbert Harman, "Moral Philosophy Meets Social Psychology: Virtue Ethics and the Fundamental Attribution Error," *Proceedings of the Aristotelian Society* 99 (1999): 315–31. It is also common to refer to the Milgram experiments to underline the effects of situation over character. Kevin Timpe and Craig A. Boyd, introduction to *Virtues and Their Vices*, ed. Kevin Timpe and Craig A. Boyd (Oxford: Oxford University Press, 2014), 11–12.

we should not attribute too much weight to our character, situationism contends, because the environment seems to have such a strong influence on us.

According to the situationist critique, humans do not possess stable character traits. However, we may develop habits of acting in particular ways in some situations so that we consistently act honestly with our best friends, for example; but this does not have an effect on our behavior toward other groups of people. Stability is context specific.[18]

If our performance is heavily dependent on environment, it follows that it is not reasonable to think that our virtues could form an interconnected whole. In other words, situationists reject the unity-of-virtue thesis, which claims that virtuous persons cannot only have some virtues, they must have them all. Instead, situationists claim that our moral characters are fundamentally fragmented, and there is therefore no necessary connection between virtues.

How should these claims be answered? First, an immediate problem concerns the definition of "environment" and "situation," and consequent difficulties concern how to measure them. While it has been acknowledged in personality psychology that people do not act in a vacuum and that their context has a significant effect, it has been extremely difficult to provide any consistent account of what counts as "situation," and how this might be separated from personality in the first place.[19] Situationism's critics have also pointed out how empirical studies do not warrant the leap from the data to a situationist denial of the existence of character traits. First, studies usually put the test subject into a conflicted situation, which complicates the interpretation of the situation. The classic example of this is Daniel Batson's "Good Samaritan test," where he examined Princeton Theological Seminary students' willingness as they were on their way to a lecture to help a man lying on the ground. The result was that one's sense of hurry was the

---

18. For example, when moral behavior of young children was investigated, they could act honestly among their peers while being dishonest toward their parents. See Hugh Hartshorne and Mark A. May, *Studies in the Nature of Character*, vol. 1, *Studies in Deceit* (New York: Macmillan, 1928).

19. Robert Hogan points out that the way the agent perceives the situation is itself partly a product of the agent. Thus the agent has an effect on the situation where they are; the situation is not something that is "out there," waiting to influence us. Robert Hogan, "Much Ado about Nothing: The Person-Situation Debate," *Journal of Research in Personality* 43 (2009): 249. See also John T. Jost and Lawrence T. Jost, "Virtue Ethics and the Social Psychology of Character: Philosophical Lessons from the Person-Situation Debate," *Journal of Research in Personality* 43 (2009): 253–54. See also Christian B. Miller, *Character and Moral Psychology* (Oxford: Oxford University Press, 2014), 85–107.

most successful indicator for helping the man and not, for example, one's self-reported level of religiosity. However, here the students were conflicted between virtues of punctuality and benevolence (the students were told that they were late and that they had to hurry). Similar conflict exists in Milgram's obedience experiments, in which participants were given an order to give supposedly lethal electric shocks to the test subjects. The experiments are often used to discredit traditional virtue theories since only a few were able to resist the order. However, here we have a similar conflict of virtues. Many people regard it as a good thing to trust scientists because they must know what they are doing even if this might cause harm to someone else. The Milgram experiments prove that people are prone to follow authorities, but this does yet prove the stronger situationist claim.

Second, test subjects and observers may have different ideas regarding what counts as a virtue in a given situation. For example, is putting an abandoned coin in one's pocket a theft, or is it a completely legitimate act based on the rule "finders keepers"? Third, some test cases examine a virtue that is marginal or ambiguous and not a representative case of virtuous action. For example, we often see people lying on the ground in a park and choose to do nothing because we have learned that some people just choose to drink too much and pass out, for example, and in most cases nothing bad happens to them.

Fourth, the cases at hand measure acts that happen in a given moment. In order to establish the bold conclusion required for total situationism, we would have to gather data on a person's performance for some time and observe how he or she performs in various situations. *Then* we could put that person into a test scenario and see how he or she behaves. One-off tests simply do not give us enough data to conclude that character traits do not exist.

Last, I comment on the unity-of-virtue thesis. The thesis is nowadays criticized because it seems to contradict our intuitions. Wasn't Martin Luther King Jr. a virtuous man, even if he had extramarital affairs? Didn't Oskar Schindler act heroically when saving lives of countless Jews, even if he was a scoundrel both in his professional and private life? It seems empirically verifiable that a person may hold some virtues to a greater degree compared to other people, yet fail in other areas. Of course, one way to solve the problem is to brush it off as mere semantics. Does it really matter whether we want to call the person "virtuous" or a "good person who had significant flaws"? However, the actual point of the unity-of-virtues thesis goes deeper.[20]

20. See Craig Steven Titus, "Moral Development and Connecting the Virtues: Aquinas,

The unity-of-virtues position has been defended by pointing out that even if a person is, for example, generous but has problems with his or her temper, that person can act generously but a lack of virtues will hinder that person from acting generously in all those situations when he or she should so act. Likewise, a person who is loyal and courageous but who does not have a sense of justice lacks something important, which prevents that person, for example, from being courageous for the right cause. The problems that are caused by the disunity of virtues are well illustrated by G. K. Chesterton, who claims that promoting just one virtue and forgetting all the others will lead to vicious behavior:

> The modern world is not evil; in some ways the modern world is far too good. It is full of wild and wasted virtues. When a religious scheme is shattered (as Christianity was shattered at the Reformation), it is not merely the vices that are let loose. The vices are, indeed, let loose, and they wander and do damage. But the virtues are let loose also; and the virtues wander more wildly, and the virtues do more terrible damage. The modern world is full of the old Christian virtues gone mad. The virtues have gone mad because they have been isolated from each other and are wandering alone. Thus some scientists care for truth; and their truth is pitiless. Thus some humanitarians only care for pity; and their pity (I am sorry to say) is often untruthful. . . . Torquemada tortured people physically for the sake of moral truth. Zola tortured people morally for the sake of physical truth. But in Torquemada's time there was at least a system that could to some extent make righteousness and peace kiss each other. Now they do not even bow. But a much stronger case than these two of truth and pity can be found in the remarkable case of the dislocation of humility.[21]

I conclude that the strongest situationist arguments against traditional virtue theory fail. However, the contemporary received view is that human action is highly complex and hard to measure since the influences are so numerous. Nevertheless, it is best to argue that our actions are a composition of our character and the situations in which we live.

Porter and the Flawed Saint," in *Ressourcement Thomism: Sacred Doctrine, the Sacraments, and the Moral Life*, ed. Reinhard Hütter and Matthew Levering (Washington, DC: Catholic University of America Press, 2010), 330–52; Timpe and Boyd, introduction, 7–8. See also Gopal Sreenivasan, "Disunity of Virtue," *Journal of Ethics* 13 (2009): 195–212.

21. G. K. Chesterton, *Orthodoxy* (Charlotte: Saint Benedict Press, 2006), 26–27.

But can we learn virtues? Obviously, the same problems that make situationist critiques inadequate make the studying of virtues difficult. In order to have conclusive facts, we would need substantial data on the performance of persons in various situations and over a long period of time. These kinds of studies are difficult to come by, and there are also serious ethical problems in subjecting people to this kind of surveillance.[22] However, recent empirical research has been able to provide evidence for cross-contextual stability of character traits and discredit earlier eliminative situationist claims.[23]

Christian Miller offers an account of "mixed character traits," by which he means that very few people actually possess perfected virtues or vices. On the one hand, few of us are able to stand against group pressure. On the other hand, most of us are not pathological liars or completely untrustworthy.[24] Even if we do not stand out because of our virtues or vices, people are relatively consistent in their behavior. Miller's account seeks to accommodate the fluctuation in human behavior without denying the existence of character traits. Our behavior is elusive because our actions are affected by several factors. Miller argues that in order for virtuous action to *take* place, several things need to happen:

1. Background influences in a situation: when action x is possible, there are factors that either prevent or encourage action x.
2. Activation of the moral norms and moral sentiments a person recognizes.
3. Conscious reasons to abide by recognized moral norms.
4. Alternative courses of action, such as the option of leaving x undone or the assumption that someone else will do x.
5. Activation of a mixed character trait: an estimation of the relation between action x and moral principles.[25]

22. Another reason for the lack of these kinds of studies has been the preoccupation of psychology to concentrate on mental disease and treating malfunctions of the human mind. There has not been similar attention in psychology paid to human flourishing and those ways in which improvement of overall well-being might be possible to achieve. Everett L. Worthington et al., "Virtue in Positive Psychology," in Timpe and Boyd, *Virtues and Their Vices*, 433.

23. Miller, *Character and Moral Psychology*; Miller, *Moral Character: An Empirical Theory* (Oxford: Oxford University Press, 2013); Jonathan Webber, "Virtue, Character and Situation," *Journal of Moral Philosophy* 3 (2006): 190–213.

24. Miller, *Character and Moral Psychology*, 1–61; Miller, *Moral Character*, 1–26. See also Miller, "Which Beliefs Contribute to Virtuous Behavior?," *Big Questions Online*, June 15, 2012, https://www.bigquestionsonline.com/content/which-beliefs-contribute-virtuous-behavior.

25. Miller, *Character and Moral Psychology*, 24–57, 81–97.

Miller's theory allows one to acknowledge that a person's choices can be both fragmentary and coherent. For example, a person can act in two separate, closely related situations in differing ways, but the difference can be explained by other factors that can affect a person's choices. Let us think about the following example. Three people, Jane, Joy, and Jean, are walking through Central Park. On their way, they see a man lying on the ground. How each person perceives the situation is affected by her background conditions, like things that either enable or hinder the action in various degrees. The person is likely to revisit (often unconsciously) those beliefs, moral codes, and behavioral patterns that pertain to the given case. Before the action is carried out, there still exists a set of factors that may cause the person not to take action. For example, she may think that it is not wrong to turn one's back on a person in need if she has good reason to believe that someone else will help him or can help him better. If everything that was listed here supports the action, the person very likely performs it, but turning away may be caused by a very minor thing. Nevertheless, this does not as such mean that the person lacks compassion.

In our example, Jane stops and helps the man, but Joy and Jean go past him. Joy has just received a message from her friend who has told her that she is considering committing suicide. Jean, seeing the man, also spots a park guard and thinks that the guard can help the man more than she can. Jean is also small, and she has recently been assaulted by a drunkard, so she is afraid to approach the man. Jane, Joy, and Jean all share factors 2 and 3, but they differ in factors 1, 4, and 5. Based on these differences, we cannot really say that these three people are morally different, or that Joy and Jean are less moral than Jane.[26]

Miller argues that humans do not act like machines; our action patterns change all the time. Nevertheless, our actions do not fluctuate widely between extremes but are relatively predictable. In fact, classical virtue theory does not presuppose that most people are able to act in a near-perfect manner. Instead, virtue is an ideal, toward which we are called to strive. Virtue theory requires only that virtues are possible, not that they are usual.

Miller thinks that it is possible for people to improve their behavior and to move closer to the virtuous ideal, even if reaching it will likely fail. In order to assess how to become good, we need to monitor and train several factors that have an effect on our behavior. First, our beliefs, desires, and

26. On the other hand, human action that superficially looks virtuous is not necessarily so because it can be motivated by nonvirtuous causes, like self-interest or guilt.

emotions guide our actions. It is not enough that I have a correct moral belief, since my emotions should fall in line with judgments of reason so that they produce correct action. If this does not take place, we suffer from the weakness of the will (*akrasia*): I know how I should behave, but my desires are stronger than my will or reason. Thus in order to perform well I need to have a deeply ingrained and correct moral conviction: I need not only to recognize the moral norm as a generally good rule to follow but also to make it a personal norm. It is of no use to think that it is good that people give money to charities; I need to personally make this my way of conduct.

Second, we need good moral examples that exemplify to us higher ideals and help us to imitate them. These moral exemplars cause the feeling of elevation in the rest of us, which contributes to our willingness to imitate their behavior.[27] Related to this is how we feel about ourselves as moral agents. It is easier for us to behave well if we perceive ourselves as good people. Often if we are tagged with virtuous labels we start acting like we are actually as virtuous as we have been told.[28] This relates to our sense of moral identity. If certain ideals and norms are salient in our sense of self, we are more likely to follow them. Our moral identity often needs scaffolding so that if we dwell in a proper environment (meaning that it supports virtuous behavior and constantly reminds us about the correct norms), following these norms becomes easier. Religious activities like attending Mass or meditating on the Ten Commandments are likely to strengthen virtuous behavioral patterns.[29]

To summarize the problems of virtuous habituation, we can list the following obstacles based on what has been said so far:

1. Virtues are related to our personality and character, which develop often in ways that are beyond our direct control.

---

27. Jonathan Haidt, "The Positive Emotion of Elevation," *Prevention and Treatment* 3 (2000): http://faculty.virginia.edu/haidtlab/articles/haidt.2000.the-positive-emotion-of-eleva tion.pub020.pdf. Miller (*Moral Character*, 80) discusses Haidt's intuitivist model, where the role of emotions is decisive. Haidt acknowledges that emotion is more salient in third-person moral conclusions, whereas in first-person conclusions ("what *I* should do") the role of deliberation of other relevant factors becomes more important.

28. Miller, *Character and Moral Psychology*, 179.

29. Among youth, religious attendance correlates negatively with, e.g., drug use or misbehavior and positively with altruistic activities. Of course, it is hard to measure whether "good people" are those who choose to go to church (or make their children go to church), or whether going to church makes people good. See Miller, "Which Beliefs."

2. Some virtues can be inhibited by personality disorders.
3. Some virtues appear to be related to hemisphere symmetry.
4. All virtues are dependent on experience.
5. The learning and practicing of virtues is sometimes dependent on one's supporting environment.
6. Many virtues ask for sacrifice, create cognitive dissonance, or cause some other unpleasant state.
7. Some institutional structures, for example, academia and the business world, effectively block the virtuous way of life.

However, overcoming these challenges is not impossible, even if all of us cannot excel in virtues in all possible ways. Learning virtuous behavioral patterns takes time and effort, and it requires that we know how human beings make decisions. As has been stated before, our decision-making is mostly intuitive and unconscious; sometimes our intuitions are correct, sometimes they are false. Clearly, we cannot bypass intuitions, but we can to some extent improve our intuitions through reflection, experience, and practice. However, the extent to which we can actually improve our cognitive performance is a matter of debate.[30]

One major obstacle is the fact that we often resist debiasing and do not want to hear criticism or insinuations that we are not thinking or acting as we should. Especially when the contested matter is close to our hearts, we may even react aggressively to such allegations. On the other hand, some methods of debiasing are not that easy or natural to use, and not necessarily even available to everybody. Some debiasing methods can also be counter-productive and trigger some other harmful biases.[31] If we set debiasing in the framework of dual-process theory, it basically means training of type 2 cognition and especially the reflective mind.[32] The general problem with

30. See Richard P. Larrick, "Debiasing," in *Blackwell Handbook of Judgment and Decision Making*, ed. Derek Koehler and Nigel Harvey (Oxford: Blackwell, 2004), 316–37; Pat Croskerry et al., "Cognitive Debiasing 2: Impediments to and Strategies for Change," *BMJ Quality and Safety: The International Journal of Healthcare Improvement* 22 (2015): 65–72. Philip Johnson-Laird, *How We Reason* (Oxford: Oxford University Press, 2006), 292. See especially Larrick's article for the empirical studies that support the possibility of debiasing.
31. Larrick, "Debiasing," 331.
32. Keith Stanovich, *Rationality and the Reflective Mind* (Oxford: Oxford University Press, 2010). See also Miller, *Moral Character*, 309–13; Robert C. Roberts, *Emotions in Moral Life* (Cambridge: Cambridge University Press, 2013); James A. Van Slyke, "Moral Psychology, Neuroscience, and Virtue," in Timpe and Boyd, *Virtues and Their Vices*, 476.

biases is that they are subconscious and not under our direct voluntary control. Intuitive, type 1 cognition takes care of most of our mental processes; it is rare that we need to resort to the deliberative functions of type 2 cognition. However, if we are given time and opportunity to train our type 2 thinking, we can learn to spot the dysfunctional override when type 1 takes control when it shouldn't. Debiasing seeks to alter our cognitive behavior by (1) making us aware of the reasons behind our convictions and the causes of our moods; and (2) helping us balance reason and emotion in decision-making.

How can this kind of change be brought about? We already discussed some of the factors that Miller perceives to be of importance. In debiasing literature, it is customary to list some particular practices or strategies that strengthen the wanted models of conduct. The basic debiasing strategies include the following considerations.[33]

Rewards and sanctions: Just offering a prize for doing our thinking conscientiously or punishing for carelessness has very little beneficial value for our cognitive performance. However, rewards and punishment do help if we have preexisting abilities and faculties to perform well in the first place. Rewards may motivate us to use our currently held abilities, but they do not improve those abilities. Another way of using rewards is to make people accountable for their choices. If they need to explain to others why they have made certain decisions, it can motivate them to use their skills, but it may lead to distortions if they accommodate their views to match what they believe others want to hear.

Consider the opposite: Merely listing the reasons for the view that one already has does not help, because people tend to overestimate the force of the arguments that support their currently held convictions. Self-serving biases can be encountered by making people adopt different viewpoints. This simply means asking the question: Is there something that might have influenced my judgment in negative ways? Honestly addressing this question may open the subject to wider sources of evidence, and this can help to engage in self-criticism.

Think with others: The general problem with harmful biased thinking is that it stays below our cognitive radar: we are not aware when we perform suboptimally. Merely acknowledging that I am biased does not really help because even if I grant that I am not always right, I am often unable to reach outside my own convictions. Still, acknowledging our biases may help us to

33. Larrick, "Debiasing," 321–24.

recognize them and prepare in advance for when we see that we are drawn into situations where biases are likely to arise.

Thinking about the problems in groups can help, but the group needs to be diverse enough so that no particular view dominates the group. In order to prevent peer pressure and "groupthink," it is important for differing ideas and convictions to be brought forth simultaneously and without the fear of negative reactions. If successful, thinking with others automatically enables the consideration of alternative views and more informed decision-making. Moreover, the group enables effective fact-checking and spotting possible errors, when people with different backgrounds interact.[34]

Nothing that has been said above necessarily ensures that person x will perform better in situation s if he or she follows these suggestions. Humans are more complicated than that. However, if x actually develops more virtuous habits, this is very likely the route that he or she has gone through. If successful, debiasing proceeds as shown in figure 4.

In the best-case scenario, our potentially harmful biases are replaced with less harmful ones, and they are then replaced with even less harmful ones, and so on. Recent studies on brain plasticity suggest that our brains are malleable and that they react to our experiences by strengthening those areas that are put to use. A classic study on London taxi drivers demonstrated growth in the hippocampus (an area of the brain that is related to memory), which correlated with the experience and the service years of the drivers. Constant use also strengthens synaptic connections and neural circuits.[35] This is called bootstrapping, and it proceeds through the stages outlined in figure 5.[36]

It is widely acknowledged that our brain can become more effective in finding our way through the streets of London, but can we become wiser? Even if we could improve our intelligence, that would not itself make us any better persons or shield us from the harmful effects of biases. Intelligence and wisdom are not necessarily correlated.[37] In Aristotelian virtue theory, experience is supposed to grant us wisdom, but we all are aware of old people who are not all that wise. This suggests that experience as such is not

34. Larrick, "Debiasing," 326–27.

35. Leslie Paul Thiele, *The Heart of Judgment: Practical Wisdom, Neuroscience, and Narrative* (Cambridge: Cambridge University Press, 2006), 86–89; Van Slyke, "Moral Psychology," 460–66.

36. Thiele, *Heart of Judgment*, 114–15.

37. Daniel Kahneman, *Thinking, Fast and Slow* (London: Allen Lane, 2011), 48–49; Stanovich, *Rationality and the Reflective Mind*, 37–38.

Figure 4. The process of debiasing

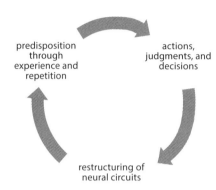

Figure 5. Bootstrapping

enough by itself. Current research supports the view that our intentional stance toward experiences affects the way they influence us.[38] If experience is to be beneficial to us, it needs to be reflected and subjected to the faculty of judgment. Mere existence of different "happenings" in our lives is not enough if we do not act on and process them. This explains why, for example, the experiences of suffering have differing effects on different people. There is nothing valuable in suffering as such, but some people are able to react to it in ways that enable them to survive the suffering and come through the trials stronger than before.

James A. Van Slyke offers a possible angle for understanding the generation of virtuous behavior through imitation and simulation.[39] Imitation is natural for human beings. Young children learn by imitating others, and this propensity stays with us when we grow, even though its applications change.[40] Imitation does not concern only outward behavior such as facial movements;

38. Thiele, *Heart of Judgment*, 94.
39. Van Slyke, "Moral Psychology," 460–67.
40. Imitation is often automatic and unconscious, and the machinery behind it can be to some extent explained by the mirror neuron system (MSN). Briefly, observing the behavior of someone, our brain imitates the brain states of the observed person by firing the same neurons as the object's brain.

it involves emotions and other kinds of mind reading that are typically linked to theory of mind. Simulation takes place when someone is able to "simulate the reasons, motives, and feelings of the moral exemplar until those states become their own and the moral learner acts based on their own internalized characteristics."[41] Imitation and simulation employ both type 1 and type 2 thinking, and they involve both cognition and emotion. As has been stated, type 1 and type 2 thinking should not be seen as separate modules but as parts of machinery that affect each other. Therefore, the virtuous action can be seen as an excellent use of reason, control of emotions, gut feelings, and elaborate thinking that is able to bring forth a form of action that reflects the content of as many virtues as possible. Our natural ability to imitate and simulate behavior of exemplars forms the material basis for the appropriate kind of intentional stance that allows virtues to develop.[42]

At this point, the weakest part of my narrative should be obvious. To put it succinctly: Why should we resort to virtues to help us correct the poorly functioning human mind if the virtues themselves are products of this same poorly functioning machinery?

First, my intention is not to claim that we could easily educate people to act more virtuously. That is not a reasonable aim, although it clearly is something that we should strive for. After all, what would be the option? To *not* teach people about virtues? We will fail in many ways in this endeavor, but this does not diminish our obligation to strive for ideal performance.

Second, poor human cognitive performance does not mean that everyone performs poorly all the time. The psychological data suggest that humans are prone to make mistakes, but this does not mean that no one ever performs well. Those who are able to perform well are our moral exemplars, whom we are called to imitate. In the center of classical virtue theory is the Aristotelian concept of the practically wise person, the *phronimos*. These persons have the skill "to see the world and themselves through the eyes of another without threat to their identity."[43] It is up to them to translate the nature of conflict to the members of their respective communities and engage in extended dialogue with practically wise persons of the other party. If conflict is resolved, it takes place through dialogue that is embodied in the exchange between practically wise persons of each group. Now, it must be recognized that resolving

41. Van Slyke, "Moral Psychology," 460.
42. Van Slyke, "Moral Psychology," 476.
43. Linda Trinkaus Zagzebski, *Divine Motivation Theory* (Cambridge: Cambridge University Press, 2004), 371.

the conflict does not necessarily mean (and it rarely does) that group *a* simply decides to agree with group *b*. Often the result is that opposing propositions retain their original force. However, it is possible that the persons who are in dialogue change. The hold that people have on their convictions may change. They become more self-reflective; they understand better the reasons they hold their beliefs and why these beliefs appear strange to others; they see the problems inhering in their own belief systems and the ways they might be improved with the help of others; and so on. Often this is enough.

Third, the simplistic person-situation juxtaposition should be avoided. More precisely, we should not think we have to make a choice between trying to improve people and trying to improve the institutions and contexts where people make their choices. We need to pay attention to both. However, even if we were to adopt a grimmer picture of human nature and argue that the situationist option seems more reasonable, we still need to ask what criteria we adopt to improve our decision-making contexts and institutions. The obvious answer is that the ideal situation is characterized by virtues and supports virtuous action. Therefore, we need to resort to virtues anyway. Admittedly, this is not a revolutionary theory that will change the way we deal with conflicts. Instead, it is an affirmation of certain human ideals. Perceived from another angle, the virtues are the way conflicts are solved if they are solved at all.

In the following, I will briefly look at three different virtues: open-mindedness, intellectual humility, and intellectual courage, examining the data we have regarding our ability to learn these virtues. I will then discuss tolerance in more detail.

4.2. Virtues of Disagreement

Open-Mindedness

Open-mindedness is a natural choice for a virtue that has special relevance for disagreement, as it controls the dialectic between our currently held beliefs and the beliefs of the other. Jason Baehr defines an open-minded person as someone who "is characteristically willing and (within limits) able to transcend a default cognitive standpoint in order to take up or take seriously the merits of a distinct cognitive standpoint."[44] Open-mindedness

---

44. Baehr, *Inquiring Mind*, 152. See also Peterson and Seligman, *Character Strengths and Virtues*, 143–45; Roberts and Wood, *Intellectual Virtues*, 139.

requires a conscious act of will that lifts its holder outside the box, as we say. Because of our cognitive biases, we often have a comfortable default position, which resists change. An open-minded person is able to transcend this.[45]

Let us note here a minor detail. First, sometimes open-mindedness is exemplified by attitudes like the following statement: "I hold these beliefs but, hey, I might be wrong." This is not open-mindedness; this is simply lazy thinking. Instead, thinking outside the box entails engaging a serious thought exam: even if I hold these beliefs, I will try to inhabit a different mode of thinking that is not common to me. Second, an open-minded person engages in dialectical deliberation by reflecting the strengths and weaknesses of both his or her own and opposing position(s). Third, open-mindedness entails that we must sometimes remain in a state of uncertainty and avoid drawing hasty conclusions. These same questions were discussed in the previous chapter in relation to doubt and belief.

When should we be open-minded? Obviously, being open-minded all the time and toward everything can be a vice; excessive open-mindedness is in danger of turning into skepticism or shoddiness.[46] Baehr suggests that open-mindedness is a virtue when we have a good reason to believe that being open-minded will lead us toward truth. Baehr's more detailed definition of open-mindedness reads as follows:

> (OM) It is "reasonable" for person S to think that being open-minded in context C may be helpful for reaching the truth is generally a function of the comparative strength of S's grounds concerning: (1) the claim P itself; (2) S's own reliability relative to the propositional domain to which P belongs; and (3) the reliability of the source of the argument or evidence against it.[47]

In other words, if S knows well the subject at hand and has good reasons to doubt the counterarguments for P, it might not be reasonable for S to be open-minded, according to Baehr's account. In some cases OM is clearly a good principle. If, for example, my three-year-old son starts to give me cooking advice, I had better not be very open-minded. Yet OM tends to be

45. Baehr, *Inquiring Mind*, 149.
46. C. S. Lewis, *The Abolition of Man* (San Francisco: HarperSanFrancisco, 2001), 60: "An open mind, in questions that are not ultimate, is useful. But an open mind about the ultimate foundations either of Theoretical or of Practical Reason is idiocy. If a man's mind is open on these things, let his mouth at least be shut."
47. Baehr, *Inquiring Mind*, 161.

a merely descriptive account of what we do anyway. It does not tell us when we *should* be open-minded. For example, there are cases when I cannot objectively evaluate (3) because the other is so far off that I cannot recognize the rationale of their counterarguments, given our mutual distance.

Consider the following scenario. A European right-wing party makes a proposal that would make it easier for local farmers to sell their products directly from their farm. This would entail that the shape and curve of the cucumbers need not conform to EU standards, they would not be properly packed in plastic, and there would be less government regulation in the process in general. How might a left-wing party read this proposal? Quite likely, they would have reason to suspect the reliability of this particular source, as it embodies everything they detest. Also, the left-wing party will in all likelihood have a high view of their own reliability regarding how farms should be run.

As it stands, OM does not allow us to show open-mindedness in cases when the alternative view comes from a great distance from our own position. It is not only the issue between left and right political positions, but basically every paradigmatic shift in human sciences would have been an epistemic crime if we had taken OM as our only normative criteria. Clearly, the epistemic worry here is that we do not want to give outlandish or dangerous ideas a free pass. But sometimes it is precisely those outlandish and dangerous ideas that turn out to be right!

A very general answer to the question of when to be open-minded would be: in those cases when being open-minded increases our likelihood to achieve some intellectual good, like truth or understanding. But how can we tell when we are in such a situation? A possible answer would go like this: In inquiries in the different fields of science and human life, we are guided by some set of desiderata. These may include simplicity, explanatory power, moral virtues, epistemic virtues, correspondence, coherency, scope, beauty, truthfulness, and effectiveness, to name a few. To be sure, some of these may, and will, be in conflict with each other, but that does not matter at this point. Our ability to recognize the worth of an alien intellectual system is dependent on our ability to identify these desiderata. I assume that there is no system in human societies that does not latch on to at least some of these. This would entail that we have an a priori duty to take seriously everything that displays some set of desiderata that we are able to recognize, and we need to search for these desiderata, as they may not be immediately obvious to us. Against this background, we can formulate two normative principles: (1) we have an epistemic duty to seek for common desiderata that we are able to recognize as good; (2) we must attempt to give a true account of the alien system, which includes a description of its central desiderata and how they might or might not fit with our system.

But how easy is this? In psychology, open-mindedness can be tested as an application of two distinct notions: differentiation and integration. Differentiation means the ability to apply different perspectives to a particular issue, while integration refers to a person's ability to see connections between and among divergent perspectives.[48] A person is said to have integrative complexity if he or she encompasses both of these aspects to a high degree. Contrariwise, lacking these aspects results in rigid, one-dimensional views and an inability to consider alternative viewpoints.

Below, I have text samples from a test where subjects were asked to offer a short yet comprehensive account of the abortion debate. The answers were graded so that a score of one was given to answers that completely lacked integrative complexity and scores from five to seven were given for optimal complexity.

- Score 1: Abortion is a basic right that should be available to all women. To limit a woman's access to an abortion is an intolerable infringement on her civil liberties. Such an infringement must not be tolerated. To do so would be to threaten the separation of church and state so fundamental to the American way of life.
- Score 3: Many see abortion as a basic liberty that should be available to any woman who chooses to exercise this right. Others, however, see abortion as infanticide.
- Score 5: Some view abortion as a civil liberties issue—that of the woman's right to choose; others view abortion as no more justifiable than murder. Which perspective one takes depends, in large part, on when one views the organism developing within the mother as a human being.[49]

The answers' complexity increases as we move downward. We gain an increasingly wider understanding of both sides of the issue, which is expressed in a neutral way. It is worthwhile to note that integrative complexity does not manifest everything that pertains to open-mindedness: it is a necessary but not sufficient condition for genuine open-mindedness. The answer that re-

48. Peterson and Seligman, *Character Strengths and Virtues*, 148.
49. Peterson and Seligman, *Character Strengths and Virtues*, 148–49.

ceived five points demonstrates understanding, but it does not tell anything about the way the person thinks and acts.

How do we humans generally perform, then? It is possible to distinguish three groups that hold different epistemic attitudes about questions, such as how sure people are about their own beliefs, whether experts can know the truth about the matter, whether it is rational and possible to hold different views, and whether they might all be correct in some sense.[50]

Absolutists hold on to their beliefs, and what they perceive as expert opinions, with a high degree of certainty. Also, absolutism naturally means that other relevant options are not viable. *Multiplists* are of the opinion that experts can be wrong and several theories might get it right, but we cannot really compare different theories because, for example, experiences and emotions play such a strong role in belief formation. *Evaluative* theorists hold that several theories can be true, experts can err, and they themselves might not get it right. But, in spite of this, we can still evaluate and compare different theories and engage in some kind of reasonable exchange of views that strives for the truth. The majority of people are absolutist by default. Of the college students that participated in this test, only 14 percent were able to reach the evaluative mind-set; what is worse, of those who had not attended college, only 5 percent were in the evaluative group. Against this background, it is no wonder that reasonable conversation is so difficult.

In light of these sobering findings, it is worth asking, can we learn open-mindedness? If we focus on my-side bias, it seems that people are able to consider the opposite point of view with some help, and, in so doing, the effects of bias are reduced, but not much. People are generally able to produce the arguments that support their own cause, yet they are unable and/or unwilling to produce the arguments for the other side without good incentive. Posing an argument for the contrary side does not take place automatically, only with sufficient motivation. Moreover, this kind of forcing does not have a long-lasting influence. If debiasing is momentary, the effects of debiasing are usually short-lived as well. Afterward, people go about their lives as if nothing had happened.

Nevertheless, consistent education may increase our ability to think outside our own bias.[51] In a study by D. N. Perkins, it was found that it

50. Deanna Kuhn, Eric Amsel, and Michael O'Loughlin, *The Development of Scientific Thinking Skills* (San Diego: Harcourt, Brace, 1988). See also Peterson and Seligman, *Character Strengths and Virtues*, 150–52.

51. However, just thinking outside of one's own position as such is not a sign of virtuous thinking. Often there are not that many options, which leads just to another kind of conform-

is possible to decrease my-side bias among graduate students (the education appeared not to have any effect on college or high school students).[52] In this case, the time used for observation was limited, but when students participated in a sixteen-hour course where several controversial issues were discussed from multiple angles, the results were more positive. When continuously instructed to take into account and engage both sides of the argument, the graduate students were able to come up with accounts that displayed more integration. Of all disciplines, philosophy graduate students scored highest, which may reflect the nature of the discipline, which forces one to engage all kinds of arguments.[53]

Humility

A general definition of humility is an ability to avoid overestimation and underevaluation of one's own position, including power, status, skills, gifts, knowledge, and the like. In other words, humility is a virtue that enables its holder to view oneself as one truly is.[54] June Price Tangney lists the following key features in the definition of humility:[55]

- An accurate (not underestimated) sense of one's abilities and achievements.
- The ability to acknowledge one's mistakes, imperfections, gaps in knowledge, and limitations (often with reference to a "higher power").

---

ism. This is the reason, for example, all hipsters (who try to be anticonformists) look exactly the same. Jonathan Touboul, "The Hipster Effect: When Anticonformists All Look the Same," *Arxiv.org.* October 29, 2014, http://arxiv.org/pdf/1410.8001v1.pdf.

52. D. N. Perkins, "Postprimary Education Has Little Impact on Informal Reasoning," *Journal of Education Psychology* 77 (1985): 562–71.

53. Peterson and Seligman, *Character Strengths and Virtue*, 158. Helen de Cruz, "Irrelevant Influences and Philosophical Practice: A Qualitative Study" (forthcoming), has also argued that based on self-reports of the philosophers of religion, studying philosophy has tempered their religious views.

54. For a general account on humility, see Andrew Pinsent, "Humility," in *Being Good: Christian Virtues for Everyday Life*, ed. Michael Austin and R. Douglas Geivett (Grand Rapids: Eerdmans, 2011), 245–46. Roberts and Wood, *Intellectual Virtues*, 236–57; Peterson and Seligman, *Character Strengths and Virtues*, 461–75.

55. June Price Tangney, "Humility," in *Handbook of Positive Psychology*, ed. C. R. Snyder and Shane J. Lopez (New York: Oxford University Press, 2002), 411–19. Cited in Peterson and Seligman, *Character Strengths and Virtues*, 462.

- An openness to new ideas, contradictory information, and advice.
- The ability to keep one's abilities and accomplishments in perspective.
- A relatively low focus on the self or an ability to "forget the self."[56]
- An appreciation of the value of all things, as well as the many different ways that people and things can contribute to our world.

However, humility is not typically listed among the classical virtues. It is absent from the standard lists of Aristotle and Plato, for example. In fact, in heroic pre-Christian societies, humility and submission were closer to vices than virtues.[57] Even today, humility is not fashionable. The culture of competition prevalent in the business world and academia does not promote and value humility. More generally, when all kinds of societal and individual problems are attributed to low self-esteem, humility is not a virtue that has high demand. Instead of humility, it is suggested, we need pride (which is, in the classic Christian virtue literature, the very opposite of humility). In our culture, humility is seen as a sign of weakness and passivity, resulting from shame and reflecting a pathological devaluing of the self.[58]

On the other hand, it is rather fashionable to tout "epistemic humility," but few people have actually defined what it means.[59] Typically, it is taken to imply doubt, but for the reasons I have already mentioned, this is not a good idea. Instead, I propose the following definition:

(EH) A person is epistemically humble when he or she is able to (1) articulate the strengths and weaknesses of his or her own beliefs, (2) correctly

56. C. S. Lewis, *Mere Christianity* (San Francisco: HarperSanFrancisco, 2001), 128: "Do not imagine that if you meet a really humble man he will be what most people call 'humble' nowadays: he will not be a sort of greasy, smarmy person, who is always telling you that, of course, he is nobody. . . . He will not be thinking about humility: he will not be thinking about himself at all."

57. Early Christian theologians, especially Augustine, saw the pagan virtue of magnanimity as a form of pride that should be replaced with Christian humility. Herdt, *Putting on Virtue*, 45–71.

58. Peterson and Seligman, *Character Strengths and Virtues*, 463, 469–70. However, several studies demonstrate that a false sense of pride is linked with personality disorders, and in the worst cases, narcissism. Consequently, narcissists show higher levels of aggression, a will to dominate and control others, and many other negative features. Even if high self-esteem, in which narcissists excel, does have some health benefits, both mentally and physically the overall sum is negative.

59. For discussion and several perspectives on the issue, see James Kraft and David Basinger, eds., *Religious Tolerance through Humility: Thinking with Philip Quinn* (Farnham, UK: Ashgate, 2008); James Kraft, "Religious Tolerance through Religious Diversity and Epistemic Humility," *Sophia* 45 (2006): 114.

understand the strengths and weaknesses of an alien belief, and (3) relate his or her own beliefs with the alien belief in a constructive manner, which means either proper accommodation of the two ways of believing or a well-argued negative response to the alien view.

This short overview of two central epistemic virtues demonstrates that open-mindedness and epistemic humility can be achieved without invoking the concept of doubt. Doubt does appear in the description of an epistemically humble individual, but in a more refined form. Such a person doubts only those things he or she has reason to doubt.[60] Epistemic humility coupled with a desiderata approach should be able to provide conceptual tools that help us to articulate how tolerant attitudes should be expressed and applied.

Let us, then, consider again the practical question: Can we become more humble? This question is not easily answered. There are no existent, reliable methods to measure how humble people in fact are. Self-reporting is manifestly inaccurate, and sometimes what appears to observers as humility can be something else entirely. Moreover, different cultures have different takes on humility. Asian cultures, for example, typically foster a different kind of humility and modesty than Western cultures. Humility may also have different societal functions, which can be complex, and which will make assessing one's level of humility challenging.

Nevertheless, there are some indirect ways to observe these aforementioned personality traits. One of them is to track the absence of narcissistic traits. Another is to map out those factors that people typically refer to as the sources of humility in their own lives. Of course, we do not know whether these things actually make people humble, since this is just what they think makes them humble. The list is as follows:

- Reality-based feedback about one's strengths and weaknesses, conveyed in an atmosphere of care and respect.
- Awe-inspiring experiences.
- Educational approaches that emphasize the limits of human knowledge.
- Experiences of failure and disappointment.[61]

60. The first thing to do is locate what we are actually "doubting": is it our beliefs, our ways of coming to believe things and how we hold on to our convictions, or is it the results of those beliefs? It is wise to "doubt" all of these every now and then, but we should be conscious about what we are actually doing and why. And we cannot question all three spheres at the same time. The boat needs to be fixed while we are sailing in it.

61. Peterson and Seligman, *Character Strengths and Virtues*, 470–71.

This suggests that quite a lot depends on our environment. In the case of humility, it seems that early childhood plays a central role as secure attachment to parents gives a person a means of realistic self-evaluation in a safe context. This relates to the meaning of an intentional stance on our behavior that was already noted earlier. If we do not reflect and act on our experiences, they will not have humility-inducing value.[62]

It is clear that we cannot simply force people into contexts where they are supposed to learn humility, as they can have a negative response and learn nothing from it. What if, for example, I do not want to wash my neighbor's feet? And if I do, this single act does not help me if it is not transformed into a way of life. An additional problem is related to feedback. It requires character to internalize negative feedback in a way that actually helps us. And in some cases, internalizing positive feedback may be challenging too.

Courage

If open-mindedness and humility help us avoid attributing too high a certainty to our beliefs, intellectual courage should enable us to hold our ground when we are challenged.[63] By courage we usually mean a voluntary state of mind that involves conscious judgment to act in proper ways in the face of danger. Baehr's general definition of intellectual courage is as follows:

> (IC) Intellectual courage is a disposition to persist in or with a state or course of action aimed at an epistemically good end despite the fact that doing so involves an apparent threat to one's own well-being.[64]

Baehr explains his definition by making a distinction between moral and intellectual courage. It is possible to be intellectually courageous without being morally virtuous. For example, if I am motivated by vainglory in my research, I may display courage in the face of criticism, but if the main reason for pursuing research is self-centered, I am not properly virtuous.

62. Thiele, *Heart of Judgment*, 94.
63. For discussion, see Baehr, *Inquiring Mind*, 163–90; Daniel McInerny, "Fortitude and the Conflict of Frameworks," in Timpe and Boyd, *Virtues and Their Vices*, 75–92; Peterson and Seligman, *Character Strengths and Virtues*, 213–28.
64. Baehr, *Inquiring Mind*, 177.

Epistemic virtue also differs from moral virtue in that it has an epistemic, knowledge-related goal. Being intellectually courageous requires both the willingness and ability to act in courageous ways. The success component is in this case more important than in some other cases. The word "state" in IC refers to more stable belief states, whereas "course of action" refers to active inquiry or communication of knowledge.[65]

Aquinas explains how courage in general is dependent on two sets of qualities.[66] On the one hand, a courageous person has *magnanimitas* and *magnificentia*. The former refers to an initial attitude of trust that one is able to secure something good through one's actions. The latter is the quality of an actual courageous deed, how it is planned and carried out.[67] The second set includes *patientia* and *perseverantia*. A courageous person needs to be patient in the face of evils so as not to become disheartened. A patient person decides to hold his or her ground even when all hope seems lost. Patience is strengthened by perseverance, which enables the person to sustain this state of mind.

Of course, courage needs to be informed by prudence; sometimes it is a sign of courage to back down. Daniel McInerny argues that humility "encourages us to have a true estimate of our various weaknesses, an estimate that should often lead us to temper our attacks by stepping back from our own opinions and reflecting on the opinions of others."[68] For Aquinas, courage is perfected through the theological virtues of faith, love, and hope. Acts of courage need to be formed by these virtues in order to reflect the highest ideal of good. For example, acts of courage need to be motivated by the love of neighbor and the love of God, not love of one's self or honor. In some cases, martyrdom is the end of courage, as it is the highest expression of love: there is nothing higher that anyone can give than his or her own life.[69]

65. Baehr, *Inquiring Mind*, 163–64, 177–79.
66. McInerny, "Fortitude," 84–85; McInerny, *The Difficult Good: A Thomistic Approach to Moral Conflict and Human Happiness* (New York: Fordham University Press, 2006), 160–62. See *ST* II-II.128. Aquinas concentrates on moral courage, but the same things apply to intellectual courage as well.
67. Courage typically refers to deeds that everyone can see. Therefore, the treatment of intellectual courage is easily taken to refer to the public expressions of conviction. There is nothing especially praiseworthy in holding a belief in private, even though this belief may be a result of intellectually virtuous inquiry. It is acting on this belief that makes it possibly intellectually virtuous in the full sense of the word.
68. McInerny, *Difficult Good*, 160–61.
69. McInerny, "Fortitude," 75–81, 85–86.

Even if one does not give one's life in following the courageous path, several other harms may take place. Among the typical consequences of standing one's ground are "depression and anxiety, feelings of isolation and powerlessness, increased distrust in others, declining physical health, financial decline, and familial problems."[70] Interestingly, those who perform courageous acts are the sort of persons who have a high tolerance for such negative effects. Decorated soldiers, for example, stand out from the crowd in terms of social maturity, self-confidence, risk taking, low stress levels under pressure, intelligence, emotional stability, and a lack of physical or mental complaints.[71]

Although the aforementioned individual characteristics correlate with courage, the virtue itself has close relations to communal thinking. First of all, those who endanger themselves typically have a sense of belonging to a greater humanity; that is, they have an experience of unity with other people and are prosocially orientated. Moreover, community is also a salient enabling factor. If the context supports courage through acts and speech and also expects courageous actions, it is easier to behave courageously. Strong leadership, mutual trust, and bonding among community members also enable courage.[72]

When should we be intellectually courageous? If we consider the actions of people such as Holocaust deniers, it seems that they portray significant levels of courage when publicly proclaiming their convictions. But should we consider these expressions as signs of true intellectual courage? It all depends how they go about holding their beliefs in the face of disagreement. It must be granted that person *a*, who has lived all her life in a community where it is widely believed that the Holocaust never happened and who has never encountered significant challenges to her belief, does not do anything wrong, even though she holds a false belief. However, if she meets person *b* who offers an argument against what she has learned, then her situation changes. She is suddenly presented with a new piece of evidence about the Holocaust that needs to be evaluated. Again, we can presume that she acts virtuously if she approaches this new evidence with suspicion. But if she neglects the new evidence by not seriously engaging it, she becomes epistemically culpable.

Trent Dougherty suggests that in these kinds of cases, in which some

---

70. Peterson and Seligman, *Character Strengths and Virtues*, 219.

71. Peterson and Seligman, *Character Strengths and Virtues*, 222.

72. Peterson and Seligman, *Character Strengths and Virtues*, 221.

people are presented with novel information, the problem is that they are not attentive to the evidence; other concerns get in the way.[73] Thus they are not interested in truth as the ultimate value. This can be a result of either moral failure or practical irrationality. Here the unity of virtues helps to analyze the situation. They display some intellectual virtues, but because the virtues are not connected in the right way, the act of courage fails to express genuine virtue.

Baehr suggest that the proper place of intellectual courage is the situation when the goods that could be secured through steadfastness outweigh the harm that results from standing one's ground.[74] As it was with open-mindedness, intellectual courage needs to be balanced so that one picks the right battle. Not every single iota is worth a fight. On the other hand, it is a sign of poor judgment if one does not recognize the right moments of resistance. The following quote from Martin Niemöller (1892–1984), who stood against the Nazi regime and spent seven years in concentration camps, illustrates this lack of wisdom well:

> First they came for the Socialists, and I did not speak out—Because I was not a Socialist. Then they came for the Trade Unionists, and I did not speak out—Because I was not a Trade Unionist. Then they came for the Jews, and I did not speak out—Because I was not a Jew. Then they came for me—and there was no one left to speak for me.[75]

The type of speech Niemöller yearns for is called *parrhēsia*, truthful and courageous speech. Recently, Michel Foucault has provided an analysis of the concept. Foucault argues that the *parrhēsiastēs*, the one who uses *parrhēsia*, speaks everything in his or her mind: "In *parrhesia*, the speaker is supposed to give a complete and exact account of what he has in mind so that the audience is able to comprehend exactly what the speaker thinks."[76]

---

73. Trent Dougherty, "Reducing Responsibility: An Evidentialist Account of Epistemic Blame," *European Journal of Philosophy* 20 (2010): 534–47. See also Jason Baehr, "Evidentialism, Vice, and Virtue," in *Evidentialism and Its Discontents*, ed. Trent Dougherty (Oxford: Oxford University Press, 2011), 88–101.

74. Baehr, *Inquiring Mind*, 186–90.

75. Niemöller used this quote in several postwar lectures, and it appears in various forms.

76. Michel Foucault, "The Meaning and Evolution of the Word Parrhesia," in *Discourse and Truth: The Problematization of Parrhesia*, ed. Joseph Pearson, *Foucault, Info*, 1999, http://foucault.info/doc/documents/parrhesia/foucault-dt1-wordparrhesia-en-html.

But something more is needed; the speaker also needs to speak the truth since only truth is worthy to be spoken in this way. However, the truth often hurts. Thus the *parrhēsiastēs* always risks something. Foucault mentions as examples the possibility of ruining friendships and, in the case of politicians, ruining their careers. Yet voicing the opinions people hold as true is a test case for genuine freedom. As George Orwell states, "Freedom is the right to tell people what they do not want to hear."[77] Paradoxically, in Western culture, which has cherished the ideal of freedom, this is not taken for granted anymore. I will return to this troubling phenomenon shortly.

Reinhard Hütter has adopted Foucault's analysis for theological discourse, especially in the context of ecumenical theology where disagreeing Christian bodies address each other. He notes how the idea of courageous, truthful discourse is built in to Christian identity. The concept appears often in the Letter to the Hebrews, such as in 3:6: "We are [Christ's] house if we hold firm the confidence and the pride that belong to hope." Therefore Hütter claims, "Any individual practitioner of Christian theology must be a *parrhēsiastēs*."[78]

4.3. Tolerance as a Virtue

I have offered brief accounts of some central virtues that are needed to confront the lived reality of disagreement. Next, I will look at tolerance, which is often named the most important, or even the only, virtue of our time. Tolerance gets a longer treatment because what we have learned from the history of philosophy and the human mind tells us that disagreements are not going to disappear, and those ideas that we do not like are not going away.

In democracies, the decisions to change current policies or adopt completely new ones are very likely to leave some segments of the population disgruntled, which then will form new minorities, since Western societies make laws to satisfy the views of the majority of the population.[79] It is possible to disagree on all kind of things, even after extensive debate—and including after political decisions have been made in favor of some particular view

77. George Orwell, "The Freedom of the Press," preface to *Animal Farm* (New York: Penguin, 2000).
78. Reinhard Hütter, *Bound to Be Free: Evangelical Catholic Engagements in Ecclesiology, Ethics, and Ecumenics* (Grand Rapids: Eerdmans, 2004), 12–13.
79. Of course, our societies sometimes make laws precisely to protect the minorities against the majorities or other minorities.

or other. This, of course, can create frustration and tension. The question of John Rawls and many others is how we are able to create and sustain a stable and just society that consists of citizens divided by their basic beliefs and values.

In this section, I shall first examine the differing uses and meanings of the concept of "toleration," and how most of the uses actually fail to be instances of virtue. Second, I will consider how it might be possible to understand tolerance (and intolerance) as a virtue. And last, I consider whether "virtuous tolerance" could be a viable possibility in public life.

Discourses of Tolerance

The concept of "tolerance" is used frequently in both popular and political discourse. It can have various meanings, and it can be used to embody various public attitudes. As a working hypothesis, I refer to a general definition: tolerance is "the deliberate decision to refrain from prohibiting, hindering, or otherwise coercively interfering with conduct that one disapproves, although one has the power to do so."[80] Tolerance thus needs three coexisting components:

> T1 Genuine disagreement
> T2 The power to hinder the conduct of the other
> T3 Deliberate refraining from hindering

I will revisit this formulation later, but for now it can function as a working hypothesis, which illuminates some crucial, but not necessarily all, elements of genuine toleration. Before redefining the meaning of tolerance, I will highlight the different ways people use the concept and distinguish six different uses, which are as follows:

1. Tolerance as self-congratulation, or a despising attitude toward the other
2. Tolerance as relativism
3. Tolerance as vice

80. See, e.g., John Horton, "Toleration," in *Routledge Encyclopedia of Philosophy*, ed. Edward Craig (London: Routledge, 1998), 9:862; Andrew J. Cohen, "What Toleration Is," *Ethics* 115 (2004): 69; Paul Ricoeur, "The Erosion of Tolerance and the Resistance of the Intolerable," *Diogenes* 44, no. 4 (1996): 189; T. M. Scanlon, *The Difficulty of Tolerance: Essays in Political Philosophy* (Cambridge: Cambridge University Press, 2003), 187.

4. Tolerance as approval
5. Tolerance as negligence
6. Tolerance as virtue

Tolerance is often used in a laudatory way. I take this to mean that contemporary Western people have a high regard for tolerance. They like to perceive themselves as tolerant. Indeed, tolerance is widely considered an important virtue.[81] However, tolerance can be used to express self-congratulation, which has as its counterpart a despising attitude toward those who think differently (e.g., "I am tolerant, while you are closed-minded bigots"). The person who says statements like this may satisfy the aforementioned criteria, but something is clearly amiss. Of course, situations like this can be complex, but one possible scenario is that if it were in one's power to stop others from acting according to their views, one would do so. Furthermore, this kind of use does not reflect greater variety or the unity of virtues. Consequently, tolerance can appear in the form of hatred and seek to promote antagonism.

The second use is another example of a careless use of terms. We may use the term *tolerance* to express imprecise, relativist attitudes. Here the concept works as a slogan, as when one says, "We need to tolerate difference." The odd thing is that nobody actually tolerates unqualified difference. Furthermore, toleration does not here mean toleration but something like putting everything on par. It is almost like saying "We do not have to tolerate *x* because everything is the same after all." This attitude thus excises and hides actual differences, leaving nothing left to tolerate.[82] It is not clear that there is any disagreement at all, and when the disagreement is absent there is no need for toleration. All the aforementioned elements of tolerance are thus missing. Here the meaning of tolerance is the same as that of acceptance.

The third use of the concept is tolerance as vice. When the other is saying or doing something we want to proscribe, we say something like "This cannot be tolerated!" Elements T1 and T2 are present, but T3 is not. Here tolerance is something negative because it is feared that giving room to those who disagree with us will enable them to grow in number and turn against us. This use points to something that is in fact vicious in that par-

81. Thus, among others, Ricoeur, "Erosion of Tolerance," 189.
82. This problem has been pointed out by, e.g., Peter Jonkers, "Can Freedom of Religion Replace the Virtue of Tolerance?," in *From Political Theory to Political Theology: Religious Challenges and the Prospects of Democracy*, ed. Peter Losonczi and Aakash Singh (London: Continuum, 2010), 74–76. On similar criticisms made by Slavoj Žižek, see Marcus Pound, *Žižek: A (Very) Critical Introduction* (Grand Rapids: Eerdmans, 2008), 96–97, 134–37.

ticular context, making intolerance the virtuous course of action in certain given situations. The problem, of course, is to offer arguments when some particular belief or action is so bad that it cannot be tolerated.

The following two examples are interesting because they involve all three elements but still fail to portray a virtuous attitude. The first of these is complacent approval ("Let them do what they like; it's not that bad"). One may think there is something problematic about a particular belief or action, and could stop it, but one lets it happen. In so doing, one approves it.

The second way, tolerance as negligence, is somewhat similar to approval, but it expresses more clearly neglect and lack of interest. One may think there is something not quite right with a particular belief or action, but for whatever reason one is not willing to engage the issue in detail, and ends up putting it out of mind. The difference between these two examples is that while the first expresses general approval, the other is merely negligent about the matter. However, it could be argued that the component T1 dissolves when nobody cares about the disagreement anymore, and these two examples thus fail to represent tolerance in a virtuous way.

Supplementing Tolerance

This brings us to the crux of the matter. The aforementioned components are unable to sustain the attitude I call *virtuous tolerance*. As we saw in the previous examples, the problem of tolerance is that it easily backslides into negligence or approval, or fails otherwise to sustain the critical attitude. Alasdair MacIntyre recognizes this predicament as follows: "Toleration . . . is not in itself a virtue and too inclusive a toleration is a vice. Toleration is an exercise of virtue just in so far as it serves the purposes of a certain kind of rational enquiry and discussion, in which the expression of conflicting points of view enables us through constructive conflict to achieve certain individual and communal goods. And intolerance is also an exercise of virtue when and in so far as it enables us to achieve those same goods."[83] In other words, tolerance should be used to create a space for sustained encounter and discussion between disagreeing parties. Thus I suggest that our earlier definition of tolerance needs the additional principle:

83. Alasdair MacIntyre, "Toleration and Goods in Conflict," in *Selected Essays*, vol. 2, *Ethics and Politics* (Cambridge: Cambridge University Press, 2006), 223. See also John Bowlin, "Tolerance among the Fathers," *Journal of the Society of Christian Ethics* 26 (2006): 8-10.

T4 Maintaining a critical attitude and public conversation.

T4 helps to realize the presence of T1. When there exists a genuine disagreement about a certain matter, it is not virtuous to pretend that it does not exist, or that we should just let it be. Nor is it virtuous if we engage the other party with disrespect or hate. Virtuous tolerance entails keeping up the public conversation and the public expression of critique.[84]

The first example of the use of tolerance illustrates a case where the critical attitude remains, but it is motivated by scorn and disdain. Of course, when we do not recognize the other as our epistemic peer, or when the opinion seems false, it is hard to avoid negative reactions. For example, the atheist critique of religion sometimes displays this kind of attitude: religion is a delusion, and people who defend it are mad, evil, or intellectually substandard. Clearly, the plea for rational encounter and dialogue seems to be in vain if you a priori regard the other as incapable of rationality. That is why we need a fifth component:

T5 Conversation and dialogue has to express intellectual virtues.

By intellectual virtues, I mean such qualities as discretion, humility, wisdom, interpretive sensitivity, prudence, coachability, tenacity, open-mindedness, honesty, and the like. Tolerance is not usually listed among intellectual or moral virtues. The reason for this may be its ambiguity, and also that the goals of tolerance can be gained through other virtues, such as patience, truthfulness, and open-mindedness.

But how can intellectual virtues help us understand the nature of tolerance? Of course, there is no necessary connection between these two. It is easy to come up with examples where an action is not virtuous (smoking in a crowd of people, for example) but tolerable. On the other hand, some actions are argued with philosophical rigor, but they are still cruel and possibly illegal (for example, when a postmodernist performance artist tortures a living animal in order to expose the nihilist vocation of our society). Vir-

---

84. Ricoeur, "Erosion of Tolerance," 201. Likewise, John Rawls's (*Political Liberalism* [New York: Columbia University Press, 1996], xxii) model of liberalism does not try to "attack or criticize, much less reject, any particular theory of truth of moral judgments." Thus his model does not aim at consensus but conviviality. He believes that disagreements, when handled well (that is, when they follow "public reason"), can be instructive and cultivating for societies. My argument here is only to make a footnote to Rawls's theory by proposing explicit virtue language as one possible way of giving visible form to Rawls's aims.

tues as such do not give a solution to the question of what can be tolerated. However, virtues might give us guidance about how we should live and act when we are in a state of perplexity and persistent disagreement. Virtues can also illuminate how we should reach the decision regarding what can be tolerated and what ought not be.

What happens when we come across something we do not like or agree with? MacIntyre distinguishes four attitudes toward the claims of others. First, we may take the other perspective as reinforcing our views or helping us to reformulate our point better. Second, it may compel us to adopt another point of view that differs from our previous views. Third, we see no way of regarding the other view as beneficial for us, but we nevertheless recognize its force. We feel compelled to give due answer, for example, by trying to demonstrate the flaws or misunderstandings within the argument, or convincing the other that adopting our view does not have the implications they are afraid of. And fourth, there is also the possibility that the other's opinion is formulated in such a way that there is no alternative to excluding them, temporarily or permanently, from discussion. MacIntyre, however, immediately recognizes that the line between justified intolerance (the expelling of the other) and unjustified suppression of opinion is a line drawn in water.[85]

Paul Ricoeur invokes the concept of "harm" in this context, which entails both physical and mental injury.[86] But the concept is rather vague, since "harm" can be extended to cover public discussion about a controversial topic if somebody ends up feeling hurt or discriminated against as a result of said conversation. In cases of disagreement, hurt seems unavoidable. In our current political climate, these kinds of moral arguments can be used to ban discussion about delicate matters.[87] Ricoeur seems to acknowledge this problem when he resists, and ask his readers to resist, the charm of consensus in moral matters. Instead, the wisdom, he claims, lies in being "content with fragile compromises" and "recognition of reasonable disagreements." Additionally, we should not be impatient and try to reach premature consensus in disputed matters. (Ricoeur singles out abortion and euthanasia as

85. MacIntyre, "Toleration," 206.

86. Ricoeur, "Erosion of Tolerance," 198, 201. See also Jonkers, "Freedom of Religion," 82.

87. This is also the concern in Frank Furedi, *On Tolerance: A Defence of Moral Independence* (London: Continuum, 2011). In contemporary political discourse, tolerance is sometimes criticized as a suboptimal concept compared to recognition. For discussion, see Olli-Pekka Vainio and Aku Visala, "Tolerance or Recognition? What Can We Expect?," *Open Theology* (forthcoming); Bradley Campbell and Jason Manning, "Microaggressions and Moral Cultures," *Comparative Sociology* 13 (2014): 692–726.

concrete examples.) In these kinds of cases, the conflict should be regarded as important and, for the time being, unsolvable, by mutual recognition of all parties to the dispute. Virtue language might prove to be beneficial in these kinds of fragile situations: What are the moral and intellectual goods that are, or are not, secured by different viewpoints?

The Viability of Tolerance

How viable is this concept of tolerance? Critics of tolerance have claimed that it is inherently utopian and therefore impossible. As a political principle it sets the bar too high; if we try to be virtuously tolerant we are doomed to fail. Living in a fallen world takes up a lot of mental resources and requires a mentally and morally robust character, which is, unfortunately, rare. Additionally, intellectually virtuous belief formation requires philosophical acumen and familiarity with arguments, which requires time—a luxury we do not have. A further problem is that religious and political traditions that should provide us with needed virtues are not very effective in motivating us to virtuous action in large masses. Of course, people embrace their traditions to different degrees and in different ways, and only a small number of them can attain the level of perfect, or near-perfect, virtue.

However, we should distinguish between the ideals that nobody can attain and the ones most cannot attain. Clearly, everybody cannot be virtuous, but some can, and even those who cannot are able to recognize virtues when they see them performed (although they might not necessarily appreciate them). Partly, the viability of virtuous tolerance hangs on the ability of at least some people to recognize and appreciate virtues, which is something that can be improved by education and a deeper understanding of our intellectual and religious traditions, which are tightly intertwined.

Of course, religion can be associated with both deep wisdom and utter stupidity, but that description fits equally well with secular affiliations. For that matter, very few institutions are completely evil or completely good. Robert Merrihew Adams argues that mid-level social affiliations (families, neighborhoods, schools, workplaces, religious institutions, etc.) and social roles (parent, friend, teacher, supervisor, citizen, etc.) are crucial components for the constitution of moral character and a virtuous way of life. However, he remains doubtful about the possibilities of the state to be able to fulfill the functions of moral education and argues that moral development requires a church, or an institution that resembles a church by providing a space for sustained discourse on ethical issues and a context of mutual care between the members of the community.[88] Adams's model suggests that instead of pushing religion into the private sphere, churches and religions should be brought to the public sphere because they have the best possible sources and instruments for moral development. More particularly, because of its long history, including various moral successes and failures, and its venerable tradition of moral deliberation, the Christian religion has immense resources for internal critique. Despite the many examples of abuses and betrayals of central Christian commitments, the instruments needed for its correction are found within the tradition.

Tolerance is a difficult virtue, and the difficulties in achieving it lie not only in us but also in the structures that surround us. MacIntyre notes, for example, that the rhetorical modes of rational inquiry are profoundly at odds with the rhetorical modes of contemporary, commercialistic political culture.[89] The future of virtuous tolerance looks quite grim. But what are the alternatives? Should we ditch the idea of tolerance because it is too hard?

The idea of virtuous tolerance has some benefits over its alternatives, which gives at least some pragmatic reasons for pushing toward the goal, even if it turns out to be beyond our reach. First, virtuous tolerance exposes the false view that the world is simple. Second, it enables the critical movement and engagement with other stories that the strongly consensual systems are not able to provide, thus making the slide into apathy and complacency more difficult. Third, it takes pluralism seriously and forces us to understand the other from their point of view. And fourth, the alternatives effectively present either brute power or mediocrity as a moral aim.

4.4. Religious Disagreement and Virtue

In this final section I wish to address different forms of religious disagreement, relating them to the taxonomy I provided in the beginning.

1. Religious disagreements in the public sphere
   a. Violent clashes between religions and worldviews (ideologically motivated violence and war)

---

88. Adams, *A Theory of Virtue*, 138–43, 228–29. See also John Bowlin, "Nature, Grace, and Toleration: Civil Society and the Twinned Church," *Annual of the Society of Christian Ethics* 21 (2001): 85–104. Cf. Rawls, *Political Liberalism*, lviii–lix.

89. MacIntyre, "Toleration," 223.

    b. Clashes between ideologically motivated values (arguments about abortion, euthanasia, marriage, etc.)

2. Intrareligious disagreements
    a. Disagreements between members of the same community in a smaller scale (such as the Anglican Communion crisis or the Great Schism of 1054)
    b. Disagreements between the members of neighboring communities (ecumenical debates)

3. Personal conflicts
    a. Disagreements among family members and other close peers
    b. Individual feelings of cognitive dissonance

I will address the above questions by following three focal points: community, ideology, and personal identity. These focal points latch on to the aforementioned levels of conflict in various ways, as will become apparent.

Communities

When we look at the problem of disagreement from the viewpoint that pertains to communal elements, we are talking about levels 1a, 1b, 2a, and 2b. In these cases, we have distinct groups that have conflicting relationships with one another. These disagreements typically create frustration at the personal level, but here I will concentrate on what happens at the communal level if participants in the dispute seek resolution.

The existence of several distinct communities within the same social space is a phenomenon that marks our contemporary Western world. Most of the time these communities coexist peacefully, but sometimes the situation can take a problematic turn. Harvey Whitehouse argues that our group-forming strategies can help us to make sacrifices for our own group, and persuade us to work for the common good. Yet these same cognitive models can turn us against our neighbors if we are provoked. Changing this fundamental state of affairs would "require near eradication of between-group competition and exceptionally high levels of affluence and existential security."[90] Whitehouse suggest (with his tongue in cheek, pre-

---

90. Harvey Whitehouse, "Religion, Cohesion and Hostility," in *Religion, Intolerance, and Conflict: A Scientific and Conceptual Investigation*, ed. Steve Clarke, Russell Powell, and Julian Savulescu (Oxford: Oxford University Press, 2013), 45.

sumably) that this is only possible in Scandinavia, where the government provides a safety net for everyone, thus lowering the pressure for violent outbursts. However, even this state has a paradoxical nature: "As soon as we can afford to be pluralists, the irony is we actually all become the same."[91] Even if we could create small enclaves where this kind of peaceful state is possible, it is not reasonable (given our human nature) to expect that this is a viable prospect for humanity in general. Therefore, we need some guidelines on how to manage the plurality of human existence.

I will follow here Linda Zagzebski, who offers some principles that draw our attention to central cognitive stances that are required when seeking mutual understanding.[92]

> *The need-to-resolve-conflict principle*: It is a demand of rationality for a community to attempt to resolve putative conflicts between its beliefs and the beliefs of other communities.
>
> *The cultural-sensitivity principle*: People should treat members of other cultures and religions as though they were prima facie as rational as themselves.
>
> *The recognition-of-conscientiousness principle*: If our community's belief is conscientious, its conscientiousness is recognizable, in principle, by persons in other communities whose conscientiousness we recognize as a community.

These principles illustrate the nature of ideal communication between disagreeing parties. Of course, these kinds of settings can be hard to come by, and our pluralistic societies are trying to find ways of constructing such spaces. Zagzebski's philosophical work offers a robust theoretical back-

91. Whitehouse, "Religion, Cohesion and Hostility," 45. This is parodied in Lukas Moodysson's movie *Together* (2000), when one of the characters compares Swedish life to porridge: "You could say that we are like porridge. First we're like small oat flakes—small, dry, fragile, alone. But then we're cooked with the other oat flakes and become soft. We join so that one flake can't be told apart from another. We're almost dissolved. Together we become a big porridge that's warm, tasty, and nutritious and yes, quite beautiful, too. So we are no longer small and isolated but we have become warm, soft, and joined together. Part of something bigger than ourselves. Sometimes life feels like an enormous porridge, don't you think?" The same issue was also the theme in *The Invasion* (2007), a remake of the sci-fi classic *The Invasion of the Body Snatchers*.

92. Zagzebski develops these principles in *Divine Motivation Theory*, 368–72; and Zagzebski, *Epistemic Authority: A Theory of Trust, Authority, and Autonomy in Belief* (Oxford: Oxford University Press, 2012), 222–28.

ground, which helps us to see the crucial elements involved in successful attempts at reconciliation.

First, it has not always been recognized that conflicts need to be negotiated and solved. Not that long ago, several cultures and communities held it as self-evident that they were superior and the opinions of others did not need to be taken into account. If we are hoping for a peaceful resolution, both parties need to subscribe to the need to resolve conflict.

Second, the principle of cultural sensitivity prevents us from dodging the criticism a priori. It is common to think that others are somehow intellectually deficient, and subject to various biases and both intellectual and moral vices. Of course, it is possible that this is actually the case. Yet the point of the principle is to make sure that we do not make this judgment before investigating the case and its roots.

The third principle attempts to make the reasons of disagreement mutually transparent to all parties. If we have done our job well in constructing our convictions, it should be evident to outsiders. Likewise, if the other party has also performed conscientiously, this should be apparent to us. Again, it is possible that neither of the parties performs conscientiously. But if they have done their job well, they can trust that the other party will recognize their conscientiousness.

How does this recognition take place? One natural way would be through recognizing virtues and vices. A genuine virtuous action bears the marks of a well-executed process, which necessarily reflects the central intellectual virtues of thoroughness, honesty, clarity, and the like. Furthermore, the vices are visible in similar ways. This point provides us with a normative request: if we wish to be taken seriously, we must try harder. Not even the fact that the other party does not reflect all the necessary virtues can take away this obligation because the other party may still be able to display virtues in their respective action.

As already indicated, nothing here suggests that all conflicts can be resolved. Sometimes it can be a failure on our part and we need to assume at least part of the blame. Sometimes we do our best but nothing changes. In this case, our conscience is free and we need to find other ways of keeping the conflict from escalating and minimize the damage, while trying simultaneously to find points of agreement in the hope that something happens in the future.

Here we face an obvious problem that is often discussed in relation to virtue theories. Virtue theorists such as Adams and MacIntyre point out that the natural places for growing in virtues are found in the immediate sur-

---

roundings where people live their lives: families, sport clubs, churches, and other similar civil societies. These are the spaces where virtues are learned and practiced.[93] However, our societies are torn in two opposite directions as they try to find public policies that could function in our ever-diversifying situations. On the one hand, we should see plurality as a good thing, but on the other hand, plurality creates a need for more control. The uncritical embrace of plurality would lead to anarchy, while similar attitudes toward order would lead to totalitarianism.

In lived reality, cultural diversity means the existence of mutually opposed civil societies, religions, and other similar groups. This leads us to think that because these groups are the problem, they cannot be the solution. However, giving absolute power to Leviathan makes tolerance redundant: we do not need to tolerate difference because our legislation allows only one particular way of conduct. This leaves us in an uneasy situation. Tolerance means taking a risk, and there are many voices that tell us not to take that risk. The obvious question that follows is this: Does religion make it easier or harder for us to form and re-form our beliefs in ways that the aforementioned virtues are manifested in the process?

Ideologies

An ideology is a set of beliefs and practices that gives shape to a certain group of people. Ideology is not coterminous with community since within the same community there can be different ideologies, and people with the same ideology do not necessarily form a community of their own. Thus ideologies can create conflicts both within a community and between communities. In my taxonomy, ideological conflicts are possible at all levels. Here I cannot offer a substantial account of conflicts in all these levels; I will, instead, approach the issue through a single example.

In his sociological study, Jon Shields observed and analyzed organizations on the Christian Right, especially those involved in abortion debates. Shields, who identifies himself as a liberal Protestant, argues that contrary to widely held beliefs according to which the Christian Right is the movement that endangers the foundations of American democracy, it is first and

93. Adams, *A Theory of Virtue*, 138–43, 228–29; Luke Bretherton, "Religion and the Salvation of Urban Politics," in *Exploring the Postsecular: The Religious, the Political and the Urban*, ed. Arie Molendijk, Justin Beaumont, and Christoph Jedan (Leiden: Brill, 2010), 207–22.

foremost the Christian Right that has been able to mobilize a marginalized minority, challenge mainstream consciousness, and raise the level of debate on matters such as the definition of a human person and the ontological basis for human dignity (goals typically associated with the Left). Shields argues that of all contemporary movements, those associated with the Christian Right teach their members central democratic, deliberative norms, and quite effectively ensure that these norms are maintained in their public appearances. These norms include:

1. The practice of civility and respect.
2. The cultivation of real dialogue by listening and asking questions.
3. The rejection of appeals to theology.
4. The practice of careful moral reasoning.
5. Openness to alternative points of view.[94]

Shields found out that the first four norms are promoted and practiced far more than we are usually led to believe. However, there is a twist. The fifth norm, which is often included among the aforementioned norms by political scientists, is not widely and explicitly encouraged, although there are notable exceptions. For example, pro-life activists can say that they are willing to change their minds if they are given a good argument that demonstrates that there is a fundamental difference between a fetus and a newborn child. Of course, this is a conversation-stopper, since there is no such argument currently available. Nevertheless, Shields contrasts this with pro-choice organizations' statements, according to which they do not engage in dialogue with pro-life groups because abortion is, in their view, a basic human right and therefore not open to debate or negotiation. According to Shields's study, we have reason to believe that, in some contexts, conservative Christian beliefs can foster epistemic and democratic values (at least when compared to the opposing groups) that can be universally recognized, even if the moral values in question are not shared.[95]

Moreover, there are several things about the fifth deliberative norm that need to be understood properly. As we saw in the previous chapter, several political theorists advocate skeptical attitudes when dealing with complicated public matters. According to these views, we should hold our beliefs tentatively and entertain the real possibility that we can be wrong. I

---

94. Jon Shields, *The Democratic Virtues of the Christian Right* (Princeton: Princeton University Press, 2009), Kindle ed. loc. 295 of 2888.

95. Of course, there are also pro-life atheists and members of other religions.

have already partly discussed this issue from the epistemic point of view in the previous chapter, so I will not revisit those aspects again. Suffice it to say, in order to further a public cause, we simply need to sustain relatively high levels of certainty in order to act in the first place. If we are skeptical, we will do nothing, thereby letting the status quo prevail. If people act, they will act with confidence, and there should be nothing wrong with that—if they are able live according to the first four norms.

In fact, it could be argued that following the fifth norm should be a natural consequence of the first four norms. Even if they are not willing to admit that they might actually be wrong, they can show open-mindedness by promoting civilized norms of conversation, which may lead to belief revision at some point. As argued before, we should be open to alternative viewpoints only if we have good reason to do so. Acting otherwise would be a clear violation of our epistemic norms.

This connects with the recent debates on "civility." In the current American and European discussion concerning free speech and its limits, there have been suggestions that freedom of expression should be limited by civility.[96] Thus anything whatsoever cannot be said because one's message must fulfill certain criteria. I can see the motivation behind this suggestion, and I think the virtue of civility should, of course, be endorsed. But the suggestion has some obvious problems as it stands. Critics have already pointed out how civility itself is a relatively opaque virtue and that it can be effectively used to silence dissent—by labeling it as "hate speech." If the message of group *a* is categorized as uncivil or hateful, their right to have a voice is denied—this has already happened. Consequently, some topics that should be discussed in public become almost impossible to discuss in a reasonable manner. As G. K. Chesterton noted, "The old restriction meant that only the orthodox were allowed to discuss religion. Modern liberty means that nobody is allowed to discuss it. Good taste, the last and vilest of human superstitions, has succeeded in silencing us where all the rest have failed."[97]

In several UK universities, there have been so-called No Platform votes for all kinds of groups and societies. For example, several pro-life student organizations have experienced attempts to limit their access to student happenings, like the Fresher's Fair, and University College London banned

96. See, e.g., Henry Reichman, "Civility and Free Speech," *Inside Higher Ed*, October 12, 2011, https://www.insidehighered.com/views/2014/10/14/essay-argues-recent-statements-college-leaders-about-civility-are-threat-academic.

97. G. K. Chesterton, *Heretics*, in *Collected Works*, vol. 1, *Heretics, Orthodoxy, The Blatchford Controversies* (San Francisco: Ignatius, 1986), 41.

the Nietzsche Club as a harmful institution.[98] In 2014, journalist Brendan O'Neill was supposed to argue for the pro-choice view in an Oxford debate, but the debate was canceled due to student protests. Looking back at the discussion surrounding the debate that never took place, O'Neill observes that the students believe they have "a right to feel comfortable." He calls this group of young people "Stepford students" to signify their remarkable likeness to post-1960s right-wing movements that tried to pursue similar goals by censoring movies, music, television programs, and plays that they found offensive. Ironically, the Left now cherishes these same attitudes.[99]

Perplexingly, the will to promote particular virtues seems to have created this situation, which is far from virtuous. Yet again, the problem seems to be the disunity of virtues. Stepford students recognize a limited set of virtues, which skews their approach to contested issues. Effectively, they fail to represent several civic virtues by resorting to shaming and manipulation.

An additional problem here is the arbitrariness of civility in this context. Why should we choose this particular virtue and not, for example, conscientiousness? Why is "the right to feel comfortable" considered higher than the obligation to foster epistemic practices that aim toward truth and understanding? It is blatantly obvious that avoiding information that makes one uncomfortable is a vicious epistemic practice. Naturally, there are times when people are within their rights to avoid such situations, for example, when their psychological state is incapable of handling cognitive dissonance, but as a general policy it is hard to see it as anything but dangerous. The reason is simple: avoiding uncomfortable information is not a truth-tracking epistemic process, while exposing oneself to contrary positions is.

Concentrating on merely one particular virtue tends to escalate the conflict. As noted, it would be better to approach the problem from the point of view of the unity of virtues. If several other virtues are present, we should be able to suffer from incivility or forms of speech that make us uncomfortable. Against this purview, it is sometimes possible to use indecorous modes of speech. Of course, here one should be able to distinguish between anger and wrath, the latter being a vicious form of anger. Anger can

---

98. A funny detail concerning the Nietzsche ban was that the person seeking the ban was the president of the University College Marxist Society. Nico Hines, "University College London's Nietzsche Club Is Banned," June 5, 2014, http://www.thedailybeast.com/arti cles/2014/06/05/university-college-london-s-nietzsche-club-is-banned.html.

99. Brendan O'Neill, "Free Speech Is So Last Century," *The Spectator*, November 22, 2014, http://www.spectator.co.uk/features/9376232/free-speech-is-so-last-century-todays -students-want-the-right-to-be-comfortable/.

be virtuous if it does not create negative reaction that shuts down dialogue or create more resentment than understanding. There must be a reasonable chance of success. Contrariwise, wrath or vicious anger is impulsive and does not express conscious reflection.[100] An example of virtuous anger is Martin Luther King Jr.'s famous "I have a dream" speech, which has a section where he goes on the offensive.[101] Here, King takes a risk and gets personal. Yet, all things considered, he manifests a wide array of civic virtues.

Identities

Last, I want to consider the reality of disagreement from the viewpoint of an individual person. This angle pertains to all levels of disagreement in the taxonomy. What I have in mind is illustrated by Rowan Williams.

> If another Christian comes to a different conclusion and decides in different ways from myself, and if I can still recognize their discipline and practice as sufficiently like mine to sustain a conversation, this leaves my own decisions to some extent under question. I cannot have absolute subjective certainty that this is the only imaginable reading of the tradition; I need to keep my reflections under critical review. This, I must emphasise again, this is not a form of relativism; it is a recognition of the element of putting oneself at risk that is involved in any serious decision-making or any serious exercise of discernment (as any pastor or confessor will know). But this is only part of the implication of recognizing the differences and risks of decision-making in the Body of Christ. If I conclude that my Christian brother or sister is deeply and damagingly mistaken in their decision, I accept for myself the brokenness in the Body that this entails.[102]

100. Zac Cogley, "A Study of Virtuous and Vicious Anger," in Timpe and Boyd, *Virtues and Their Vices*, 199–24.

101. Martin Luther King Jr., *I Have A Dream: Writings and Speeches That Changed the World*, ed. James M. Washington (San Francisco: HarperSanFrancisco, 1992), 105. "I have a dream that one day, down in Alabama, with its vicious racists, with its governor having his lips dripping with the words of interposition and nullification, that one day, right here in Alabama, little black boys and black girls will be able to join hands with little white boys and white girls as sisters and brothers."

102. Rowan Williams, "Making Moral Decisions," in *The Cambridge Companion to Christian Ethics*, ed. Robin Gill, 2nd ed. (Cambridge: Cambridge University Press, 2012), 11.

Williams argues that this attitude persists as long as we are able to recognize the other as a speaker of the same language and engaging "the same given data of faith." Being a member of the body of Christ means being a member of a broken body, where we see numerous errors. As concrete examples, Williams lists Christians who have supported slavery, torture, and the execution of heretics. It is not an option (although it is a temptation) to renounce them and remove them from the membership of the body, but that is not a sustainable solution because they have manifestly engaged in the same practices and argued for their cause using the same sources as the so-called genuine members of the body.[103]

Living in a broken body requires a virtuous mind-set. It is not easy, however, and often we would like to avoid this situation. Stimulatingly, Nigel Biggar asks, are not these *the* moments when the church should be able to offer witness to the world, how it deals with disagreements? Biggar argues, "The way churches conduct their own internal controversies is a vital test of their own integrity, a vital part of their witness to the rest of the world, and a vital part of their contribution to its wellbeing." Controversies are thus "major opportunities for the Christian churches to become what they should be, to embody what they believe, to bear theological witness in the manner of their being, and to offer a salutary and hopeful example to the rest of the world."[104]

But what if I cannot recognize the other as engaging in the same activities? Then the voice we hear comes to us from a distance. But this does not mean the voice is meaningless or that we are allowed to brush it aside. Granted, hearing the voice may require great effort from us, some of which does not come easily. Biggar offers a list of practices that illustrate well how debiasing should work.

> The Christian will regard the other as a fellow creature who also stands in relationship to God, but whose relationship is immediate, inimitable, and different from her own. She will recognize that the other's vocation is uniquely the other's. She will cede the other space, acknowledging his difference. She will approach him as a potential prophet, as one who might yet mediate a true word of God. In this theological sense, there-

---

103. Williams, "Making Moral Decisions," 10–13. See also Wesley A. Kort, *Bound to Differ: The Dynamics of Theological Discourse* (University Park: Pennsylvania State University Press, 1992), 121–42.

104. Nigel Biggar, *Behaving in Public: How to Do Christian Ethics* (Grand Rapids: Eerdmans, 2011), 76–77.

fore, she will respect the other as equal—and yet not the same. She will not assume that he has nothing worth saying. She will not presume to know what the other thinks before she has first bothered to inquire and listen. She will not stereotype or caricature him. She will not assimilate him to some ideal type, for example, "liberal," or "modernist" or "conservative" or "fundamentalist." Instead, she will listen to his particular, complex, idiosyncratic, and unpredictable views, which refuse easy accommodation in any prefabricated box. She will respect the other by taking him as he actually comes.[105]

Williams and Biggar offer a view of communication between members of a shared fallen world. The view is not rose-colored, and its requirement is not easy. However, we cannot hope for anything better. Given what we know about our history, and ourselves as thinkers, ending disagreements is not an option. What we are left with is a fragile hope, which often seems utopian, yet sometimes it surprises us through the examples of those of us who have mastered the art of wisdom.

105. Biggar, *Behaving in Public*, 72.

Bibliography

Adams, Robert Merrihew. *A Theory of Virtue. Excellence in Being for the Good.* Oxford: Oxford University Press, 2006.

Allport, G. W., and Ross, J. M. "Personal Religious Orientation and Prejudice." *Journal of Personality and Social Psychology* 5 (1967): 432–43.

Alston, William. *Beyond "Justification": Dimensions of Epistemic Valuation.* Ithaca, NY: Cornell University Press, 2005.

Anderson, Craig A., Mark R. Lepper, and Lee Ross. "Perseverance of Social Theories: The Role of Explanation in the Persistence of Discredited Information." *Journal of Personality and Social Psychology* 39 (1980): 1037–49.

Aristotle. *De Anima.* Translated by D. W. Hamlyn. Oxford: Clarendon, 1968.

———. *Introductory Readings.* Translated by Terence Irwin. Indianapolis: Hackett Publishing, 1966.

———. *Nicomachean Ethics.* Translated by J. A. K. Thomson. London: Penguin, 1955.

———. *Politics.* Translated by Benjamin Jowett. Blacksburg: Virginia Tech, 2001.

Atran, Scott. *Talking to the Enemy: Violent Extremism, Sacred Values and What It Means to Be Human.* London: Allen Lane 2010.

Audi, Robert. *The Architecture of Reason: The Structure and Substance of Rationality.* Oxford: Oxford University Press, 2001.

———. "Cognitive Disparities: Dimensions of Intellectual Diversity and the Resolution of Disagreements." In *The Epistemology of Disagreement: New Essays*, edited by David Christensen and Jennifer Lackey, 205–22. Oxford: Oxford University Press, 2013.

———. *Rationality and Religious Commitment.* New York: Oxford University Press, 2011.

Augustine. *The City of God.* In *A Select Library of Nicene and Post-Nicene Fathers of the Church.* Vol. 2, series 1, *St. Augustin's "City of God" and "Christian Doctrine."* Edited by Philip Schaff. Translated by Marcus Dods. 1886–1889. Reprint, Peabody, MA: Hendrickson, 1994.

———. *Confessions.* Translated by Albert C. Outler. 1955. Reprint, New York: Barnes & Noble Classics, 2007.

———. *On Christian Teaching*. Translated by R. P. H. Green. Oxford: Oxford University Press, 1997.

Aukst-Margetić, B., and B. Margetić. "Religiosity and Health Outcomes: Review of Literature." *Collective Anthropology* 29 (2005): 365–71.

Austen, Ben. "Public Enemies: Social Media Is Fueling Gang Wars in Chicago." *Wired*. September 17, 2013. http://www.wired.com/underwire/2013/09/gangs-of-social-media/all/.

Austin, Greg, Todd Kranock, and Thom Oommen. "God and War: An Audit and an Exploration." BBC. 2003. http://news.bbc.co.uk/2/shared/spl/hi/world/04/war_audit_pdf/pdf/war_audit.pdf.

Babcock, Linda, and George Loewenstein. "Explaining Bargaining Impasse: The Role of Self-Serving Biases." *Journal of Economic Perspectives* 11 (1997): 109–26.

Bacon, Francis. *Selected Philosophical Works*. Edited by Rose-Mary Sargent. Indianapolis: Hackett, 1999.

Baehr, Jason. "Evidentialism, Vice, and Virtue." In *Evidentialism and Its Discontents*, edited by Trent Dougherty, 88–101. Oxford: Oxford University Press, 2011.

———. *The Inquiring Mind: On Intellectual Virtues and Virtue Epistemology*. Oxford: Oxford University Press, 2011.

Baron-Cohen, Simon. "I Cannot Tell a Lie." *In Character* 3 (Spring 2007): 53–55.

Barrett, Justin L. *Cognitive Science, Religion, and Theology: From Human Minds to Divine Minds*. West Conshohocken, PA: Templeton Press 2011.

———. *Why Would Anyone Believe in God?* Walnut Creek, CA: Altamira, 2004.

Basinger, David. *Religious Diversity: A Philosophical Assessment*. Burlington, VT: Ashgate, 2002.

Batson, C. Daniel. "Individual Religion, Tolerance and Universal Compassion." In *Religion, Intolerance, and Conflict: A Scientific and Conceptual Investigation*, edited by Steve Clarke, Russell Powell, and Julian Savulescu, 88–106. Oxford: Oxford University Press, 2013.

———. *Religion and the Individual: A Social-Psychological Perspective*. Oxford: Oxford University Press, 1993.

Bayer, Oswald. *A Contemporary in Dissent: Johann Georg Hamann as a Radical Enlightener*. Grand Rapids: Eerdmans, 2012.

Berger, Peter. *The Heretical Imperative: Contemporary Possibilities of Religious Affirmation*. Garden City, NY: Anchor, 1980.

———. "Introduction: Between Relativism and Fundamentalism." In *Between Relativism and Fundamentalism: Religious Resources for a Middle Position*, edited by Peter Berger, 1–16. Grand Rapids: Eerdmans, 2009.

Berger, Peter L., and Anton J. Zijverfeld. *In Praise of Doubt: How to Have Convictions without Becoming a Fanatic*. San Francisco: HarperOne, 2009.

Bergmann, Michael. "Rational Disagreement after Full Disclosure." *Episteme* 6 (2009): 336–53.

Berker, Selim. "The Normative Insignificance of Neuroscience." *Philosophy and Public Affairs* 37, no. 4 (2009): 293–329.

Berlin, Isaiah. *The Magus of the North: J. G. Hamann and the Origins of Modern Irratio-nalism*. London: Fontana, 1994.

Betz, John. *After Enlightenment: The Post-secular Vision of J. G. Hamann*. Oxford: Wi-ley-Blackwell, 2009.

Biggar, Nigel. *Behaving in Public: How to Do Christian Ethics*. Grand Rapids: Eerdmans, 2011.

Biggar, Nigel, and Linda Hogan. *Religious Voices in Public Places*. Oxford: Oxford Uni-versity Press 2009.

Bogardus, Tomas. "The Vindication of Equal Weight View." *Episteme* 6 (2009): 324–35.

Boghossian, Paul. *Fear of Knowledge: Against Relativism and Constructivism*. Oxford: Oxford University Press, 2007.

Botterill, George, and Peter Carruthers. *The Philosophy of Psychology*. Cambridge: Cam-bridge University Press, 1999.

Bowlin, John. "Nature, Grace, and Toleration: Civil Society and the Twinned Church." *Annual of the Society of Christian Ethics* 21 (2001): 85–104.

———. "Tolerance among the Fathers." *Journal of the Society of Christian Ethics* 26 (2006): 3–36.

Brandom, Robert B., ed. *Rorty and His Critics*. Oxford: Blackwell, 2000.

Bretherton, Luke. "Religion and the Salvation of Urban Politics." In *Exploring the Post-secular: The Religious, the Political and the Urban*, edited by Arie Molendijk, Justin Beaumont, and Christoph Jedan, 205–21. Leiden: Brill, 2010.

Buchak, Lara. "Rational Faith and Justified Belief." In *Religious Faith and Intellectual Virtue*, edited by Laura F. Callahan and Timothy O'Connor, 49–75. Oxford: Oxford University Press, 2014.

Bullens, Lottie, Frenk van Harreveld, and Jens Förster. "Keeping One's Options Open: The Detrimental Consequences of Decision Reversibility." *Journal of Experimental Social Psychology* 47 (2011): 800–805.

Byrne, Peter. *God and Realism*. Aldershot: Ashgate, 2003.

Campbell, Bradley, and Jason Manning. "Microaggressions and Moral Cultures." *Com-parative Sociology* 13 (2014): 692–726.

Cary, Phillip. *Outward Signs: The Powerlessness of External Things in Augustine's Thought*. New York: Oxford University Press, 2008.

———. "United Inwardly by Love: Augustine's Social Ontology." In *Augustine and Pol-itics*, edited by John Doody, Kevin L. Hughes, and Kim Paffenroth, 3–33. Lanham MD: Lexington, 2004.

Cavanaugh, William T. *The Myth of Religious Violence*. Oxford: Oxford University Press, 2009.

Chambers, Simone. "Who Shall Judge? Hobbes, Locke and Kant on the Construction of Public Reason." *Ethics and Global Politics* 2, no. 4 (2009): 349–68.

Chesterton, G. K. *Collected Works*. Vol. 1, *Heretics, Orthodoxy, The Blatchford Controver-sies*. San Francisco: Ignatius, 1986.

———. *Orthodoxy*. Charlotte: Saint Benedict Press, 2006.

Chignell, Andrew. "'As Kant Has Shown . . .': Analytic Theology and the Critical Philosophy." In *Analytic Theology: New Essays in the Philosophy of Theology*, edited by Oliver Crisp and Michael Rea, 117–35. Oxford: Oxford University Press, 2009.

Christensen, David, and Jennifer Lackey, eds. *The Epistemology of Disagreement: New Essays*. Oxford: Oxford University Press, 2013.

Clark, Kelly James. "Calling Abraham's Children." In *Abraham's Children: Liberty and Tolerance in an Age of Religious Conflict*, edited by Kelly James Clark, 1–20. New Haven: Yale University Press, 2012.

Clark, Maudemarie. *Nietzsche on Truth and Philosophy*. Cambridge: Cambridge University Press, 1990.

Clarke, Steve. *The Justification of Religious Violence*. Malden, MA: Wiley-Blackwell, 2014.

Clarke, Steve, Russell Powell, and Julian Savulescu, eds. *Religion, Intolerance, and Conflict: A Scientific and Conceptual Investigation*. Oxford: Oxford University Press, 2013.

Cleveland, Christena. *Disunity in Christ: Uncovering the Hidden Forces that Keep Us Apart*. Downers Grove: IVP Books, 2013.

Clor, Harry. *On Moderation: Defending an Ancient Virtue in a Modern World*. Waco: Baylor University Press, 2008.

Coady, C. A. J. "Violence and Religion." *Revue International de Philosophie* 265 (2013): 237–57.

Cogley, Zac. "A Study of Virtuous and Vicious Anger." In *Virtues and Their Vices*, edited by Kevin Timpe and Craig Boyd, 199–224. Oxford: Oxford University Press, 2012.

Cohen, Andrew J. "What Toleration Is." *Ethics* 115 (2004): 68–95.

Collins, Randall. *Sociology of Philosophies: The Global Theory of Intellectual Change*. Cambridge, MA: Belknap Press of Harvard University Press, 1998.

Conee, Earl. "Peerage." *Episteme* 6 (2009): 313–23.

Copan, Paul, and Matt Flanagan. *Did God Really Command Genocide? Coming to Terms with the Justice of God*. Grand Rapids: Baker Books, 2014.

Coxon, A. H. *The Fragments of Parmenides*. Assen: Van Gorcum, 1986.

Craig, William Lane. "Is Uncertainty a Sound Foundation for Religious Tolerance?" In *Religious Tolerance through Humility*, edited by James Kraft and David Basinger, 13–28. Farnham, UK: Ashgate, 2008.

Danziger, Shai, Jonathan Levav, and Liora Avnaim-Pesso. "Extraneous Factors in Judicial Decisions." *Proceedings of the National Academy of Sciences* 108, no. 17 (2011): 6889–92.

De Cruz, Helen. "Irrelevant Influences and Philosophical Practice: A Qualitative Study." (forthcoming; available for download at https://www.academia.edu/14876793/Irrelevant_influences_and_philosophical_practice_A_qualitative_study).

———. "Religious Disagreement: An Empirical Study among Academic Philosophers." *Episteme* (2015): 1–17.

Denyer, Nicholas. *Language, Thought and Falsehood in Ancient Greek Philosophy*. London: Routledge, 1991.

Descartes, René. *Discourse on the Method of Rightly Conducting One's Reason and Seeking Truth in the Sciences*. Translated by Jonathan Bennett. Some Texts from Early Modern Philosophy. Last revised 2007. http://earlymoderntexts.com/assets/pdfs/descartes1637.pdf.

————. *Principles of Philosophy*. Translated by Jonathan Bennett. Some Texts from Early Modern Philosophy. Last revised 2012. http://earlymoderntexts.com/assets/pdfs/descartes1644.pdf.

Doris, John. *Lack of Character: Personality and Moral Behavior*. Cambridge: Cambridge University Press, 2002.

Dougherty, Trent. "Reducing Responsibility: An Evidentialist Account of Epistemic Blame." *European Journal of Philosophy* 20 (2010): 534–47.

Elgin, Catherine. "Persistent Disagreement." In *Disagreement*, edited by Richard Feldman and Ted Warfield, 53–68. Oxford: Oxford University Press, 2010.

Elliot, Anthony. *Concepts of the Self*. 2nd ed. Cambridge: Polity, 2009.

Evans, Jonathan St. B. T. "Dual-Processing Accounts of Reasoning, Judgment, and Social Cognition." *Annual Review of Psychology* 58 (2008): 255–78.

————. "In Two Minds: Dual-Process Accounts of Reasoning." *Trends in Cognitive Science* 10 (2003): 454–59.

Evans, Jonathan St. B. T., and Keith E. Stanovich. "Dual-Process Theories of Higher Cognition: Advancing the Debate." *Perspectives on Psychological Science* 8 (2013): 223–41.

Eze, Emmanuel Ugwudi. *On Reason: Rationality in a World of Cultural Conflict and Racism*. Durham: Duke University Press, 2008.

Feldman, Richard. "Reasonable Religious Disagreements." In *Philosophers without Gods: Meditations on Atheism and the Secular Life*, edited by Louise M. Antony, 194–214. New York: Oxford University Press, 2010.

Feldman, Richard, and Ted A. Warfield, eds. *Disagreement*. Oxford: Oxford University Press, 2010.

Feltz, Adam, and Edward Cokely. "Predicting Philosophical Disagreements." *Philosophy Compass* 8, no. 10 (2013): 978–89.

Ferguson, Christopher J., and Cheryl K. Olson. "Video Game Violence among 'Vulnerable' Populations: The Impact of Violent Games on Delinquency and Bullying among Children with Clinically Elevated Depression or Attention Deficit Symptoms." *Journal of Youth and Adolescence* 43 (2014): 127–36.

Foucault, Michel. "The Meaning and Evolution of the Word Parrhesia." In *Discourse and Truth: The Problematization of Parrhesia*, edited by Joseph Pearson. *Foucault, Info*. 1999. http://foucault.info/doc/documents/parrhesia/foucault-dt1-wordparrhesia-en-html.

Fricker, Miranda. *Epistemic Injustice*. Oxford: Oxford University Press, 2007.

Gaita, Raimond. *A Common Humanity: Thinking about Love and Truth and Justice*. London: Routledge, 2000.

Gigerenzer, Gerd. "Bounded and Rational." In *Contemporary Debates in Cognitive Science*, edited by Robert J. Stainton, 115–33. Oxford: Blackwell, 2006.

————. *Rationality for Mortals: How People Cope with Uncertainty*. Oxford: Oxford University Press, 2010.

Gioia, Luigi. *The Theological Epistemology of Augustine's "De Trinitate."* Oxford: Oxford University Press, 2008.

Goodreau, John R. "Kant's Contribution to the Idea of Democratic Pluralism." In *Reas-*

sessing the Liberal State: Reading Maritain's "Man and the State," edited by Timothy Fuller and John P. Hittinger, 99–126. Washington, DC: Catholic University of America Press, 2006.

Gough, John Wiedhoft. "The Development of Locke's Belief in Toleration." In *John Locke, "A Letter Concerning Toleration" in Focus*, edited by John Horton and Susan Mendus, 57–77. London: Routledge, 1991.

Graham, Jesse, Jonathan Haidt, and Brian A. Nosek. "Liberals and Conservatives Rely on Different Sets of Moral Foundations." *Journal of Personality and Social Psychology* 96 (2009): 1029–46.

Gregory, Eric. "Before the Original Position: The Neo-orthodox Theology of the Young John Rawls." *Journal of Religious Ethics* 35 (2007): 179–206.

———. *Politics and the Order of Love: An Augustinian Ethic of Democratic Citizenship.* Chicago: University of Chicago Press, 2010.

Griffiths, Paul J. "How Reasoning Goes Wrong: A Quasi-Augustinian Account of Error and Its Implications." In *Reasons and the Reasons of Faith*, edited by Paul J. Griffiths and Reinhard Hütter, 145–59. New York: T&T Clark, 2005.

Griffiths, Paul E., and John S. Wilkins. "Evolutionary Debunking Arguments in Three Domains: Fact, Value, and Religion." In *A New Science of Religion*, edited by Gregory W. Dawes and James Maclaurin, 133–46. New York: Routledge, 2013.

Grigoriev, Serge. "Rorty, Religion and Humanism." *International Journal for Philosophy of Religion* 70 (2011): 187–201.

Gutting, Gary. *What Philosophers Know.* Cambridge: Cambridge University Press, 2009.

Haidt, Jonathan. "The Positive Emotion of Elevation." *Prevention and Treatment* 3 (2000): http://faculty.virginia.edu/haidtlab/articles/haidt.2000.the-positive -emotion-of-elevation.pub020.pdf.

———. *The Righteous Mind: Why Good People Are Divided by Politics and Religion.* London: Allen Lane, 2012.

Hamann, Johann Georg. *Aesthetica in Nuce.* In *Writings on Philosophy and Language.* Translated by Kenneth Hayes. Cambridge Texts in the History of Philosophy. Cambridge: Cambridge University Press, 2007.

Harman, Gilbert. "Moral Philosophy Meets Social Psychology: Virtue Ethics and the Fundamental Attribution Error." *Proceedings of the Aristotelian Society* 99 (1999): 315–31.

———. "Practical Aspects of Theoretical Reasoning." In *The Oxford Handbook of Rationality*, edited by Alfred E. Mele and Piers Rawling, 45–56. Oxford: Oxford University Press, 2004.

Harrison, Peter. *The Fall of Man and the Foundations of Science.* Cambridge: Cambridge University Press, 2007.

———. "Original Sin and the Problem of Knowledge in Early Modern Europe." *Journal of the History of Ideas* 63 (2002): 239–59.

Harrison, Victoria. "Religious Diversity." In *The Routledge Companion to Theism*, edited by Charles Taliaferro, Victoria S. Harrison, and Stewart Goetz, 477–90. London: Routledge, 2013.

Hart, David Bentley. *The Experience of God: Being, Consciousness, Bliss*. New Haven: Yale University Press, 2014.

Hart, Paul T. *Groupthink in Government: A Study of Small Groups and Policy Failure*. Baltimore: Johns Hopkins University Press, 1994.

Hartshorne, Hugh, and Mark A. May. *Studies in the Nature of Character*. Vol. 1, *Studies in Deceit*. New York: Macmillan, 1928.

Haskins, Ekaterina. "Endoxa, Epistemological Optimism, and Aristotle's Rhetorical Project." *Philosophy and Rhetoric* 37 (2004): 1–20.

Hauerwas, Stanley. *Hannah's Child: A Theologian's Memoir*. Grand Rapids: Eerdmans, 2010.

Helm, Paul. *Faith with Reason*. Oxford: Oxford University Press, 2000.

Herdt, Jennifer. *Putting on Virtue: The Legacy of the Splendid Vices*. Chicago: University of Chicago Press, 2008.

Hermans, Hubert. "The Dialogical Self." In *The Oxford Handbook of the Self*, edited by Shaun Gallagher, 671–77. Oxford: Oxford University Press, 2011.

Hermans, Hubert, and Agnieszka Hermans-Konopka. *Dialogical Self Theory: Positioning and Counter-positioning in a Global Society*. Cambridge: Cambridge University Press, 2012.

Hines, Nico. "University College London's Nietzsche Club Is Banned." *Daily Beast*. June 5, 2014. http://www.thedailybeast.com/articles/2014/06/05/university-college-london-s-nietzsche-club-is-banned.html.

Hobbes, Thomas. *Leviathan*. Edited by J. C. A. Gaskin. Oxford: Oxford University Press, 1996.

Hogan, Robert. "Much Ado about Nothing: The Person-Situation Debate." *Journal of Research in Personality* 43 (2009): 249.

Horton, John, "Toleration." In *Routledge Encyclopedia of Philosophy*, ed. Edward Craig, 9:429–33. London: Routledge, 1998.

Hunter, James Davison. "Fundamentalism and Relativism Together: Reflections on a Genealogy." In *Between Relativism and Fundamentalism: Religious Resources for a Middle Position*, edited by Peter Berger, 17–34. Grand Rapids: Eerdmans, 2009.

———. *To Change the World: The Irony, Tragedy, and Possibility of Christianity in the Late Modern World*. New York: Oxford University Press, 2010.

Hursthouse, Rosalind. "Virtue Ethics." In *Stanford Encyclopedia of Philosophy*, edited by Edward N. Zalta. Fall 2013 ed. http://plato.stanford.edu/archives/fall2013/entries/ethics-virtue/.

Hütter, Reinhard. *Bound to Be Free: Evangelical Catholic Engagements in Ecclesiology, Ethics, and Ecumenics*. Grand Rapids: Eerdmans, 2004.

———. "The Directedness of Reasoning and the Metaphysics of Creation." In *Reason and the Reasons of Faith*, edited by Paul Griffiths and Reinhard Hütter, 160–93. London: T&T Clark, 2005.

Hyussteen, Wentzel van, and Erik Wiebe. *In Search of the Self: Interdisciplinary Perspectives in Personhood*. Grand Rapids: Eerdmans, 2011.

Inwagen, Peter van. "Is It Wrong Everywhere, Always, and for Everyone to Believe Anything on Insufficient Evidence?" In *Faith, Freedom, and Rationality*, edited by Jeff

Jordan and Daniel Howard-Snyder, 137–53. Lanham, MD: Rowman & Littlefield, 1996.

———. *The Problem of Evil*. Oxford: Oxford University Press, 2006.

———. "We're Right. They're Wrong." In *Disagreement*, edited by Richard Feldman and Ted Warfield, 10–28. Oxford: Oxford University Press, 2010.

Jaeggi, Susanne M., Martin Buschkuehl, John Jonides, and Walter J. Perrig. "Improving Fluid Intelligence with Training on Working Memory." *Proceedings of the National Academy of Sciences* 28 (2008): 6829–33.

———. "Short- and Long-Term Benefits of Cognitive Training." *Proceedings of the National Academy of Sciences* 108 (2011): 10081–86.

Jeeves, Malcolm, and Warren S. Brown. *Neuroscience, Psychology and Religion: Illusions, Delusions, and Realities about Human Nature*. West Conshohocken, PA: Templeton Press, 2009.

Jenkins, Philip. *The New Anti-Catholicism: The Last Acceptable Prejudice*. New York: Oxford University Press, 2003.

John Paul II. *Fides et Ratio*. The Vatican website. 1998. http://w2.vatican.va/content/john-paul-ii/en/encyclicals/documents/hf_jp-ii_enc_14091998_fides-et-ratio.html.

Johnson-Laird, Philip. *How We Reason*. Oxford: Oxford University Press, 2006.

Jong, Jonathan, and Aku Visala. "Evolutionary Debunking Arguments against Theism, Reconsidered." *International Journal of Philosophy of Religion* (2014): 243–58.

Jonkers, Peter. "Can Freedom of Religion Replace the Virtue of Tolerance?" In *From Political Theory to Political Theology: Religious Challenges and the Prospects of Democracy*, edited by Peter Losonczi and Aakash Singh, 73–84. London: Continuum, 2010.

Jost, John T., and Lawrence T. Jost. "Virtue Ethics and the Social Psychology of Character: Philosophical Lessons from the Person-Situation Debate." *Journal of Research in Personality* 43 (2009): 252–54.

Juergensmeyer, Mark. *Terror in the Mind of God: The Global Rise of Religious Violence*. Berkeley: University of California Press, 2000.

Kahan, Dan M., Ellen Peters, Maggie Wittlin, Paul Slovic, Lisa Larrimore Ouellette, Donald Braman, and Gregory Mandel. "The Polarizing Impact of Science Literacy and Numeracy on Perceived Climate Change Risks." *Nature Climate Change* 2 (2012): 732–35.

Kahane, Guy. "Evolutionary Debunking Arguments." *Nous* 45 (2010): 103–25.

Kahneman, Daniel. *Thinking, Fast and Slow*. London: Allen Lane, 2011.

Kant, Immanuel. *Critique of Pure Reason*. Translated by Francis Haywood. London: Living Time Press, 2004.

———. *Political Writings*. Edited by H. S. Reiss. Cambridge Texts in the History of Political Thought. Cambridge: Cambridge University Press, 1991.

———. *Religion within the Bounds of Bare Reason Alone*. Translated by Werner S. Pluhar. Indianapolis: Hackett, 2009.

———. "Toward Perpetual Peace." In *"Toward Perpetual Peace" and Other Writings on Politics, Peace, and History*, edited by Pauline Kleingeld. Translated by David L. Coldclasure. New Haven: Yale University Press, 2006.

Kearney, Richard. *On Paul Ricoeur: The Owl of Minerva*. Aldershot: Ashgate, 2004.

Kelly, Thomas. "Disagreement, Dogmatism, and Belief Polarization." *Journal of Philosophy* 105 (2008): 611–33.

Kenny, Anthony. *A New History of Western Philosophy*. Oxford: Oxford University Press, 2011.

Keren, Gideon, and Yaachoc Schul. "Two Is Not Always Better Than One." *Perspectives on Psychological Science* 6 (2009): 533–50.

Khan, Carrie-Ann Biondi. "Aristotle's Moral Expert: The *Phronimos*." In *Ethics Expertise: History, Contemporary Perspectives and Applications*, edited by Lisa Rasmussen, 39–53. Dordrecht: Springer, 2005.

Kidd, Ian J. "Epistemic Vices in Public Debate: The Case of 'New Atheism.'" In *New Atheism's Legacy: Critical Perspectives from Philosophy and the Social Sciences*, edited by Christopher Cotter and Philip Quadrio. Dordrecht: Springer, forthcoming.

Kim, Joseph. *Reformed Epistemology and the Problem of Religious Diversity*. Eugene, OR: Pickwick, 2011.

King, Nathan. "Disagreement: What's the Problem? Or A Good Peer Is Hard to Find." *Philosophy and Phenomenological Research* 85 (2012): 249–72.

———. "Religious Diversity and Its Challenges to Religious Belief." *Philosophy Compass* 4 (2008): 830–53.

Kiper, Jordan, and Richard Sosis. "Moral Intuitions and the Religious System: An Adaptationist Account." *Philosophy, Theology and the Sciences* 2 (2014): 172–99.

Kirk, G. S., J. E. Raven, and M. Schofield. *The Presocratic Philosophers: A Critical History with a Selection of Texts*. 2nd ed. Cambridge: Cambridge University Press, 1983.

Klosko, George. "Plato's Political Philosophy." In *The Routledge Companion to Social and Political Philosophy*, edited by Gerald Gaus and Fred D'Agostino, 3–13. London: Routledge, 2013.

Knepper, Timothy D. *Negating Negation: Against the Apophatic Abandonment of the Dionysian Corpus*. Eugene, OR: Cascade, 2014.

Koenig, Harold G., Dana E. King, and Verna Benner Carson. *Handbook of Religion and Health: A Century of Research Reviewed*. New York: Oxford University Press, 2001.

Kornblith, Hilary. "Belief in the Face of Controversy." In *Disagreement*, edited by Richard Feldman and Ted A. Warfield, 29–52. Oxford: Oxford University Press, 2010.

Kort, Wesley A. *Bound to Differ: The Dynamics of Theological Discourse*. University Park: Pennsylvania State University Press, 1992.

Kuhn, Deanna, Eric Amsel, and Michael O'Loughlin. *The Development of Scientific Thinking Skills*. San Diego: Harcourt, Brace, 1988.

Kurzban, Robert. *Why Everyone (Else) Is a Hypocrite: Evolution and the Modular Mind*. Princeton: Princeton University Press, 2010.

Kraft, James. "Religious Tolerance through Religious Diversity and Epistemic Humility." *Sophia* 45 (2006): 101–16.

Kraft, James, and David Basinger, eds. *Religious Tolerance through Humility: Thinking with Philip Quinn*. Farnham, UK: Ashgate, 2008.

Kristjánsson, Kristján. *Virtues and Vices in Positive Psychology*. Cambridge: Cambridge University Press, 2013.

Kruglanski, Arie W., Antonio Pierro, Lucia Mannetti, and Eraldo De Grada. "Groups as Epistemic Providers: Need for Closure and the Unfolding of Group-Centrism." *Psychological Review* 113 (2006): 84–100.

Kruglanski, Arie W., and Gerd Gigerenzer. "Intuitive and Deliberative Judgments Are Based on Common Principles." *Psychological Review* 118 (2011): 97–109.

Kvanvig, Jonathan. "Affective Theism and People of Faith." *Midwest Studies in Philosophy* 27 (2013): 109–28.

Lackey, Jennifer. "Taking Religious Disagreements Seriously." In *Religious Faith and Intellectual Virtue*, edited by Laura Frances Callahan and Timothy O'Connor, 299–316. Oxford: Oxford University Press, 2014.

Larrick, Richard P. "Debiasing." In *The Blackwell Handbook of Judgment and Decision Making*, edited by Derek Koehler and Nigel Harvey, 316–37. Oxford: Blackwell, 2004.

Leiter, Brian. "Perspectivism in Nietzsche's *Genealogy of Morals*." In *Nietzsche, Genealogy, Morality: Essays on Nietzsche's "On the Genealogy of Morals,"* edited by Richard Schacht, 334–54. Berkeley: University of California Press, 1994.

Levin, Shana, and Jim Sidanius. "Social Dominance and Social Identity in the United States and Israel: Ingroup Favoritism or Outgroup Derogation." *Political Psychology* 20 (1999): 99–126.

Lewis, C. S. *The Abolition of Man.* San Francisco: HarperSanFrancisco, 2001.

———. "De Futilitate." In *Essay Collection: Literature, Philosophy, and Short Stories.* London: HarperCollins, 2000.

———. *Mere Christianity.* San Francisco: HarperSanFrancisco, 2001.

———. *Surprised by Joy: The Shape of My Early Life.* London: Harcourt, Brace, 1955.

Lightbody, Brian. "Nietzsche, Perspectivism, Anti-realism: An Inconsistent Triad." *European Legacy* 15, no. 4 (2010): 425–38.

Lloyd, S. A. "Hobbes." In *The Routledge Companion to Social and Political Philosophy*, edited by Gerald Gaus and Fred D'Agostino, 59–70. London: Routledge, 2013.

Locke, John. *The Conduct of the Understanding.* Edited by Peter Millican. Some Texts from Early Modern Philosophy. 2015. http://earlymoderntexts.com/assets/pdfs/locke1706.pdf.

———. *An Essay Concerning Human Understanding.* Edited by Alexander Fraser. 2 vols. New York: Dover, 1959.

———. *A Letter Concerning Toleration.* Edited by Jonathan Bennett. Some Texts from Early Modern Philosophy. 2010. http://earlymoderntexts.com/assets/pdfs/locke1689b.pdf.

———. *Some Thoughts Concerning Education.* Edited by John W. Yolton & Jean S. Yolton. Oxford: Clarendon, 2000.

Louthan, Stephen. "On Religion—A Discussion with Richard Rorty, Alvin Plantinga and Nicholas Wolterstorff." *Christian Scholar's Review* 27 (1996): 177–83.

Lovejoy, Arthur O. *The Great Chain of Being.* Cambridge, MA: Harvard University Press, 1978.

MacDonald, Scott. "Theory of Knowledge." In *The Cambridge Companion to Aquinas,* edited by Norman Kretzman and Eleonore Stump, 160–95. Cambridge: Cambridge University Press, 1993.

MacIntyre, Alasdair. "Aquinas and the Extent of Moral Disagreement." In *Selected Essays*. Vol. 2, *Ethics and Politics*, 64–84. Cambridge: Cambridge University Press, 2006.

———. *God, Philosophy, Universities: A Selective History of the Catholic Philosophical Tradition*. London: Continuum, 2009.

———. "Philosophy Recalled to Its Tasks: A Thomistic Reading of 'Fides et Ratio.'" In *Selected Essays*. Vol. 1, *The Tasks of Philosophy*, 179–98. Cambridge: Cambridge University Press, 2006.

———. *Selected Essays*. Vol. 1, *The Tasks of Philosophy*. Cambridge: Cambridge University Press, 2006.

———. *Selected Essays*. Vol. 2, *Ethics and Politics*. Cambridge: Cambridge University Press, 2006.

———. "Some Enlightenment Projects Considered." In *Selected Essays*. Vol. 2, *Ethics and Politics*, 172–85. Cambridge: Cambridge University Press, 2006.

———. "Toleration and Goods in Conflict." In *Selected Essays*. Vol. 2, *Ethics and Politics*, 205–23. Cambridge: Cambridge University Press, 2006.

———. *Whose Justice? Which Rationality?* Notre Dame: University of Notre Dame Press, 1988.

Marsh, Jason. "Do the Demographics of Theistic Belief Disconfirm Theism? A Reply to Maitzen." *Religious Studies* 44 (2006): 465–71.

Martin, David. *Does Christianity Cause War?* Oxford: Clarendon, 2002.

Marty, Martin. *Politics, Religion and the Common Good: Advancing a Distinctly American Conversation about Religion's Role in Our Shared Life*. San Francisco: Jossey-Bass, 2000.

Matheson, David. "Bounded Rationality and the Enlightenment Picture of Cognitive Virtue." In *Contemporary Debates in Cognitive Science*, edited by Robert J. Stainton, 134–44. Oxford: Blackwell, 2006.

Mathewes, Charles. *A Theology of Public Life*. Cambridge Studies in Christian Doctrine. Cambridge: Cambridge University Press, 2008.

Mazar, Nina, and Chen-Bo Zhong. "Do Green Products Make Us Better People?" *Psychological Studies* 21 (2010): 494–98.

McClendon, James William. *Biography as Theology*. Eugene, OR: Wipf and Stock, 1974.

McGilchrist, Ian. *The Master and His Emissary: The Divided Brain and the Making of the Western World*. New Haven: Yale University Press, 2009.

McGinn, Colin. *Problems in Philosophy*. Oxford: Blackwell, 1993.

McInerny, Daniel. *Difficult Good: A Thomistic Approach to Moral Conflict and Human Happiness*. New York: Fordham University Press, 2006.

———. "Fortitude and the Conflict of Frameworks." In *Virtues and Their Vices*, edited by Kevin Timpe and Craig A. Boyd, 75–92. Oxford: Oxford University Press, 2014.

McKim, Robert. *On Religious Diversity*. Oxford: Oxford University Press, 2012.

———. *Religious Ambiguity and Religious Diversity*. Oxford: Oxford University Press, 2000.

McKnight, Stephen A. "Religion and Francis Bacon's Scientific Utopianism." *Zygon* 42 (2007): 463–86.

McMahan, Jeff. "Challenges to Human Equality." *Journal of Ethics* 12 (2008): 81–104.

McNab, Chris. *The History of the World in 100 Weapons*. London: Osprey, 2014.

Melby-Lervåg, Monica, and Charles Hulme. "Is Working Memory Training Effective? A Meta-analytic Review." *Developmental Psychology* 49 (2012): 270–91.

Merritt, Anna C., Daniel A. Effron, and Benoît Monin. "Moral Self-Licensing: When Being Good Frees Us to Be Bad." *Social and Personality Psychology Compass* 5 (2010): 344–57.

Midgley, Mary. *Myths We Live By*. London: Routledge, 2004.

Milbank, John. *Theology and Social Theory*. Oxford: Blackwell, 1990.

Miller, Christian B. "Which Beliefs Contribute to Virtuous Behavior?" *Big Questions Online*. June 15, 2012. https://www.bigquestionsonline.com/content/which-beliefs-contribute-virtuous-behavior.

———. *Moral Character: An Empirical Theory*. Oxford: Oxford University Press, 2013.

———. *Character and Moral Psychology*. Oxford: Oxford University Press, 2014.

Mouffe, Chantal. "The Limits of John Rawls's Pluralism." *Journal of International Political Theory* 3 (2007): 109–28.

Mummendey, Amélie, Andreas Klink, and Rupert Brown. "Nationalism and Patriotism: National Identification and Out-Group Rejection." *British Journal of Social Psychology* 40 (2011): 159–72.

Murphy, Nancey, and Christopher C. Knight, eds. *Human Identity at the Intersection of Science, Technology and Religion*. Farnham, UK: Ashgate, 2010.

Murray, Michael J., and Andrew Goldberg. "Evolutionary Accounts of Religion: Explaining and Explaining Away." In *The Believing Primate: Scientific, Philosophical, and Theological Reflections on the Origin of Religion*, edited by Jeffrey Schloss and Michael J. Murray, 179–199. Oxford: Oxford University Press, 2009.

Nietzsche, Friedrich. *The Gay Science*. Translated by Walter Kaufmann. New York: Vintage, 1969.

———. *On the Genealogy of Morals*. Translated by Ian Johnston. Arlington, VA: Richer Resources, 2010.

Niiniluoto, Ilkka. *Scientific Critical Realism*. Oxford: Clarendon, 1999.

Nisula, Timo. *Augustine and the Functions of Concupiscence*. Leiden: Brill, 2012.

Norenzayan, Ara. *Big Gods: How Religion Transformed Co-operation and Conflict*. Princeton: Princeton University Press, 2013.

Nussbaum, Martha. *The Fragility of Goodness*. Cambridge: Cambridge University Press, 1986.

O'Neill, Brendan. "Free Speech Is so Last Century." *The Spectator*. November 22, 2014. http://www.spectator.co.uk/features/9376232/free-speech-is-so-last-century-todays-students-want-the-right-to-be-comfortable/.

O'Neill, Onora. "The Public Use of Reason." *Political Theory* 14, no. 4 (1986): 523–51.

Oppy, Graham. "Disagreement." *International Journal of Philosophy of Religion* 68 (2010): 183–99.

Orwell, George. "The Freedom of the Press." Preface to *Animal Farm*. New York: Penguin, 2000.

Oviedo, Lluis. "Religious Cognition as a Dual-Process: Developing the Model." *Method and Theory in the Study of Religion* (2013): 31–58.

Pals, Daniel. *Seven Theories of Religion*. Oxford: Oxford University Press, 1996.

Pape, Robert. *Dying to Win: The Strategic Logic of Suicide Terrorism*. Carlton North, Australia: Scribe, 2005.

Pasnau, Robert. *Metaphysical Themes, 1274–1671*. New York: Oxford University Press, 2011.

Peels, Rik. "Epistemic Desiderata and Epistemic Pluralism." *Journal of Philosophical Research* 35 (2010): 193–207.

Perkins, D. N. "Postprimary Education Has Little Impact on Informal Reasoning." *Journal of Education Psychology* 77 (1985): 562–71.

Perry, John. *The Pretenses of Loyalty*. Oxford: Oxford University Press, 2011.

Perry, John, and Nigel Biggar. "Religion and Intolerance: A Critical Commentary." In *Religion, Intolerance, and Conflict: A Scientific and Conceptual Investigation*, edited by Steve Clarke, Russell Powell, and Julian Savulescu, 253–61. Oxford: Oxford University Press, 2012.

Persson, Ingmar, and Julian Savulescu. "The Limits of Religious Tolerance: A Secular View." In *Religion, Intolerance, and Conflict: A Scientific and Conceptual Investigation*, edited by Steve Clarke, Russell Powell, and Julian Savulescu, 236–52. Oxford: Oxford University Press, 2012.

Peterson, Christopher, and Martin E. P. Seligman. *Character Strengths and Virtues*. Oxford: Oxford University Press, 2004.

Pettit, Philip. *Made with Words: Hobbes on Language, Mind, and Politics*. Princeton: Princeton University Press, 2008.

Phillips, Charles, and Alan Axelrod, eds. *Encyclopedia of Wars*. New York: Facts on File, 2004.

Pinsent, Andrew. "Humility." In *Being Good: Christian Virtues for Everyday Life*, edited by Michael Austin and R. Douglas Geivett. Grand Rapids: Eerdmans, 2011.

Plantinga, Alvin. *Warranted Christian Belief*. New York: Oxford University Press, 2000.

Plato. *Complete Works*. Edited by John M. Cooper. Indianapolis: Hackett, 1997.

Plous, Scott. *Psychology of Judgment and Decision-Making*. Philadelphia: Temple University Press, 1993.

Porter, Jean. *Nature as Reason*. Grand Rapids: Eerdmans, 2005.

Pound, Marcus. *Žižek: A (Very) Critical Introduction*. Grand Rapids: Eerdmans, 2008.

Powell, Russell, and Steve Clarke. "Religion, Tolerance, and Intolerance: Views from across the Disciplines." In *Religion, Intolerance, and Conflict: A Scientific and Conceptual Investigation*, edited by Steve Clarke, Russell Powell, and Julian Savulescu, 1–35. Oxford: Oxford University Press, 2013.

Rawls, John. *Political Liberalism*. New York: Columbia University Press, 1996.

Reginster, Bernard. "Perspectivism, Criticism and Freedom of Spirit." *European Journal of Philosophy* 8 (2000): 40–62.

Reichman, Henry. "Civility and Free Speech." *Inside Higher Ed*. October 12, 2011. https://

www.insidehighered.com/views/2014/10/14/essay-argues-recent-statements
-college-leaders-about-civility-are-threat-academic.

Ricoeur, Paul. "The Erosion of Tolerance and the Resistance of the Intolerable." *Diogenes* 44, no. 4 (1996): 189–201.

Ridder, Jeroen de, and Mathanja Berger. "Shipwrecked or Holding Water? In Defense of Plantinga's Warranted Christian Believer." *Philo* 16 (2013): 42–61.

Riggs, Wayne D. "Understanding 'Virtue' and the Virtue of Understanding." In *Intellectual Virtue: Perspectives from Ethics and Epistemology*, edited by Michael DePaul and Linda Zagzebski, 203–26. Oxford: Oxford University Press, 2003.

Rist, John. "Faith and Reason." In *The Cambridge Companion to Augustine*, edited by Norman Kretzman and Eleonore Stump, 26–39. Cambridge: Cambridge University Press, 2001.

Roberts, Robert C., and W. Jay Wood. *Intellectual Virtues: An Essay on Regulative Epistemology*. Oxford: Clarendon, 2008.

Roberts, Robert C., *Emotions in Moral Life*. Cambridge: Cambridge University Press, 2013.

Rorty, Richard. *Philosophy and Social Hope*. London: Penguin, 2000.

———. "Religion in the Public Square: A Reconsideration." *Journal of Religious Ethics* 31, no. 1 (2003): 141–49.

Rubin, Mark, and Constantina Badea. "They're All the Same! . . . But for Several Different Reasons: A Review of the Multicausal Nature of Perceived Group Variability." *Current Directions in Psychological Science* 21 (2012): 367–72.

Ryan, Alan. "Hobbes's Political Philosophy." In *The Cambridge Companion to Hobbes*, edited by Tom Sorell, 67–80. Cambridge: Cambridge University Press, 1996.

Saarinen, Risto. *Weakness of the Will in Medieval Thought: From Augustine to Buridan*. Leiden: Brill, 1994.

Samuels, Richard, Stephen Stich, and Michael Bishop. "Ending the Rationality Wars: How to Make Disputes about Human Rationality Disappear." In *Common Sense, Reasoning and Rationality*, edited by Renee Elio, 236–68. New York: Oxford University Press, 2002.

Scanlon, T. M. *The Difficulty of Tolerance. Essays in Political Philosophy*. Cambridge: Cambridge University Press, 2003.

Schloss, Jeffrey. "Introduction: Evolutionary Theories of Religion." In *The Believing Primate: Scientific, Philosophical, and Theological Reflections on the Origin of Religion*, edited by Jeffrey Schloss and Michael J. Murray, 14–25. Oxford: Oxford University Press, 2009.

Slone, D. Jason. *Theological Incorrectness: Why Religious People Believe What They Shouldn't*. New York: Oxford University Press, 2004.

Smith, Christian. *American Evangelicalism: Embattled and Thriving*. Chicago: University of Chicago Press, 1998.

———. *Moral, Believing Animals*. Oxford: Oxford University Press, 2009.

———. *What Is a Person?* Chicago: University of Chicago Press, 2010.

Sosis, Richard. "Does Religion Promote Trust? The Role of Signaling, Reputation and Punishment." *Interdisciplinary Journal of Research on Religion* 1 (2005): 1–30.

Sosis, Richard, and Eric Bressler. "Cooperation and Commune Longevity: A Test of the Costly Signaling Theory of Religion." *Cross-Cultural Research* 37 (2003): 211–39.

Sosis, Richard, and Bradley J. Ruffle. "Religious Ritual and Cooperation: Testing for a Relationship on Israeli Religious and Secular Kibbutzim." *Current Anthropology* 44 (December 2003): 713–22.

Spruit, Leen. *Species Intelligibilis: From Perception to Knowledge*. Vol. 1, *Classical Roots and Medieval Discussions*. Leiden: Brill 1994.

Sreenivasan, Gopal. "Disunity of Virtue." *Journal of Ethics* 13 (2009): 195–212.

Stainton, Robert J., ed. *Contemporary Debates in Cognitive Science*. Oxford: Blackwell, 2006.

Standage, Tom. *A History of the World in Six Glasses*. New York: Atlantic Books, 2005.

———. *An Edible History of Humanity*. New York: Atlantic Books, 2010.

Stanovich, Keith. *Rationality and the Reflective Mind*. Oxford: Oxford University Press, 2010.

Stark, Rodney. "Atheism, Faith, and the Social Scientific Study of Religion." *Journal of Contemporary Religion* 14 (1999): 41–62.

———. *The Triumph of Christianity: How the Jesus Movement Became the World's Largest Religion*. San Francisco: HarperOne, 2011.

Stein, Edith. *On the Problem of Empathy*. Translated by Waltrau Stein. Washington, DC: ICS Publications, 1989.

Stenmark, Mikael. *Rationality in Science, Religion and Everyday Life*. Notre Dame: University of Notre Dame Press, 1995.

Stout, Jeffrey. *Democracy and Tradition*. Princeton: Princeton University Press, 2005.

———. "Folly of Secularism." *Journal of American Academy of Religion* 76 (2008): 533–44.

Street, Sharon. "A Darwinian Dilemma for Realist Theories of Value." *Philosophical Studies* 127 (2006): 109–66.

Stump, Eleonore. *Aquinas*. London: Routledge, 2013.

Swinburne, Richard. "Why Hume and Kant Were Mistaken in Rejecting Natural Theology." In *Knowledge, Action, Pluralism: Contemporary Perspectives in Philosophy of Religion*, edited by Sebastian T. Kołodziejczyk, 31–48. Frankfurt: Lang, 2013.

Tangney, June Price. "Humility." In *Handbook of Positive Psychology*, edited by C. R. Snyder and Shane J. Lopez, 411–22. New York: Oxford University Press, 2002.

Taylor, Charles. *A Secular Age*. Cambridge, MA: Belknap Press of Harvard University Press, 2008.

Thiele, Leslie Paul. *The Heart of Judgment: Practical Wisdom, Neuroscience and Narrative*. Cambridge: Cambridge University Press, 2006.

Thomas Aquinas. *Commentary on the "Posterior Analytics" of Aristotle*. Translated by Fabian R. Larcher, OP. Albany, NY: Magi Books, 1970.

———. *Summa Theologiae*. Translated by the Fathers of the English Dominican Province. Edited and revised by Kevin Knight. New Advent. 2008. newadvent.org/summa.

Thune, Michael. "Partial Defeaters and the Epistemology of Disagreement." *Philosophical Quarterly* 60 (2010): 355–72.

———. "Religious Belief and the Epistemology of Disagreement." *Philosophy Compass* 5 (2010): 712–24.

Thurow, Joshua. "Religion, 'Religion,' and Tolerance." In *Religion, Intolerance, and Conflict: A Scientific and Conceptual Investigation*, edited by Steve Clarke, Russell Powell, and Julian Savulescu, 146–62. Oxford: Oxford University Press, 2013.

Tillich, Paul. *The Courage to Be*. Glasgow: Collins, 1986.

Timpe, Kevin, and Craig A. Boyd. Introduction to *Virtues and Their Vices*, edited by Kevin Timpe and Craig A. Boyd, 1–36. Oxford: Oxford University Press, 2014.

Titus, Craig Steven. "Moral Development and Connecting the Virtues: Aquinas, Porter, and the Flawed Saint." In *Ressourcement Thomism: Sacred Doctrine, the Sacraments, and the Moral Life*, edited by Reinhard Hütter and Matthew Levering, 330–52. Washington, DC: Catholic University of America Press, 2010.

Toft, Monica Duffy. "Religion, Terrorism, and Civil Wars." In *Rethinking Religion and World Affairs*, edited by Timothy Shah, Alfred Stepan, and Monica Duffy Toft, 127–48. Oxford: Oxford University Press, 2011.

Touboul, Jonathan. "The Hipster Effect: When Anticonformists All Look the Same." *Arxiv.org*. October 29, 2014. http://arxiv.org/pdf/1410.8001v1.pdf.

Turner, Leon. *Theology, Psychology and Plural Self*. Farnham, UK: Ashgate, 2008.

Trigg, Roger. *Religious Diversity: Philosophical and Political Dimensions*. Cambridge: Cambridge University Press, 2014.

Tutu, Desmond. *No Future without Forgiveness*. London: Rider, 2000.

Vainio, Olli-Pekka. *Beyond Fideism: Negotiable Religious Identities*. Aldershot: Ashgate, 2010.

———. "Salvation and Religious Diversity: Christian Perspectives." *Religion Compass* 10 (2016): 27–34.

———. "What Does Theology Have to Do with Religion? Dual-Process Accounts, Cognitive Science of Religion and a Curious Blind Spot in Contemporary Theorizing." *Open Theology* 2 (2016): 106–12.

Vainio, Olli-Pekka, and Aku Visala. "Tolerance or Recognition? What Can We Expect?" *Open Theology* (forthcoming).

Van Der Schaar, Maria. "Locke on Judgment and Religious Toleration." *British Journal for the History of Philosophy* 20 (2012): 41–68.

Van Slyke, James A. "Moral Psychology, Neuroscience and Virtue." In *Virtues and Their Vices*, edited by Kevin Timpe and Craig A. Boyd, 459–80. Oxford: Oxford University Press, 2014.

Visala, Aku. *Naturalism, Theism and the Cognitive Study of Religion*. Farnham, UK: Ashgate, 2011.

Visala, Aku, and David Leech. "Naturalistic Explanations for Religious Belief." *Philosophy Compass* 8 (2010): 552–63.

Ward, Keith. *Is Religion Dangerous?* Oxford: Lion, 2006.

Webber, Jonathan. "Virtue, Character and Situation." *Journal of Moral Philosophy* 3 (2006): 190–213.

West, R. F., R. J. Meserve, and K. E. Stanovich. "Cognitive Sophistication Does Not Attenuate the Bias Blind Spot." *Journal of Personality and Social Psychology* 4 (2012): 506–19.

White, Nicholas. *Plato on Knowledge and Reality*. Indianapolis: Hackett, 1976.

————. "Plato's Metaphysical Epistemology." In *The Cambridge Companion to Plato*, edited by Richard Kraut, 277–310. Cambridge: Cambridge University Press, 1992.

Whitehouse, Harvey. "Religion, Cohesion, and Hostility." In *Religion, Intolerance, and Conflict: A Scientific and Conceptual Investigation*, edited by Steve Clarke, Russell Powell, and Julian Savulescu, 36–47. Oxford: Oxford University Press, 2013.

Williams, Rowan. "Making Moral Decisions." In *The Cambridge Companion to Christian Ethics*, edited by Robin Gill, 3–15. 2nd ed. Cambridge: Cambridge University Press, 2012.

Willoughby, Teena, Paul J. C. Adachi, and Marie Good. "A Longitudinal Study of the Association between Violent Video Game Play and Aggression Among Adolescents." *Developmental Psychology* 48, no. 4 (2011): 1044–57.

Wolfson, Adam. "Toleration and Relativism: The Locke-Proast Exchange." *Review of Politics* 59, no. 2 (1997): 213–31.

Wolterstorff, Nicholas. "An Engagement with Rorty." *Journal of Religious Ethics* 31 (2003): 129–39.

————. "Is It Possible and Desirable for Theologians to Recover from Kant?" *Modern Theology* 14, no. 1 (1998): 1–18.

————. *John Locke and the Ethics of Belief*. Cambridge Studies in Religion and Critical Thought. Cambridge: Cambridge University Press, 1996.

————. *The Mighty and the Almighty: An Essay in Political Theology*. Cambridge: Cambridge University Press, 2012.

————. *Understanding Liberal Democracy: Essays in Political Philosophy*. Edited by Terence Cuneo. Oxford: Oxford University Press, 2012.

Worthington, Everett L., Jr., Caroline Lavelock, Daryl R. Van Tongeren, David J. Jennings II, Aubery L. Gartner, Don E. Davis, and Joshua N. Hook. "Virtue in Positive Psychology." In *Virtues and Their Vices*, edited by Kevin Timpe and Craig A. Boyd, 433–58. Oxford: Oxford University Press, 2014.

Xenasis, Jason. "Plato on Ethical Disagreement." *Phronesis* 1 (1955): 50–57.

Yong, Ed. "Replication Studies: Bad Copy." *Nature* 485 (2012): 298–300.

Zagzebski, Linda Trinkaus. *Divine Motivation Theory*. Cambridge: Cambridge University Press, 2004.

————. *Epistemic Authority: A Theory of Trust, Authority, and Autonomy in Belief*. Oxford: Oxford University Press, 2012.

Zock, Hetty. "Voicing the Self in Postsecular Society: A Psychological Perspective on Meaning-Making and Collective Identities." In *Exploring the Postsecular: The Religious, the Political and the Urban*, edited by Arie Molendijk, Justin Beaumont, and Christoph Jedan, 131–44. Leiden: Brill, 2010.

Index

Abortion, xiii, 107, 160–61, 174–75, 180–81

Adams, Robert Merrihew, 139–40, 175–76, 179–80

agnosticism, 119, 124, 128

akrasia (weakness of the will), 12, 45, 151

Allport, G. W., 104

Alston, William, 117–18, 127, 135–36

Aquinas, Saint Thomas 1, 15–20, 141, 166

Aristotle, 7–10, 13, 16, 27, 53, 140–41, 163

Atran, Scott, 99

Audi, Robert, 123, 130–33, 135

Augustine, Aurelius, 10–15, 18, 141, 163n57

Babcock, Linda, 70

Bacon, Francis, 20–23, 28n82

Baehr, Jason, 157–58, 165

Barrett, Justin L., 81n74, 83

Batson, C. Daniel, 104, 146

Bayer, Oswald, 39

Belief formation, 30, 46: and evidence, 121, 132–33, 136 166–67; and human cognition, 80–84, 94–98, 105n44, 161; and personal limitations, 52, 175.

Berger, Peter, 123–24, 129

Bergmann, Michael, 135

Betz, John, 38

Biases, x, xii–xiii, 48, 144, 158, 179:

Debiasing, x, 60, 73, 84, 103, 138, 152–55, 161–62, 185; Hobbes on, 26; and human cognition, 60–65, 69–73, 81–84; Locke on, 31.

Biggar, Nigel, 185–86

Blake, William, 85

Brain, 62–64, 69, 73–74, 154–55

Cause, definition of, 108–9

Cavanaugh, William, xin6, 102

Chambers, Simone, 32

Character trait, 146–49

Chesterton, G. K., 148, 182

Clarke, Steve, 101, 107, 111–13

Cognitive ease, 60, 63, 71

Cognitive psychology, 59, 87–88

Cognitive science of religion (CSR), 82–83, 87, 99

Cokely, Edward, 82

Collins, Randall, 49–50

Conee, Earl, 134, 135

Dawkins, Richard, 75, 85, 90, 99

Debunking arguments, 90–94, 98–99

Denyer, Nicholas, 8

Descartes, Rene, 20, 23–25

Desire, xiii, 7, 10, 13–16, 18, 23–24, 38, 74, 86, 150–51

Dialogical Self Theory, 56–57

Discrimination, 107, 174

204

Diversity 68, 72, 95, 97, 98, 114*n*62, 180:
  and sense of self, 55–56
Dogmatism, 134
Doubt, 10, 24, 63, 104, 123–34, 163–64
Dougherty, Trent, 167
Dual process theory, 61–66, 73, 76*n*63,
  80–84, 152
Dylan, Bob, 57*n*25

Elgin, Catherine, 135
Eliade, Mircea, 87
Enlightenment, x, 2*n*2, 33–35, 38–43, 50,
  67–68, 87
Epistemic desiderata, 117–18, 127, 136
Epistemic injustice, 144
Epistemic vices, xv, 133
Epistemology, 2*n*2, 3, 5, 11, 41
Epistemology of disagreement, 10, 115–37
Evans, Jonathan St. B. T., 83
Exclusivism, 96–97

Feltz, Adam, 82
Foucault, Michel, 168–69
Frazer, James, 86
Fricker, Miranda, 144
Fundamentalism, 42, 58, 123–24, 133

Geertz, Clifford, 87
Gigerenzer, Gerd, 60–61, 67–69, 73, 76,
  79
Griffiths, Paul E., 93
Griffiths, Paul J., 11
Groupishness, 105–6, 109–13
Gutting, Gary, 119–20

Habituation, xv, 140, 151
Haidt, Jonathan, 77–80, 112, 138, 143,
  151*n*27
Hamann, Johann Georg, 33, 38–40
Harm, 78, 80, 101, 107–8, 174
Harrison, Peter, 25
Harrison, Victoria, 114*n*62
Hate speech 76, 182
Helm, Paul, 120–21, 133*n*109
Herdt, Jennifer, 19*n*59
Hermans, Hubert, 55–57

Hobbes, Thomas, 25–33, 41
Human nature 5, 20, 25, 34*n*102, 39, 76,
  106, 139, 145, 157, 178,
Hunter, James Davison, 104*n*43
Hursthouse, Rosalind, 142
Hütter, Reinhard, 169
Hypersensitive agency detection device
  (HADD), 88–89, 91

Idols (Baconian), 22–23
Ingroup/outgroup distinction, 70, 72,
  101, 111-12
Intelligence, 53, 63, 65–68, 72, 154, 167
Intolerance, 44*n*137, 101, 108, 133, 170,
  172, 174
Inwagen, Peter van, 118–19, 127
Irrationalism, 28*n*80, 38, 59–60, 75, 83,
  90–91, 120*n*78, 132–33, 168
Islam, 99–100, 105, 114, 142

Jong, Jonathan, 94

Kahneman, Daniel, 60–66, 71*n*53, 76
Kant, Immanuel, 31–33, 38–39, 51*n*10,
  68, 126
Kearney, Richard, 57
Knowledge acquisition, xiv: Alston
  on, 117, 127; Aquinas on, 16, 18–19;
  Aristotle on, 7–8; Augustine on, 13;
  and intelligence, 53, 65; and virtues,
  136, 143–44
Kohlberg, Lawrence, 77*n*65
Kurzban, Robert, 79*n*73

Larrick, Richard P., 152*n*30
Leech, David, 95
Lenin, V. I., 43
Lewis, C. S., xii*n*8, 46, 51, 158*n*46, 163*n*56
Liberal democracy, 40–44
Locke, John, ix*n*1, 20, 25, 29–31, 41
Loewenstein, George, 70
Love, 4, 45, 105: Aquinas on, 18–19; Au-
  gustine on, 12–13, 15; Confucius on,
  145; and virtue, 140–41, 166

MacIntyre, Alasdair, 19–20, 34–35, 42, 57, 172, 174, 176, 179
Mao Tse-tung, 43
Marty, Martin, 86
Maslow, Abraham, 89
McGilchrist, Ian, 73–76
McGinn, Colin, 118–19
McKim, Robert, 123–29
Metaphysics, 2–3, 5, 14n47, 28, 41, 45, 54, 57–58, 96, 102, 120n75, 126, 141–42
Method, 2n2, 4n9, 8, 13, 21–28, 45
Midgley, Mary, 86
Milgram, Stanley, 145n17, 147
Miller, Christian B., 149–53
Mind, 60, 64–67, 73–74, 77, 80, 86–89, 112, 118, 129n99, 149n22, 152, 156
Moodysson, Lukas, 178n91
Moral foundations theory, 77–80
Muhammad, 111
Murray, Michael J., 95

Narratives, 52, 57–59, 77, 84
Natural law, 19–20
Nelson, Adm. Horatio, 71
New Atheism, xi, xiv, 43, 75, 99, 102
Niemöller, Martin, 168
Nietzsche, Friedrich, 35–40, 42, 71, 183
9/11, xi, 99
Noncognitivism, 93, 94–96, 99, 126
Norenzayan, Ara, 111n56
Nussbaum, Martha, 5

O'Neill, Brendan, 183
O'Neill, Onora, 33
Oppy, Graham, 121
Orwell, George, 169
Otto, Rudolf, 87
Oviedo, Lluis, 83n79

Pape, Robert, 99n29
Parrhesia, 168–169
Perkins, D. N., 161–62
Perspectivism, 35–38
Persson, Ingmar, 110

Peterson, Christopher and Martin E.P. Seligman, 142n9, 163n58
Plato, 1–10, 13, 56, 140, 163
Postmodernism, 35, 40–42, 47n3, 54n20, 56, 87, 97n22, 173
Powell, Russell, 101, 113
Pragmatism, 117–21, 129, 176
Prejudice, 39, 60, 64, 103–4, 113, 143–44
Priming, 52–53

Rationality, x, 48n4, 59–69, 76, 90, 117, 120, 130–36, 173, 178
Rawls, John, 39–41, 44, 170, 173n84
"Recipe for doom," 110–14
Reginster, Bernard, 37
Relativism, 31n89, 56, 123–34, 170–71, 184
Religion: definition of, 102–3; explanations of, 88–90;
Religious orientation, modes of, 103–4
Religious right, 104n43, 180–81
Ricoeur, Paul, 57–58, 174
Rorty, Richard, 42–44
Ross, J. M., 104
Ryan, Alan, 27

Savulescu, Julian, 110
Scepticism, 10–11, 16, 23–24, 31, 56, 98, 117, 119, 124, 126n94, 134, 137, 158, 181–82
Scheler, Max, 75
Schindler, Oscar, 147
Schweder, Richard, 77n65
Secularism, xiv, 43, 50, 86, 99n29, 106, 109–10, 112, 123–24
Self, 54–59
Situationism, 145–48, 157
Slone, D. Jason, 81n74, 99
Sosis, Richard, 106, 109n54
Soul, 4n9, 5, 7, 9, 12–19, 22, 29, 57, 98
Stanovich, Keith, 59, 61n36, 64–66, 74n59, 76n63, 83
Stark, Rodney, 113
State, 9n29, 29, 32–33, 45; and multiculturalism, 110–11; and Plato, 5–6, 9; state religion, 29, 113
Stein, Edith, 58n27, 71

Stump, Eleanor, 19n61

Tangney, June Price, 162
Taylor, Charles, 49–51, 59
Theological correctness effect, 80–84
Theresa, Mother, 71
Thurow, Joshua, 102n37, 107n52
Tillich, Paul, 130
Toft, Monica Duffy, 100
Tolerance, 31n89, 44n137, 96, 126, 128–29,
    169–76, 180
Totalitarianism, 5, 138, 180

Universalism, 98

Van Der Schaar, Maria, 30
Van Slyke, James A., 155
Violence, xin6, 14, 28, 39, 45, 96, 99–112;
    and football, 106; and video games,
    52n16
Vice, xv, 19, 48, 113, 133, 139, 141–45,
    148–49, 152, 158, 163, 170–72, 179
Virtue, ix, xii, xv, 10n31, 17n56, 19n59,
    23n70, 44, 48, 52–53, 66, 68, 77, 79,

105, 112n59,115, 123, 136, 138: courage
    as a virtue, 165–69; definition of,
    139–42; humility, 162–65; learning
    virtues, 145–57; open-mindedness,
    157–62; relevance to disagreement,
    142–44, 176–86. *See also* Tolerance;
    Wisdom
Visala, Aku, 94–95
Voltaire, 128

War, 3n7, 15, 18, 21, 25, 29, 32, 64, 85,
    99-101, 107–8, 110–11, 113, 176: culture
    war, 79, 144; rationality war, x, 59
White, Nicholas, 5
Whitehouse, Harvey, 177
Wilkins, John S., 93
Williams, Rowan, 184–86
Wisdom, xii, 6n15, 20, 111, 139–43, 154,
    168, 173–75, 186
Wise (*phronimos*), 9, 53, 154–56,
Wolterstorff, Nicholas, 42–44

Zagzebski, Linda Trinkaus, 178
Zock, Hetty, 55